D1522604

Standards for Technological Literacy

The Role of Teacher Education

Editors

John M. Ritz
William E. Dugger, Jr.
Everett N. Israel

51st Yearbook, 2002

Council on Technology Teacher Education

Glencoe
McGraw-Hill

New York, New York   Columbus, Ohio   Chicago, Illinois   Peoria, Illinois   Woodland Hills, California

Glencoe/McGraw-Hill

A Division of The McGraw·Hill Companies

Send all inquiries to:
Glencoe/McGraw-Hill
3008 W. Willow Knolls Drive
Peoria, IL 61614

ISBN 0-07-829104-6

Printed in the United States of America.

1 2 3 4 5 6 7 8 9 10 070 06 05 04 03 02

Orders and requests for information about cost and availability of yearbooks should be directed to Glencoe/McGraw-Hill's Order Department, 1-800-334-7344.

Requests to quote portions of yearbooks should be addressed to the Secretary, Council on Technology Education, in care of Glencoe/McGraw-Hill at the above address, for forwarding to the current Secretary.

This publication is available in microform from

UMI
300 North Zeeb Road
Dept. P.R.
Ann Arbor, MI 48106
Phone: 1-800-521-0600, extension 2888

FOREWORD

The technology teacher education profession has grown and changed over the past 100 years. Beginning as manual and industrial arts, the technology education profession matured during the 1980s and 1990s. Through commitment of professionals and our associations, the content base for our discipline has been furthered explored. *Standards for Technological Literacy: Content for the Study of Technology (Standards for Technological Literacy)* is a synthesis of research directed by the International Technology Education Association's Technology for All Americans Project. Under the direction of William E. Dugger, the profession has developed a set of content standards and benchmarks that can lead teachers in designing programs to advance technological literacy of all students.

With *Standards for Technological Literacy*, teacher educators and supervisors need to adjust pre-service and in-service education to enable teachers to design and deliver technology education programs so that students realize the knowledge and skills offered through the standards. This yearbook is guided by this vision. The authors and editors have taken what they know about teacher education and have proposed ideas that can be used to incorporate *Standards for Technological Literacy* into the practices of all technology education teachers. It is hoped that these writings can assist our profession in taking the next step in preparing future technology education teachers.

John M. Ritz
Past-President (1996-2000)
Council on Technology Teacher Education

YEARBOOK PLANNING COMMITTEE

Terms Expiring 2002

Karen F. Zuga
The Ohio State University

G. Eugene Martin
Southwest Texas State University

Terms Expiring 2003

Linda Rae Markert
State University of New York-Oswego

John R. Wright
University of Southern Maine

Terms Expiring 2004

Cyril King
South Eastern Education and Library Board

John M. Ritz, Committee Chair
Old Dominion University

Peter H. Wright
Indiana State University

Term Expiring 2005

Patricia A. Hutchinson
TIES Magazine

Richard D. Seymour
Ball State University

Term Expiring 2006

Patrick Foster
Central Connecticut State University

Edward M. Reeves
Utah State University

OFFICERS OF THE COUNCIL

President
Rodney L. Custer
Illinois State University
Technology Department
Normal, IL 61790

Vice-President
Robert C. Wicklein
University of Georgia
Program of Technological Studies
Athens, GA 30602

Secretary
Jack W. Wescott
Ball State University
Department of Industry & Technology
Muncie, IN 47306

Treasurer
Marie C. Hoepfl
Appalachian State University
Department of Technology
Boone, NC 28608

Past President
John M. Ritz
Old Dominion University
Occupational & Technical Studies
Norfolk, VA 23529

YEARBOOK PROPOSALS

Each year, at the ITEA International Conference, the CTTE Yearbook committee reviews the progress of yearbooks in preparation and evaluates proposals for additional yearbooks. Any member is welcome to submit a yearbook proposal, which should be written in sufficient detail for the committee to be able to understand the proposed substance and format. Fifteen copies of the proposal should be sent to the committee chairperson by February 1 of the year in which the conference is held. Below are the criteria employed by the committee in making yearbook selections.

CTTE Yearbook Committee

CTTE Yearbook Guidelines

A. **Purpose:**

The CTTE Yearbook Series is intended as a vehicle for communicating major topics or issues related to technology teacher education in a structured, formal series that does not duplicate commercial textbook publishing activities.

B. **Yearbook topic selection criteria:**

An appropriate yearbook topic should:
1. Make a direct contribution to the understanding and improvement of technology teacher education;
2. Add to the accumulated body of knowledge of technology teacher education and to the field of technology education;
3. Not duplicate publishing activities of other professional groups;
4. Provide a balanced view of the theme and not promote a single individual's or institution's philosophy or practices;
5. Actively seek to upgrade and modernize professional practice in technology teacher education; and,
6. Lend itself to team authorship as opposed to single authorship.

Proper yearbook themes related to technology teacher education may also be structured to:
1. Discuss and critique points of view that have gained a degree of acceptance by the profession;
2. Raise controversial questions in an effort to obtain a national hearing; and,
3. Consider and evaluate a variety of seemingly conflicting trends and statements emanating from several sources.

C. **The yearbook proposal:**
1. The yearbook proposal should provide adequate detail for the Yearbook Committee to evaluate its merits.
2. The yearbook proposal should include the following elements:
   a) Defines and describes the topic of the yearbook;
   b) Identifies the theme and describes the rationale for the theme;
   c) Identifies the need for the yearbook and the potential audience or audiences;
   d) Explains how the yearbook will advance the technology teacher education profession and the technology education in general;
   e) Diagram symbolically the intent of the yearbook;
   f) An outline of the yearbook which includes:
      i) A table of contents;
      ii) A brief description of the content or purpose of each chapter;
      iii) At lease a three level outline for each chapter;
      iv) Identification of chapter author(s) and backup authors;
      v) An estimated number of pages for each yearbook chapter; and,
      vi) An estimated number of pages for the yearbook (not to exceed 250 pages).
   g) A timeline for completing the yearbook.

It is understood that each author of a yearbook proposal will sign a CTTE Editor/Author Agreement and comply with the Agreement.

PREVIOUSLY PUBLISHED YEARBOOKS

*1. *Inventory Analysis of Industrial Arts Teacher Education Facilities, Personnel and Programs,* 1952.
*2. *Who's Who in Industrial Arts Teacher Education,* 1953.
*3. *Some Components of Current Leadership: Techniques of Selection and Guidance of Graduate Students; An Analysis of Textbook Emphases;* 1954, three studies.
*4. *Superior Practices in Industrial Arts Teacher Education,* 1955.
*5. *Problems and Issues in Industrial Arts Teacher Education,* 1956.
*6. *A Sourcebook of Reading in Education for Use in Industrial Arts and Industrial Arts Teacher Education,* 1957.
*7. *The Accreditation of Industrial Arts Teacher Education,* 1958.
*8. *Planning Industrial Arts Facilities,* 1959. Ralph K. Nair, ed.
*9. *Research in Industrial Arts Education,* 1960. Raymond Van Tassel, ed.
*10. *Graduate Study in Industrial Arts,* 1961. R. P. Norman and R. C. Bohn, eds.
*11. *Essentials of Preservice Preparation,* 1962. Donald G. Lux, ed.
*12. *Action and Thought in Industrial Arts Education,* 1963. E. A. T. Svendsen, ed.
*13. *Classroom Research in Industrial Arts,* 1964. Charles B. Porter, ed.
*14. *Approaches and Procedures in Industrial Arts,* 1965. G. S. Wall, ed.
*15. *Status of Research in Industrial Arts,* 1966. John D. Rowlett, ed.
*16. *Evaluation Guidelines for Contemporary Industrial Arts Programs,* 1967. Lloyd P. Nelson and William T. Sargent, eds.
*17. *A Historical Perspective of Industry,* 1968. Joseph F. Luetkemeyer Jr., ed.
*18. *Industrial Technology Education,* 1969. C. Thomas Dean and N. A. Hauer, eds.; *Who's Who in Industrial Arts Teacher Education,* 1969. John M. Pollock and Charles A. Bunten, eds.
*19. *Industrial Arts for Disadvantaged Youth,* 1970. Ralph O. Gallington, ed.
*20. *Components of Teacher Education,* 1971. W. E. Ray and J. Streichler, eds.
*21. *Industrial Arts for the Early Adolescent,* 1972. Daniel J. Householder, ed.
*22. *Industrial Arts in Senior High Schools,* 1973. Rutherford E. Lockette, ed.
*23. *Industrial Arts for the Elementary School,* 1974. Robert G. Thrower and Robert D. Weber, eds.
*24. *A Guide to the Planning of Industrial Arts Facilities,* 1975. D. E. Moon, ed.
*25. *Future Alternatives for Industrial Arts,* 1976. Lee H. Smalley, ed.
*26. *Competency-Based Industrial Arts Teacher Education,* 1977. Jack C. Brueckman and Stanley E. Brooks, eds.
*27. *Industrial Arts in the Open Access Curriculum,* 1978. L. D. Anderson, ed.
*28. *Industrial Arts Education: Retrospect, Prospect,* 1979. G. Eugene Martin, ed.
*29. *Technology and Society: Interfaces with Industrial Arts,* 1980. Herbert A. Anderson and M. James Benson, eds.
*30. *An Interpretive History of Industrial Arts,* 1981. Richard Barella and Thomas Wright, eds.
*31. *The Contributions of Industrial Arts to Selected Areas of Education,* 1982. Donald Maley and Kendall N. Starkweather, eds.
*32. *The Dynamics of Creative Leadership for Industrial Arts Education,* 1983. Robert E. Wenig and John I. Mathews, eds.
*33. *Affective Learning in Industrial Arts,* 1984. Gerald L. Jennings, ed.
*34. *Perceptual and Psychomotor Learning in Industrial Arts Education,* 1985. John M. Shemick, ed.
*35. *Implementing Technology Education,* 1986. Ronald E. Jones and John R. Wright, eds.
*36. *Conducting Technical Research,* 1987. Everett N. Israel and R. Thomas Wright, eds.
*37. *Instructional Strategies for Technology Education,* 1988. William H. Kemp and Anthony E. Schwaller, eds.
*38. *Technology Student Organizations,* 1989. M. Roger Betts and Arvid W. Van Dyke, eds.
*39. *Communication in Technology Education,* 1990. Jane A. Liedtke, ed.

***40.** *Technological Literacy,* 1991. Michael J. Dyrenfurth and Michael R. Kozak, eds.
 41. *Transportation in Technology Education,* 1992. John R. Wright and Stanley Komacek, eds.
 42. *Manufacturing in Technology Education,* 1993. Richard D. Seymour and Ray L. Shackelford, eds.
***43.** *Construction in Technology Education,* 1994. Jack W. Wescott and Richard M. Henak, eds.
 44. *Foundations of Technology Education,* 1995. G. Eugene Martin, ed.
 45. *Technology and the Quality of Life,* 1996. Rodney L. Custer and A. Emerson Wiens, eds.
 46. *Elementary School Technology Education,* 1997. James J. Kirkwood and Patrick N. Foster, eds.
 47. *Diversity in Technology Education,* 1998. Betty L. Rider, ed.
 48. *Advancing Professionalism in Technology Education,* 1999. Anthony F. Gilberti and David L. Rouch, eds.
 49. *Technology Education for the 21st Century A Collection of Essays,* 2000. G. Eugene Martin
 50. *Appropriate Technology for Sustainable Living,* 2001, Robert C. Wicklein

* Out-of-print yearbooks can be obtained in microfilm and in Xerox copies. For information on price and delivery, write to Xerox University Microfilms, 300 North Zeeb Road, Ann Arbor, Michigan, 48106.

PREFACE

The stage is set! The play is ready to be written. The actors have been identified. The major group of actors has been determined. The actors of the play will determine the future of technology education.

The future for technology education has been staged by two major International Technology Education Associations (ITEA) publications: *Technology for All Americans: A Rationale and Structure for the Study of Technology and Standards for Technological Literacy: Content for the Study of Technology* (*Standards for Technological Literacy*). The editors of this yearbook feel that the time is right to write the play that will stage the future for technology education. One group of major actors in the play are technology teacher educators who will need to write the script and play a leadership role, which will result in technology education teachers becoming award winning actors; this can result in their students becoming increasing technologically literate. The theme of the play is the modification of traditional and alternative technology teacher education and in-service programs that result in graduates successfully implementing *Standards for Technological Literacy* at the K-12 grade levels

The goals of the play are to:

- Provide direction for restructuring technology teacher education programs,
- Provide ideas for alternative ways for preparing technology teachers to meet the shortage being experienced,
- Provide guidance for revising state and national certification/licensure requirements, and
- Provide direction for changing in-service education so our current population teaching technology (e.g., technology education, science, elementary) can learn how to implement *Standards for Technological Literacy*.

The play has six acts. The first act explains the role of standards in education. The second act summarizes the rationale and structure of technology education and provides an overview of *Standards for Technological Literacy*. The audience is expected to consult the *Standards for Technology Literacy* document for a more detailed explanation. The third act, which is the major section of the play, will provide insights for implementing *Standards for Technological Literacy* in technology teacher education programs. This act includes how the content standards should change the traditional and alternative teacher education programs. Models for each are provided. The fourth act will focus on certification/licensure requirements for quality technology education teachers and will outline proposed changes in ITEA/CTTE/NCATE technology teacher education program standards and guidelines based upon *Standards for Technological Literacy*. The fifth act will identify how technology teacher educators can play an active role in designing and implementing in-service education based upon *Standards for Technological Literacy*. The sixth act, a summary, will make recommendations to the technology teacher education profession for implementing the technology content found in *Standards for Technological Literacy*.

51st Yearbook Editors
John M. Ritz
William E. Dugger
Everett N. Israel

ACKNOWLEDGEMENTS

Without the guidance and development of *Standards for Technological Literacy: Content for the Study of Technology* (*Standards for Technological Literacy*) by the International Technology Education Association's Technology for All Americans Project, this yearbook would not have been envisioned or developed. Through this professional activity, teacher education has a refined knowledge base for better preparing teachers. The authors and editors wish to extend our acknowledgement to our profession for making this new knowledge available to us.

We recognize *Standards for Technological Literacy* would not have developed into its refined status without the financial support of National Science Foundation and National Aeronautics and Space Administration. We acknowledge these insightful federal agencies. The profession also acknowledges National Research Council and National Academy of Engineering for their positive reviews and support of *Standards for Technological Literacy*. Their critiques assisted our profession in expanding our visions and refining *Standards for Technological Literacy*.

The editors and authors, in addition to the members and officers of the Council on Technology Teacher Education, would like to acknowledge Glencoe/McGraw-Hill for its continued support of the Council's Yearbook Series. This yearbook, *Standards for Technological Literacy: The Role of Teacher Education,* is the Council's 51st Yearbook Edition. Without the support of Glencoe/McGraw-Hill and the efforts of Wes Coulter, Trudy Muller, and Jean Leslie, the technology education teacher profession would not have yearbooks to share ideas and provide professional development materials for its members.

The editors acknowledge the critical review and editing of our manuscripts by Lee Manning of Old Dominion University. You took the time to make us clarify our ideas in presenting this yearbook to the profession.

For all of your support, we thank you.

51st Yearbook Editors
John M. Ritz
William E. Dugger
Everett N. Israel

TABLE OF CONTENTS

SECTION 1. ROLE OF STANDARDS IN EDUCATION

Technology Education Standards: Power, Peril, and Promise

Rodger Bybee
Biological Science Curriculum Study
Colorado Springs, Colorado

Role of Standards in Different Subject Areas

Pamela Newberry
International Technology Education Association
Technology for All Americans
Blacksburg, Virginia

Linda S. Hallenbeck
Ohio Office of the Governor
Columbus, Ohio

SECTION 2. CONTENT STANDARDS FOR TECHNOLOGICAL LITERACY EDUCATION

Rationale and Structure for *Standards for Technological Literacy*

G. Eugene Martin
Southwest Texas State University
San Marcos, Texas

SECTION 4. CERTIFICATION/LICENSURE REQUIREMENTS FOR TECHNOLOGY EDUCATION TEACHERS

The Implications of *Standards for Technological Literacy* for Teacher Licensure in Technology Education

Mark E. Sanders
Virginia Tech
Blacksburg, Virginia

Len S. Litowitz
Millersville University
Millersville, Pennsylvania

Changes in Program Accreditation Guidelines for Technology Education

Anthony E. Schwaller
St. Cloud State University
St. Cloud, Minnesota

SECTION 5. DELIVERY OF IN-SERVICE TRAINING FOR IMPLEMENTING THE CONTENT STANDARDS FOR TECHNOLOGICAL LITERACY

Technology Teacher Education's In-Servicing of Technology Education Teachers

John R. Wright
University of Southern Maine
Gorham, Maine

SECTION 6. RECOMMENDATIONS FOR IMPLEMENTING THE CONTENT STANDARDS FOR TECHNOLOGICAL LITERACY EDUCATION

Technology Education Standards: Power, Peril, and Promise

Rodger Bybee
Biological Science Curriculum Study

Our society is both largely dependent on and mostly ignorant about technology, a situation that should be cause for national concern (Atkin, 1990; Selby, 1993; Raizen, et al., 1995). Technology educators have developed *Standards for Technological Literacy: Content for the Study of Technology* (*Standards for Technological Literacy*) and established technology as a new basic in American education. Within the United States, other groups, such as Project 2061 of the American Association for the Advancement of Science (AAAS) and the National Research Council (NRC), have included technology as part of their *Benchmarks for Science Literacy* (AAAS, 1993) and *National Science Education Standards* (NRC, 1996). As reported by Paul Black and Mike Atkin in *Changing the Subject* (1996), technology has emerged as a new field of study in many other countries.

Standards for Technological Literacy is accurate and thorough. At the same time, the standards will have to be educationally sound; understandable by those who have to implement policy, programs, and practice; usable by teachers and school personnel; and achievable by students in elementary, middle, and high schools. The degree to which standards meet these criteria will determine the power and promise of establishing the discipline of technology in school programs.

THE POWER OF EDUCATIONAL STANDARDS

The power of standards lies in their capacity to change fundamental components of the educational system. This assertion has several key points. First is the capacity to cause or influence changes. To be clear, standards imply change, not an affirmation of the status quo. Second, the changes are fundamental components of education. Standards influence curriculum content, instructional techniques, assessment strategies, and teacher education and professional development programs. Third, standards influence the larger educational system, as opposed to one component such as assessments. A feature of standards is that they influence the entire educational system by specifying <u>outcomes</u>, for which the concrete expression is—What should all students know and be able to do? In educational history, clarifying educational outcomes is a shift in emphasis. It varies considerably from our common emphasis of modifying <u>inputs</u> in hopes of improving educational outcomes. With reference to inputs one can change, for example, time (length of school days, years), content (additional courses), materials (new textbooks or activity-based programs), and techniques (cooperative groups, project-based learning, etc.). These inputs are meant to enhance student learning and they may do that, but there is also the reality that to be optimally effective, all educational inputs have to be directed to a common purpose. If not, there is the significant possibility of uncoordinated and unfocused changes; for example, in changing textbooks and teaching techniques with no significant change in outcomes. It should not surprise educators that after establishing standards, which are policies, practitioners ask for instructional materials, educators ask about teacher education, evaluators ask for tests, etc.

Implementing standards facilitates greater coherence among educational components. The assumption behind this position is that greater coherence will enhance student achievement. By some reports, for example, the Third International Mathematics and Science Study (TIMSS) states that most United States educational systems are incoherent. Goals are only tangential to instructional materials which are not true to assessments, which are not aligned with professional development, and the list goes on. Using a basic definition, coherence occurs when a small number of basic components are defined in a system, and other components are based on or derived from those basic components. There is an orderly and logical relationship of educational components that affords greater comprehension of the whole system. Over time, *Standards for Technological Literacy* will develop coherence by:

- Defining the knowledge and abilities of technology that all students should develop;
- Presenting criteria for judging technology education content and programs at different grade levels including learning goals, design features, instructional approaches, and assessment characteristics;
- Providing criteria for judging instructional materials, curricula, and learning experiences developed by national projects, state agencies, local districts, schools, or teachers; and
- Including standards for the preparation and continuing professional development of teachers.

THE PERILS OF NATIONAL STANDARDS

Release of *Standards for Technological Literacy* in the spring of 2000 inevitably has broadened and deepened discussions about technology education in general and of those standards, in particular. Although the community was aware of their development and opportunities for review and input, the actual standards stimulated new discussions as different factions of your community are confronted with the possibility of change. It would be false to report that these discussions will be calm, clear, and civil. Unfortunately, at best this yearbook will give you some warnings and suggest some strategies. The warnings build awareness and prepares for the inevitable criticisms. The strategies provide a plan that accommodates many, neutralizes some, and adapts to others.

Rather than convey a totally pessimistic warning of inevitable crisis and doom, the perils will be presented as paradoxes. A paradox, as opposed to a dilemma, is a seemingly contradictory statement that may be true, an apparent contradiction that may in fact be resolved in time and through effective leadership.

Paradox 1: Individuals and groups will demand to know more about standards; yet, the more they know about them, the more inadequacies they will report.

In the early stages of development, individuals want to know more, but as they develop awareness, they fail to see connections to their specific discipline, e.g., materials science, teacher education, and thus will claim the standards to be inappropriate or to not apply to them. A recommendation is to consistently send the message of what standards are, what they are not, and how they will influence and connect various factions of the technology education community.

Paradox 2: Individuals and groups will demand that standards bring about revolutionary improvement in technology education; yet, they will be reluctant to initiate change in their respective domains of technology education.

Standards for Technological Literacy identifies that there is a need for all citizens to understand technology and that technology education should have priority in schools, but individuals will find numerous reasons not to initiate even small, incremental changes to achieve this goal. A clear example of this paradox is when college and university faculty demand changes in K-12 education, but they are reluctant to change their programs. The technology education profession has to talk continually about the system and provide examples of changes in all components of the system: the "we are all in this and if it is going to work, we all have to change" approach.

Paradox 3: Individuals and groups will demand more specific and practical standards; yet, the more specific and practical you are, the more you will hear about the need for broad and general standards.

This paradox applies to just about everything. For example, some technology education teachers will want actual examples of instructional materials from the National Science Foundation (NSF) and National Aeronautics and Space Administration (NASA). When you provide the examples, there will still be requests for more detail, combined with misinterpretations, and criticisms of the examples. Each example should establish a context by indicating what the example does and does not show.

Paradox 4: Individuals and groups will ask for brief statements that express the standards; yet, any slogan you use will be taken to its most literal and unreasonable conclusion.

"Less is more" is a theme commonly heard in contemporary reform. Critics, of course, take it to the extreme—teaching less and less about more and more until students know nothing about everything! This was never the intention of the origination of the phrase. Rather, they meant something like learning fewer concepts more deeply.

No doubt, the meaning of the project, Technology for All Americans, who created *A Rationale and Structure for the Study of Technology* (*Rationale and Structure*, 1996), will suffer similar criticism—"You could not possibly mean all," critics will say. "What about severely disabled students?" The implication here is that if exceptions can be found, the profession should change the goal. Quite the opposite is the case. The exceptions demonstrate the need for the goal. Changes implied by the questions can open the door to a future of inequalities in technology education.

The technology education profession should not open the door, but stay with the slogan that will bring greater equity to all American students and society. The counterpoint to members of the profession is "justice for all." That is, given that society embraces the goal of "justice for all," it is fair to ask if the profession can find exceptions. Of course, the profession can. So, should technology education change the goal or work harder to achieve it? The answer is clear— we keep the goal and strive to achieve it.

Paradox 5: Individuals and groups will want you to achieve the goals set forth in the standards yet the more successful you are, the more you will be subject to criticism.

With success comes criticism. Unfortunately, it is not always accurate, deserved, or civil. Recognize that *Standards for Technological Literacy* (2000) will not be a perfect document, so critics will find errors and the need for improvement. Listen and learn from criticism that is clear, justified, and civil. When unjust and undue criticism comes, ignore most of it, respond vigorously and adequately to some of it, and have a larger vision than the critics. Also, it always helps to maintain a sense of humor.

FULFILLING THE PROMISE OF NATIONAL STANDARDS

In the project on *National Science Education Standards* (1996), a strategic framework for standards-based reform was established (referred to hereafter as the framework) (Burrill & Kennedy, 1997). Such a framework helped navigate the paradoxes, and it will help fulfill the promise of technology education. Table 1-1 summarizes that framework.

Research on dissemination and change clearly indicated that actions by many individuals and organizations are needed if meaningful and last-

Table 1-1. A Strategic Framework for Standards-Based Reform

REFORM

Dissemination	Goal: Developing Awareness	"Getting the word out"
Interpretation	Goal: Increasing Understanding and Support	"Getting the idea"
Implementation	Goal: Changing Policies, Programs, and Practices	"Getting the job done"
Evaluation	Goal: Monitoring and Adjusting Policies, Programs, and Practices	"Getting it right"
Revision	Goal: Improving the Efficacy and Influence of Standards	"Doing it all again"

ing changes are to occur (Hutchinson & Huberman, 1993). And, the larger the system (e.g., the nation vs. a school), the larger and more coordinated the effort needs to be. The framework provided in this section is intended as an organizing tool for standards-based reforms in education (Bybee, 1997).

Similar to many models for change and improvement, the framework (see Table 1-1) has several different dimensions, each with particular goals. In the framework, the developer of the standards plays a role, as do other participants in the educational system. National organizations, such as the International Technology Education Association (ITEA), play a major part in initial dissemination of the national standards, but they do not implement them.

The framework helps to organize the technology education profession's thinking about what strategies are needed and clarifies where responsibility and authority lie for making changes in the various components of the educational system. Although the framework is designed as a means of thinking about national technology education standards, it is equally appropriate as a means of thinking about implementing *Standards for Technological Literacy* at state and local levels.

Dissemination involves developing a general awareness of the existence of the *Standards for Technological Literacy* document among those responsible for policy making, programs, and teaching, and providing support and encouragement for the changes that will be required. It includes addressing the questions, "What are the standards?" "Why are they needed?" and "How could they be used to shape policy and practice?" Especially during dissemination, be articulate about what they can and cannot do, and why they are worth supporting. Being clear in the dissemination phase will help neutralize criticisms and build support.

Interpretation is about increasing understanding of and support for *Standards for Technological Literacy*. It involves careful analysis, dialogue, and the difficult educational task of challenging current conceptions and establishing a knowledge base that helps the community respond to critics. Deeper and richer understanding of standards is the goal. It is not too early to plan activities, publications, and a Web site that will help with questions and the interpretation of the standards for different groups in the technology education community and for different aspects of the instruction core.

Implementation involves changing policies, programs, and practices to be consistent with *Standards for Technological Literacy*. People modify the district and school technology curriculum, revise criteria for the selection of instructional materials, change teacher credentialing and recertification, and develop new assessments. Enacting new policies, programs, and practices builds new understandings that can feed back into interpretation.

In the evaluation dimension, information gathered about their impact can contribute directly to improvement. Monitoring of and feedback to various parts of the system result in modification and adjustment of policies, programs, and practices.

At some point, as a planned element of the process, revision of standards occurs. Incorporating the new knowledge developed through implementation and evaluation and drawing heavily on input and discussion generated in the technology education field by the original document reviewers will result in the revisions of the standards. It is important to identify this element of the strategy as it signals a dynamic and changing quality of the standards.

There exists some logical sequence to the dimensions. For example, people need to become aware of standards before they deepen their understanding through interpretation activities. Likewise, implementation without understanding can lead to change that is mechanical, superficial, and—in the extreme—can imperil reform with the dismissal that "it doesn't work." Effective implementation requires interpretation and understanding. Revision without adequate evaluation will not reflect what is learned from the original effort.

Although the framework may seem linear, its dimensions are intertwined. For example, because practice informs understanding, implementation can lead to a new or deeper interpretation of the standards or elements of them. Evaluation and reflection pervade all other dimensions.

The different dimensions of the framework are played out with different audiences, as shown in Table 1-2. These audiences are organized into four categories that reflect primary roles in the educational system: policy, program, practice, and political and public support.

The framework helps to address the question of how different stakeholders participate in standards-based reforms. For example, an interpretation activity for colleges and universities could be the development of a

Table 1-2. Participants in Standards-Based Education

Policy	Governors and State Legislators State Education Departments State and Local School Boards School Districts Schools
Programs	Colleges and Universities Publishers Curriculum and Assessment Developers School Districts Business and Industry Informal Educators Professional Organizations
Practices	Teachers Students
Political and Public Support	Scientists and Engineers Business and Industry Federal, State, and Local Governments Parents General Public Teacher Unions

publication that focuses on the role of design in the context of *Standards for Technological Literacy*. The publication would help post-secondary technology teacher education faculty and administrators to understand the standards more deeply so they could improve their teacher preparation programs. One challenge of standards-based reform is to strategically engage the key participants in such a way as to create the most leverage for change in the system.

Although the standards developers likely have major responsibility for dissemination, trained state agencies, special coalitions, or cadres of leaders especially can be equipped to do so. Responsibility and authority for implementation do not necessarily lie with the organizations that developed *Standards for Technological Literacy*. The organizations can provide support and expertise, as well as help in networking various implementers, but they are not always positioned to change policies and practices directly. State supervisors, curriculum developers, teacher educators, and classroom teachers assume major responsibility for implementation. Revision again becomes the responsibility of the developers, with substantial input and interaction with others in the system.

CONCLUSIONS

Standards for Technological Literacy will be an important tool in educational reform. In time, they should contribute to new perceptions of technology education within the larger educational community and a better understanding of technology by citizens. The profession need not be distracted from the vision. The technology education profession has developed the best standards possible. Now leaders of the profession must understand and establish commitment and direction within the community. They must explain to a broader public what technology standards are and why they are important, and pay very close attention to the single most important resource for achieving higher levels of technological literacy for all Americans—the classroom teachers of technology.

REFERENCES

American Association for the Advancement of Science (AAAS). (1993). *Benchmarks for science literacy.* Washington, DC: Author.

Atkin, J.M. (1990). Teach science for science's sake: For global competitiveness, try technology. *Education Week.* September 26: 32.

Black, P., & Atkin, J.M. (Eds.). (1996). *Changing the subject.* New York and London: Routledge.

Bugliarello, G. (1990). *The intelligent layman's guide to technology.* Brooklyn, NY: Polytechnic Press, Polytechnic University.

Burrill, G., & Kennedy, D. (1997). *Improving student learning in mathematics and science: The role of national standards in state policy.* Washington, DC: National Academy Press.

Bybee, R. (1997). *Achieving scientific literacy.* Portsmouth, NH: Heinemann.

Hutchinson, J., & Huberman, M. (1993, May). *Knowledge dissemination and use in science and mathematics education: A literature review.* Prepared for the Directorate of Education and Human Resources, Division of Research, Evaluation and Dissemination, National Science Foundation by the Network.

International Technology Education Association (ITEA). (1996). *A rationale and structure for the study of technology.* Reston, VA: Author.

International Technology Education Association (ITEA). (2000). *Standards for technological literacy: Content for the study of technology.* Reston, VA: Author.

National Research Council. (1996). *National science education standards.* Washington, DC: National Academy Press.

Raizen, S., Sellwood, P., Todd, R., & Vickers, M. (1995). *Technology education in the classroom.* San Francisco: Jossey-Bass.

Selby, C. (1993). Technology: From myths to realities. *Phi Delta Kappan* 74(9): 684-89.

Role of Standards in Different Subject Areas

Chapter 2

Pam Newberry
International Technology Education Association
Technology for All Americans

Linda S. Hallenbeck
Ohio Office of the Governor

A hallmark year in the reform movement of education was 1989. During that year President George Bush formed the National Education Goals Panel following the National Governors Association's endorsement of national education goals. The reform movement in education was further assisted by the publication of several key documents and the continuation of support by President William Clinton's administration.

The first publications to make a strong push for educational reform were *Everybody Counts: A Report to the Nation on the Future of Mathematics Education* by the National Research Council (NRC) and *Curriculum and Evaluation Standards for School Mathematics* by the National Council of Teachers of Mathematics (NCTM), both published in 1989. These two documents marked the beginning of the expansion of educational reform and the development of standards in other fields of study. In addition, the NCTM document demonstrated the need to open the door for participation of groups and individuals interested and responsible for the delivery of standards.

This chapter will make the reader aware that standards have been around since the late 1980s. The history of standards will enable the technology education profession to understand the context of the evolution of standards in general and learn what and what not to do for implementing *Standards for Technological Literacy: Content for the Study of Technology* (*Standards for Technological Literacy*). Also, the history identifies the interdisciplinary nature of the study of technology.

SCIENCE

History of Science Education Leading to National Science Education Standards

The American Association for the Advancement of Science (AAAS), through its Project 2061, published *Science for All Americans* in 1989 resulting in the clear call to action and the need for science literacy for all students. This publication paved the way for future developments of standards for science. Shortly after the release of *Science for All Americans*, the National Science Teachers Association (NSTA), through its Scope, Sequence, and Coordination Project, published *The Content Core*. The National Academy of Sciences (NAS) and the NRC coordinated the development of *National Science Education Standards* (Science Standards) in content, teaching, and assessment. The Department of Education (DOE) and the National Science Foundation (NSF) provided funding for the development of the science standards and the NRC established the National Committee on Science Education Standards and Assessment (NCSESA) to oversee the development of the *National Science Education Standards*.

NCSESA solicited input from large numbers of science teachers, scientists, science educators, and many others interested in science education. Numerous public presentations were made and the many suggestions for improving the drafts of the *National Science Education Standards* were collated and analyzed. Extensive revisions were made in preparation of a draft for national review. Many interpretations and statements of what all students should know and be able to do in science were based on the seminal work of AAAS Project 2061 and the publication of *Science for All Americans*, and the follow-up publication *Benchmarks for Science Literacy* (1993). After the national review by more than 18,000 individuals and 250 groups, the final publication of the *National Science Education Standards* was released in 1996.

Goals of the National Science Education Standards

The goals of school science that underlie the *National Science Education Standards* are to educate students who are able to:

- Experience the richness and excitement of knowing about and understanding the natural world;

- Use appropriate scientific processes and principles in making personal decisions;
- Engage intelligently in public discourse and debate about matters of scientific and technological concern; and
- Increase economic productivity through the use of the knowledge, understanding, and skills of the scientifically literate person in careers (NRC, 1996, p. 13).

Organization and Structure of National Science Education Standards

The *National Science Education Standards* are organized into eight chapters. Chapter 1 presents an introduction to the ideas behind the development of the *National Science Education Standards*. Chapter 2 provides the definitions of key terms and the principles and vision of science literacy for all students. The outline of the standards for science teaching is discussed in Chapter 3. These standards focus on what teachers should know and do. Chapter 4 follows with the professional development standards that outline the professional knowledge and skill needed to help in the development of science teachers. Together, Chapters 3 and 4 provide the basis for "...the conviction that scientific inquiry is at the heart of science and science learning" (NRC, 1996, p. 15). Chapter 5 provides the science education assessment standards in order to judge "...the quality of assessment practices" (NRC, 1996, p. 15). In addition, the science education assessment standards "...are also designed to be used as guides in developing assessment practices and policy. These standards apply equally to classroom-based and externally designed assessments and to formative and summative assessments" (NRC, 1996, p. 15).

The science content standards are divided into K-4, 5-8, and 9-12 grade levels and discussed in detail in Chapter 6. An underlying principle in the science content standards is the idea of inquiry. Traditional subject topics of physical, life, and earth and space sciences are discussed and provide clear expectations. In addition, the science content standards make connections between science and technology, science in personal and social perspectives, and the history and nature of science. Fundamental concepts that underlie each standard are discussed and are supplemented with information on developing student understanding of science.

The science program standards "...provide criteria for judging the quality of school and district science programs" (NRC, 1996, p. 16) and are found in Chapter 7. Chapter 8 includes the standards that reflect the criteria for the science education system beyond the school and district, reaching out to the people in the community who support schools. Examples of actual practice have been provided throughout the *National Science Education Standards* in order to demonstrate that the vision of the science standards is attainable provided students are given ample opportunity to study and learn science as it is recommended. Further, all students are represented in *National Science Education Standards*; therefore equity should be a part of all characteristics of science education.

Content of the National Science Education Standards

The *National Science Education Standards* provide six different sets of standards. Science teaching standards are covered in Chapter 3; standards for professional development for teachers of science are discussed in Chapter 4; assessment standards are covered in Chapter 5; science content standards are covered in Chapter 6; science education program standards are covered in Chapter 7; and science education system standards are depicted in Chapter 8. Table 2-1 illustrates the science content standards found in Chapter 6 and shows the main concepts to be taught by grade level cluster.

Note that Standard A, which focuses on inquiry, is treated as a content idea that is woven throughout the content standards. Also, it should be noted that the similar language of a standard does not show the various depth of coverage or building of ideas from one grade level to the next. In addition, the science content standards do not propose a curriculum, but provide a "...comprehensive vision of science education and will be most effective when used in conjunction with all of the standards described in [the *National Science Education Standards*]" (NRC, 1996, p. 103).

Throughout each of the science content standards are identified unifying concepts and processes that provide the conceptual and procedural schemes that help students develop an understanding that builds on prior experience and knowledge and helps in the connections and integration of that knowledge. The unifying concepts and processes are:

- Systems, order, and organization;
- Evidence, models, and explanation;

Table 2-1. National Science Education Standards, 1996

SCIENCE CONTENT STANDARDS	K-4	5-8	9-12
	As a result of activities in grades K–4, all students should develop	**As a result of activities in grades 5–8, all students should develop**	**As a result of activities in grades 9–12, all students should develop**
Standard A: Science as inquiry is basic to science understanding and is fundamental to all scientific experiences.	*Abilities necessary to do scientific inquiry *Understanding about scientific inquiry	*Abilities necessary to do scientific inquiry *Understandings about scientific inquiry	*Abilities necessary to do scientific inquiry *Understandings about scientific inquiry
Standard B: Comprises the physical science standard domain	*Properties of objects and materials *Position and motion of objects *Light, heat, electricity, and magnetism	*Properties and changes of properties in matter *Motions and forces *Transfer of energy	*Structure of atoms *Structure and properties of matter *Chemical reactions *Motions and forces *Conservation of energy and increase in disorder *Interactions of energy and matter
Standard C: Comprises the life science standard domain	*The characteristics of organisms *Life cycles of organisms *Organisms and environments	*Structure and function in living systems *Reproduction and heredity *Regulation and behavior *Populations and ecosystems *Diversity and adaptations of organisms	*The cell *Molecular basis of heredity *Biological evolution *Interdependence of organisms *Matter, energy, and organization in living systems *Behavior of organisms
Standard D: Comprises the earth and space science standard domain	*Properties of earth materials *Objects in the sky *Changes in earth and sky	*Structure of the earth system *Earth's history *Earth in the solar system	*Energy in the earth system *Geochemical cycles *Origin and evolution of the earth system *Origin and evolution of the universe

(Continued on next page.)

Table 2-1. National Science Education Standards, 1996 (continued)

SCIENCE CONTENT STANDARDS	K-4	5-8	9-12
	As a result of activities in grades K-4, all students should develop	As a result of activities in grades 5-8, all students should develop	As a result of activities in grades 9-12, all students should develop
Standard E: Comprises the science and technology standard domain	*Abilities of technological design *Understanding about science and technology *Abilities to distinguish between natural objects and objects made by humans	*Abilities of technological design *Understandings about science and technology	*Abilities of technological design *Understandings about science and technology
Standard F: Comprises the science in personal and social perspectives standard domain	*Personal health *Characteristics and changes in populations *Types of resources *Changes in environments *Science and technology in local challenges	*Personal health *Populations, resources, and environments *Natural hazards *Risks and benefits *Science and technology in society	*Personal and community health *Population growth *Natural resources *Environmental quality *Natural and human-induced hazards *Science and technology in local, national, and global challenges
Standard G: Comprises the history and nature of science standard domain	*Science as a human endeavor	*Science as a human endeavor *Nature of science *History of science	*Science as a human endeavor *Nature of scientific knowledge *Historical perspectives

- Change, constancy, and measurement;
- Evolution and equilibrium; and
- Form and function

The unifying concepts and processes standard can be the focus of instruction at any grade level but should always be closely linked to outcomes aligned with other content standards (NRC, 1996, p. 6).

The National Science Education Standards *Related to* Standards for Technological Literacy

Standard E: Science and Technology standard "…emphasizes developing the ability to design a solution to a problem and understanding the relationship of science and technology and the way people are involved in both" (NRC, 1996, p. 135). Standard F: Science in Personal and Social Perspectives standard emphasizes that "People continue inventing new ways of doing things, solving problems, and getting work done. New ideas and inventions often affect other people; sometimes the effects are good and sometimes they are bad" (NRC, 1996, p. 140). These two science content standards provide a starting point for science teachers to begin to incorporate the study of technology into their classrooms. In addition, the recognition for the need for technological literacy enables science and technology teachers to demonstrate the distinctions between science and technology, yet make the connections of science while minimizing the idea that technology is "applied" science.

Examination of Science Standard E and Standard F reveals a relationship with *Standards for Technological Literacy*, in particular those dealing with design and its application. Together, the two science content standards, in conjunction with *Standards for Technological Literacy*, offer an opportunity for science and technology teachers to discuss the relationships between science and technology and to clearly point out the distinctions. This enables students to build on their experiences in both science and technology laboratory-classrooms and to use the resources available to them to develop central ideas that provide the foundations for students' understandings and actions as citizens.

BENCHMARKS FOR SCIENCE LITERACY

History of AAAS, Project 2061 - Leading to Benchmarks for Science Literacy

In 1993, the AAAS Project 2061 published *Benchmarks for Science Literacy* to specify the steps necessary to increase understanding of students in K-12 in order to "develop adult literacy—what all students should know and be able to do when they leave high school" (AAAS, 1993, inside cover). As stated in the history section of the development of the *National Science Education Standards*, the ideas behind the development of *Benchmarks for Science Literacy* came from the groundwork studied and debated in the publication of Project 2061's *Science for All Americans* (AAAS, 1989) in 1989. It was recognized from the start that teachers and educators would need support and guidance in the development of "...curricula that would meet the content standards of [the *National Science Education Standards*]" (AAAS, 1993, p. 303).

Over a period of several years, the six 25-member teams consisting of teachers from elementary, middle, and high school; principals; and curriculum specialists covering subjects such as physical sciences, social studies, mathematics, technology, and other disciplines formulated the ideas of *Benchmarks for Science Literacy*. It is recognized that *Science for All Americans* deliberately omits much of the traditional content of science, mathematics, and technology found in curricula and textbooks, and contains materials that most teachers find totally unfamiliar. Few teachers have had the opportunity to become familiar with how science really works, study the history of science, explore themes that cut across disciplines, or learn engineering concepts. Moreover, there is little crossover in the education, training, and experiences of secondary school teachers in science, mathematics, and technology. Also, the background of most high school science teachers is limited to biology, earth and space, or physical sciences. It is not unusual for elementary teachers to have very little of any of these subjects in college (AAAS, 1993, p. 305).

The team members met with and interviewed a variety of scientists, engineers, mathematicians, historians, and other representatives in order to learn more about science, mathematics, and technology. They worked in cross-discipline, cross-grade discussion groups, participated in inquiry and design projects, and built upon each other's understandings to help formulate and write the steps necessary to develop science literacy for students in grade clusters K-2, 3-5, 6-8, and 9-12. To aid them in their writing, they developed a process known as "mapping." The process "…required groups to link more sophisticated ideas in later grades to the more basic ones suitable in the earlier years" (AAAS, 1993, p. 305). The team members began to ask and look for "…what would count as evidence of student understanding" (AAAS, 1993, p. 307) and learning.

The draft of *Benchmarks for Science Literacy* was available for review in the early part of 1993. More than 1,000 reviewers from groups who were asked to review the document and those who volunteered or requested an opportunity to review the document were given a chance to voice their opinions. They were asked to "…appraise the technical accuracy of the science document, the necessity and sufficiency of precursors provided to anticipate later concepts, the appropriateness of grade-level placement, the acceptability of the language, and the overall usefulness of the benchmarks" (AAAS, 1993, p. 308). After all reviews were compiled and analyzed and rewrites were completed, the document was published with the understanding that future updates and revisions would be necessary based on new findings on how children learn. Thus in the future it will be determined "…which benchmarks should be shifted, eliminated, elaborated…or even left alone" (AAAS, 1993, p. 309).

Goals of Benchmarks for Science Literacy

The goals and characteristics of *Benchmarks for Science Literacy* describe its purpose and intent. They are:

- *Benchmarks for Science Literacy* is a report from a cross-section of practicing educators.
- *Benchmarks for Science Literacy* is different from a curriculum, a curriculum framework, a curriculum design, or a plan for a curriculum.
- *Benchmarks for Science Literacy* is a compendium of specific science literacy goals that can be organized however one chooses.
- *Benchmarks for Science Literacy* specifies thresholds rather than average or advanced performance.
- *Benchmarks for Science Literacy* concentrates on the common core of learning that contributes to the science literacy of all students.
- *Benchmarks for Science Literacy* avoids technical language used for its own sake.
- *Benchmarks for Science Literacy* sheds only partial light on how to achieve the goals it recommends.

- *Benchmarks for Science Literacy* is informed by research.
- *Benchmarks for Science Literacy* is a developing product.
- *Benchmarks for Science Literacy* is but one of a family of tools being designed by Project 2061.
- *Benchmarks for Science Literacy* is a companion for *Science for All Americans*, not a substitute (AAAS, 1993, pp. xii-xiv).

Organization and Structure of Benchmarks for Science Literacy

Benchmarks for Science Literacy is organized into 16 chapters, with the first 12 discussing the benchmarks themselves. The remaining four chapters provide the background for the development of *Benchmarks for Science Literacy*. Chapters 1, 2, and 3 focus on the Nature of Science, Mathematics, and Technology, respectively. Each chapter focuses on the particular subject matter and related enterprises, taking care to clearly define and outline the experiences needed by students to develop an understanding of science, mathematics, and technology, and how they are related. Chapter 4 follows with the physical setting, covering topics related to the universe and the earth with related processes that shape the earth, the structure of matter, energy transformations, forces, and motion.

The living environment follows in Chapter 5, covering discussions on the diversity of life, heredity, and the make-up of life from cells to their evolution. Chapter 6 focuses more deeply on the human organism, in particular, and covers basic functions of bodily organs related to physical health, well being, and the learning process. The human society follows in Chapter 7, spotlighting social, political, and global behavior. Chapter 8 delves into what students should know and learn about concepts and systems in technology. Chapter 9 provides a view of the mathematical world, highlighting what is necessary for mathematical understanding, such as number sense and symbiotic relationships. A historical perspective in the history of science is covered in Chapter 10. Common themes are explored in Chapter 11. These themes, systems, models, and constancy and change, are discussed in detail. They provide a foundation for the interrelations of science, mathematics, and technology, as well as exploring their distinctions. Chapter 12 focuses on habits of the mind, encompassing how students develop computational and estimation skills, and critical thinking and response skills.

Table 2-2 provides a quick reference to the chapters. Unlike the *National Science Education Standards* and *Standards for Technological Literacy*, *Benchmarks for Science Literacy* does not include a set of standards, but contains "statements of what *all* students should know and be able to do in science, mathematics, and technology by the end of grades 2, 5, 8, and 12" (AAAS, 1993, p. xi). The word "know" implies that students can explain ideas in their own words, relate the ideas to other benchmarks and apply the ideas in novel contexts" (AAAS, 1993, p. xviii).

<u>Content of Benchmarks for Science Literacy</u>

Three sections of *Benchmarks for Science Literacy* are illustrated in Tables 2-3, 2-4, and 2-5. They show how the ideas that are conveyed are mapped and move through grades building on prior knowledge and experience. Likewise, the sections that are illustrated are those that are most aligned with the ideas expressed in *Standards for Technological Literacy*. Tables 2-3, 2-4, and 2-5 depict the benchmarks for kindergarten through grade 12 and are related to Chapters 3, 8, and 11 respectively.

<u>Benchmarks for Science Literacy *Related to* Standards for Technological Literacy</u>

A major distinction between *Benchmarks for Science Literacy* and *Standards for Technological Literacy* needs to be discussed on the outset. *Benchmarks for Science Literacy* is written with statements that identify what every student should know and be able to do in science, mathematics, and technology, kindergarten through grade 12. In contrast, *Standards for Technological Literacy* is written with standards that specify what every student should know and be able to do in technology and each standard has an accompanying list of statements for kindergarten through grade 12 that provide guidance on how the student may achieve the standard. Therefore, *Standards for Technological Literacy* uses the idea of standards from the *National Science Education Standards* and the idea of benchmarks from *Benchmarks for Science Literacy* and combines them in a presentation of technological literacy.

Table 2-2. Benchmarks for Science Literacy
Chapter Headings and Subheadings

Benchmarks Chapters	Kindergarten through Grade 12 Related Chapter Subheadings
Chapter 1: The Nature of Science	A. The Scientific World View B. Scientific Inquiry C. The Scientific Enterprise
Chapter 2: The Nature of Mathematics	A. Patterns and Relationships B. Mathematics, Science, and Technology C. Mathematical Inquiry
Chapter 3: The Nature of Technology	A. Technology and Science B. Design and Systems C. Issues in Technology
Chapter 4: The Physical Setting	A. The Universe B. The Earth C. Processes that Shape the Earth D. Structure of Matter E. Energy Transformations F. Motion G. Forces of Nature
Chapter 5: The Living Environment	A. Diversity of Life B. Heredity C. Cells D. Interdependence of Life E. Flow of Matter and Energy F. Evolution of Life
Chapter 6: The Human Organism	A. Human Identity B. Human Development C. Basic Functions D. Learning E. Physical Health F. Mental Health
Chapter 7: Human Society	A. Cultural Effects on Behavior B. Group Behavior C. Social Change D. Social Trade-Offs E. Political and Economic Systems F. Social Conflict G. Global Interdependence

Table 2-2. *Benchmarks for Science Literacy*
Chapter Headings and Subheadings (continued)

Benchmarks **Chapters**	**Kindergarten through Grade 12** **Related Chapter Subheadings**
Chapter 8: The Designed World	A. Agriculture B. Materials and Manufacturing C. Energy Sources and Use D. Communication E. Information Processing F. Health Technology
Chapter 9: The Mathematical World	A. Numbers B. Symbolic Relationships C. Shapes D. Uncertainty E. Reasoning
Chapter 10: Historical Perspectives	A. Displacing the Earth from the Center of the Universe B. Uniting the Heavens and Earth C. Relating Matter & Energy and Time & Space D. Extending Time E. Moving the Continents F. Understanding Fire G. Splitting the Atom H. Explaining the Diversity of Life I. Discovering Germs J. Harnessing Power
Chapter 11: Common Themes	A. Systems B. Models C. Constancy and Change D. Scale
Chapter 12: Habits of Mind	A. Values and Attitudes B. Computation and Estimation C. Manipulation and Observation D. Communication Skills E. Critical-Response Skills

Table 2-3. *Benchmarks for Science Literacy*, 1993, pp. 49-52

Benchmark Chapter and Subheading	Kindergarten through Grade 2	Grades 3 through 5	Grades 6 through 8	Grades 9 through 12
Chapter 3: The Nature of Technology 3b: Design and Systems	By the end of the 2nd grade, students should know that *People can use objects and ways of doing things to solve problems. *People may not be able to actually make or do everything that they can design.	By the end of the 5th grade, students should know that *There is no perfect design. Designs that are best in one respect (safety or ease of use, for example) may be inferior in other ways (cost or appearance). *Usually some features must be sacrificed to get others. How such trade-offs are received depends upon which features are emphasized and which are down-played.	By the end of the 8th grade, students should know that *Design usually requires taking constraints into account. Some constraints, such as gravity or the properties of the materials to be used, are unavoidable. Other constraints, including economic, political, social, ethical, and aesthetic ones, limit choices. *All technologies have effects other than those intended by the design, some of which may have been predictable and some not. In either case, these side effects may turn out to be unacceptable to some of the population and therefore lead to conflict between groups. *Almost all control systems have inputs, outputs, and	By the end of he 12th grade, students should know that *In designing a device or process, thought should be given to how it will be manufactured, operated, maintained, replaced, and disposed of and who will sell, operate, and take care of it. The costs associated with these functions may introduce yet more constraints on the design. *The value of any given technology may be different for different groups of people and at different points in time. *Complex systems have layers of controls. Some controls operate particular parts of the system and some control other controls. Even fully automatic systems require human control at some point.

(Continued on next page.)

Table 2-3. Benchmarks for Science Literacy, 1993, pp. 49-52 (continued)

Benchmark Chapter and Subheading	Kindergarten through Grade 2	Grades 3 through 5	Grades 6 through 8	Grades 9 through 12
Chapter 3: The Nature of Technology 3b: Design and Systems			feedback. The essence of control is comparing information about what is happening to what people want to happen and then making appropriate adjustments. This procedure requires sensing information, processing it, and making changes. In almost all modern machines, microprocessors serve as centers of performance control. *Systems fail because they have faulty or poorly matched parts, are used in ways that exceed what was intended by the design, or were poorly designed to begin with. The most common ways to prevent failure are pretesting parts and procedures, overdesign, and redundancy.	*Risk analysis is used to minimize the likelihood of unwanted side effects of a new technology. The public perception of risk may depend, however, on psychological factors as well as scientific ones. *The more parts and connections a system has, the more ways it can go wrong. Complex systems usually have components to detect, back up, bypass, or compensate for minor failures. *To reduce the chance of system failure, performance testing is often conducted using small-scale models, computer simulations, analogous systems, or just the parts of the system thought to be least reliable.

Table 2-4. *Benchmarks for Science Literacy*, 1993, pp. 188-191

Benchmark Chapter and Subheading	Kindergarten through Grade 2	Grades 3 through 5	Grades 6 through 8	Grades 9 through 12
Chapter 8: The Designed World 8b: Materials and Manufacturing	By the end of the 2nd grade, students should know that *Some kinds of materials are better than others for making any particular thing. Materials that are better in some ways (such as stronger or cheaper) may be worse in other ways (heavier or harder to cut). *Several steps are usually involved in making things. *Tools are used to help make things, and some things cannot be made at all without tools. *Each kind of tool has a special purpose. *Some materials can be used over again.	By the end of the 5th grade, students should know that *Naturally occurring materials such as wood, clay, cotton, and animal skins may be processed or combined with other materials to change their properties. *Through science and technology, a wide variety of materials that do not appear in nature at all have become available, ranging from steel to nylon to liquid crystals. *Discarded products contribute to the problem of waste disposal. Sometimes it is possible to use the materials in them to make new products, but materials differ widely in the ease with which they can be recycled. *Through mass production, the time required to make a product and its cost can be greatly reduced. Although many things	By the end of the 8th grade, students should know that *The choice of materials for a job depends on their properties and on how they interact with other materials. Similarly, the usefulness of some manufactured parts of an object depends on how well they fit together with other parts. *Manufacturing usually involves a series of steps, such as designing, obtaining product and preparing raw materials, processing the materials mechanically or chemically, and assembling, testing inspecting, and packaging. The sequence of these steps is also often important. *Modern technology reduces manufacturing costs, produces more uniform products, and creates new synthetic materials that can help reduce the depletion of some natural resources.	By the end of the 12th grade, students should know that *Manufacturing processes have been changed by improved tools and techniques based on more thorough scientific understanding, increases in the forces that can be applied and the temperatures that can be reached, and the availability of electronic controls that make operations occur more rapidly and consistently. *Waste management includes considerations of quantity, safety, degradability, and cost. It requires social and technological innovations, because waste-disposal problems are political and economic as well as technical. *Scientific research identifies new materials and new uses of known materials. *Increased knowledge of the

(Continued on next page.)

Table 2-4. *Benchmarks for Science Literacy*, 1993, pp. 188-191 (continued)

Benchmark Chapter and Subheading	Kindergarten through Grade 2	Grades 3 through 5	Grades 6 through 8	Grades 9 through 12
Chapter 8: The Designed World 8b: Materials and Manufacturing	By the end of the 2nd grade, students should know that	By the end of the 5th grade, students should know that are still made by hand in some parts of the world, almost everything in the most technologically developed countries is now produced using automatic machines. Even automatic machines require human supervision.	By the end of the 8th grade, students should know that *Automation, including the use of robots, has changed the nature of work in most fields, including manufacturing. As a result, high-skill, high-knowledge jobs in engineering, computer programming, quality control, supervision, and maintenance are replacing many routine, manual-labor jobs. Workers therefore need better learning skills and flexibility to take on new and rapidly changing jobs.	By the end of the 12th grade, students should know that molecular structure of materials helps in the design and synthesis of new materials for special purposes.

Table 2-5. *Benchmarks for Science Literacy,* 1993, pp. 264-266

Benchmark Chapter and Subheading	Kindergarten through Grade 2	Grades 3 through 5	Grades 6 through 8	Grades 9 through 12
Chapter 11: Common Themes 11a: Systems	By the end of the 2nd grade, students should know that *Most things are made of parts. *Something may not work if some of its parts are missing. *When parts are put together, they can do things that they couldn't do by themselves.	By the end of the 5th grade, students should know that *In something that consists of many parts, the parts usually influence one another. *Something may not work as well (or at all) if a part of it is missing, broken, worn out, mismatched, or misconnected.	By the end of the 8th grade, students should know that *A system can include processes as well as things. *Thinking about things as systems means looking for how every part relates to others. The output from one part of a system (which can include materials, energy, or information) can become the input to other parts. Such feedback can serve to control what goes on in the system as a whole. *Any system is usually connected to other systems, both internally and externally. Thus a system may be thought of as containing subsystems and as being a subsystem of a larger system.	By the end of the 12th grade, students should know that *A system usually has some properties that are different from those of its parts, but appear because of the interaction of those parts. *Understanding how things work and designing solutions to problems of almost any kind can be facilitated by systems analysis. In defining a system, it is important to specify its boundaries and subsystems, indicate its relation to other systems, and identify what its input and its output are expected to be. *The successful operation of a designed system usually involves feedback. The feedback of output from some parts of a system to input for other parts can be used to

(Continued on next page.)

Table 2-5. *Benchmarks for Science Literacy*, 1993, pp. 264-266 (continued)

Benchmark Chapter and Subheading	Kindergarten through Grade 2	Grades 3 through 5	Grades 6 through 8	Grades 9 through 12
Chapter 11: Common Themes **11a: Systems**	**By the end of the 2nd grade, students should know that**	**By the end of the 5th grade, students should know that**	**By the end of the 8th grade, students should know that**	**By the end of the 12th grade, students should know that** encourage what is going on in a system, discourage it, or reduce its discrepancy from some desired value. The stability of a system can be great when it includes appropriate feedback mechanisms. *Even in some very simple systems, it may not always be possible to predict accurately the result of changing some part or connection.

As stated before, there are three chapters of *Benchmarks for Science Literacy* that make direct correlations to the standards listed in *Standards for Technological Literacy*. These chapters are Chapter 3: The Nature of Technology, Chapter 8: The Designed World, and Chapter 11: Common Themes. Without listing all possible connections and relationships, the key ideas presented in Tables 2-3, 2-4, and 2-5 help to demonstrate the inter-relations between science and technology and their distinctions. In addition to the specific chapters discussed above, there are sections in other chapters that also make a connection or passing comment that is in direct correlation to or integrates the study of technology. For example, "Chapter 10: Historical Perspectives, includes a discussion of the Industrial Revolution" (AAAS, 1993, p. 42). It is to the advantage of technology teachers to be aware of the ideas and concepts presented in *Benchmarks for Science Literacy*. A clear understanding of the relationships between *Benchmarks for Science Literacy* and *Standards for Technological Literacy* will help teachers dialogue about how "...technology has been a powerful force in the development of civilization, all the more so as its link with science has been forged" (AAAS, 1993, p. 41).

MATHEMATICS

History of Mathematics Education—Leading to Principles and Standards for School Mathematics

The National Council of Teachers of Mathematics (NCTM) worked for more than three years before the 1989 historic release of their first standards, *Curriculum and Evaluation Standards for School Mathematics*. By 1991, NCTM released *Professional Standards for Teaching Mathematics*, followed by the 1995 release of the *Assessment Standards for School Mathematics*. NCTM looked to the future, and thus continued the ongoing process of evaluating the standards to improve mathematics education.

By October of 1998, NCTM had a new draft document of standards. Copies of the draft were circulated to over 30,000 readers and various associations. Readers were requested to provide feedback. In April of 2000, at the national conference, NCTM released *Principles and Standards for School Mathematics*. The 402-paged document encompasses curriculum, professional, and assessment standards in a single document as it strengthens the rigor of mathematics education and builds on the trio of standards released in 1989.

Clearly the 1989 *Curriculum and Evaluation Standards for School Mathematics* had a profound impact on mathematics education in the United States. Learned societies looked to NCTM as a model for creating standards. Mathematics educators turned to the 1989 standards to support mathematics reform. While it is too early to know the impact of *Principles and Standards for School Mathematics,* there is no doubt the standards will influence the future of mathematics education in the United States.

Goals of Mathematics Education

Principles and Standards for School Mathematics "…supplies guidance and vision while leaving specific curriculum decisions to the local level" (NCTM, 2000, p. 6). Not only does the document set goals for mathematics education for students of mathematics, as well as teachers, it also provides resources for educators teaching mathematics. *Principles and Standards for School Mathematics* can serve as a common tool or basis for communication in mathematics education.

Teachers can use *Principles and Standards for School Mathematics* to guide not only the rigor of the curriculum, but also to guide their role in the classroom, as well as the role of assessment. The standards help teachers see the connections within mathematics as well as connections to other curriculum and fields of study. Such a connection example, in the content area of measurement, inspires teachers to see that "Opportunities to use and understand measurement arise naturally during high school in other areas of mathematics, in science, and in technical education" (NCTM, 2000, p. 321).

The intent of the document is to:

- Set forth a comprehensive and coherent set of goals for mathematics for all students from pre-kindergarten through grade 12 that will orient curricular, teaching, and assessment efforts during the next decades;

- Serve as a resource for teachers, education leaders, and policy makers to use in examining and improving the quality of mathematics instructional programs;

- Guide the development of curriculum frameworks, assessments, and instructional materials; and

- Stimulate ideas and on-going conversations at the national, provincial or state, and local levels about how best to help students gain a deep understanding of important mathematics (NCTM, 2000, p. 6).

Organization and Structure of the Principles and Standards for School Mathematics

The *Principles and Standards for School Mathematics* contains six guiding principles, five content standards, and five process standards for mathematics. The eight-chapter document devotes the first chapter to the vision for school mathematics. The second chapter gives a brief overview of each of the six principles of school mathematics. These principles serve as a foundation in describing characteristics of high-quality mathematics education.

The third chapter serves as an introduction to the 10 standards for school mathematics from pre-kindergarten through grade 12, while Chapters 4, 5, 6, and 7 delve more deeply into the standards by grade bands. *Principles and Standards for School Mathematics* has designed four grade bands as: Pre-Kindergarten-2, 3-5, 6-8, and 9-12. All of the five content standards and five process standards are included in each of the four grade bands with specific expectations delineated within the given grade band as shown in Figure 2-1.

Content of the Principles and Standards for School Mathematics

"Standards are descriptions of what mathematics instruction should enable students to know and do" (NCTM, 2000, p. 28). *Principles and Standards for School Mathematics* was written with knowledge of the enormous task that lie ahead for mathematics educators, that "...teaching mathematics well is a complex endeavor, and there are no easy recipes" (NCTM, 2000, p. 17) and that the standards would be rigorous. "Ambitious standards are required to achieve a society that has the capability to think and reason mathematically" (NCTM, 2000, p. 28).

"Historically, number has been a cornerstone of the mathematics curriculum" (NCTM, 2000, p. 32), and thus begins the process in delineation in presenting *Principles and Standards for School Mathematics*.

While one may note the standards are listed for each content and process, which spread the width of all grades from Pre-Kindergarten-12, one must also be aware that each specific grade band clearly delineates more specific expectations for instructional programs for students within each standard. As indicated in Table 2-6, each standard extends throughout the grades, the depth of the studies by grade band is reflected in the number of specific expectations as well as the complexity of each. As illus-

Figure 2-1. *PSSM*, 2000, p. 30

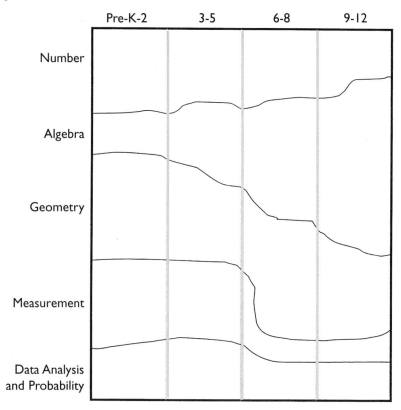

trated in the following three examples, one specific standard for instructional programs within algebra, geometry, and measurement have been taken and the expanded expectations per grade band have been cited. Thus each of the standards listed in Table 2-6 (*National Science Education Standards*) replicate the design to be shown in Tables 2-7, 2-8, and 2-9 (*Principles and Standards for School Mathematics*). That is to say, all general standards are more clearly defined as grade level expectations.

Table 2-6. *Principles and Standards for School Mathematics, 2000*

Note: Shaded areas are further developed through Tables 2-7, 2-8, and 2-9.

Mathematics Content Standards	Instructional programs from pre-kindergarten through grade 12 should enable all students to —
Number & Operations	*Understand numbers, ways of representing numbers, relationships among numbers, and number systems *Understand meaning of operations and how they relate to one another *Compute fluently and make reasonable estimates
Algebra	*Understand patterns, relations, and functions *Represent and analyze mathematical situations and structures using algebraic symbols *Use mathematical models to represent and understand quantitative relationships *Analyze change in various contents
Geometry	*Analyze characteristics and properties of two-and three-dimensional geometric shapes and develop mathematical arguments about geometric relationships *Specify locations and describe spatial relationships using coordinate geometry and other representational systems *Apply transformations and use symmetry to analyze mathematical situations *Use visualization, spatial reasoning, and geometric modeling to solve problems
Measurement	*Understand measurable attributes of objects and the units, systems, and processes of measurement *Apply appropriate techniques, tools, and formulas to determine measurement
Data Analysis & Probability	*Formulate questions that can be addressed with data and collect, organize, and display relevant data to answer them *Select and use appropriate statistical methods to analyze data *Develop and evaluate inferences and predictions that are based on data *Understand and apply basic concepts of probability
Problem Solving	*Build new mathematical knowledge through problem solving *Solve problems that arise in mathematics and in other contexts *Apply and adapt a variety of appropriate strategies to solve problems *Monitor and reflect on the process of mathematical problem solving

Table 2-6. *Principles and Standards for School Mathematics,* 2000 (cont.)

Reasoning & Proof	*Recognize reasoning and proof as fundamental aspects of mathematics *Make and investigate mathematical conjectures *Develop and evaluate mathematical arguments and proofs *Select and use various types of reasoning and methods of proof
Communication	*Organize and consolidate their mathematical thinking through communication *Communicate their mathematical thinking coherently and clearly to peers, teachers, and others *Analyze and evaluate the mathematical thinking and strategies of others *Use the language of mathematics to express mathematical ideas precisely
Connections	*Recognize and use connections among mathematical ideas *Understand how mathematical ideas interconnect and build on one another to produce a coherent whole *Recognize and apply mathematics in contexts outside of mathematics
Representation	*Create and use representations to organize, record, and communicate mathematical ideas *Select, apply, and translate among mathematical representations to solve problems *Use representations to model and interpret physical, social, and mathematical phenomena

Table 2-7. Algebra Standard Excerpt: One of Four Standards in Content Area of Algebra (PSSM, 2000)

Algebra Content Standard	Pre-K-2 Expectations	Grades 3-5 Expectations	Grades 6-8 Expectations	Grades 9-12 Expectations
	Instructional programs from prekindergarten through grade 12 should enable all students to—	Instructional programs from prekindergarten through grade 12 should enable all students to—	Instructional programs from prekindergarten through grade 12 should enable all students to—	Instructional programs from prekindergarten through grade 12 should enable all students to—
Understand patterns, relations, and functions	*Sort, classify and order objectives by size, number, and other properties; *Recognize, describe, and extend patterns such as sequence of sounds and shapes or simple numeric patterns and translate from one representation to another; *Analyze how both repeating and growing patterns are generated.	*Describe, extend, and make generalizations about geometric and numeric patterns; *Represent and analyze patterns and functions, using words, tables and graphs.	*Represent, analyze, and generalize a variety of patterns with tables, graphs, words, and when possible, symbolic rules; *Relate and compare different forms of representation for a relationship; *Identify functions as linear or nonlinear and contrast their properties from tables, graphs, or equations.	*Generalize patterns using explicitly defined and recursively defined functions; *Understand relations and functions and select convert flexibly among, and use various representations for them; *Analyze functions of one variable by investigating rates of change, intercepts, zeros, asymptotes, and local and global behavior; *Understand and perform transformations such as arithmetically combining, composing, and inverting commonly used functions, using technology to perform such operations on more complicated symbolic expressions; *Understand and compare the properties of classes of functions, including exponential, polynomial, rational, logarithmic, and periodic functions; *Interpret representations of functions of two variables.

Table 2-8. Geometry Standard Excerpt: One of Four Standards in Content Area of Geometry (PSSM, 2000)

Geometry Standard	Pre-K-2 Expectations	Grades 3-5 Expectations	Grades 6-8 Expectations	Grades 9-12 Expectations
	Instructional programs from prekindergarten through grade 12 should enable all students to—	Instructional programs from prekindergarten through grade 12 should enable all students to—	Instructional programs from prekindergarten through grade 12 should enable all students to—	Instructional programs from prekindergarten through grade 12 should enable all students to—
Use visualization, spatial reasoning, and geometric modeling to solve problems	*Create mental images of geometric shapes using spatial memory; *Recognize and represent shapes from different perspectives; *Relate ideas in geometry to ideas in number and measurement; *Recognize geometric shapes and structures in the environment and specify their location.	*Build and draw geometric objects; *Create and describe mental images of objects, patterns, and paths; *Identify and build a three-dimensional object from two-dimensional representations of that object; *Identify and build a two-dimensional representation of a three-dimensional object; *Use geometric models to solve problems in other areas of mathematics, such as number and measurement; *Recognize geometric ideas and relationships and apply them to other disciplines and to problems that arise in the classroom or in everyday life.	*Precisely describe, classify, and understand relationships among types of two- and three-dimensional objects using their defining properties; *Understand relationships among angles, side lengths, perimeters, area, volumes of similar objects; *Create and critique inductive and deductive arguments concerning geometric ideas and relationships, such as congruence, similarity, and the Pythagorean relationship.	*Analyze; *Explore relationships (including congruence and similarity) among classes of two- and three-dimensional geometric objects, make and test conjectures about them, and solve problems involving them; *Establish the validity of geometric conjectures using deduction, prove theorems, and critique arguments made by others; *Use trigonometric relationships to determine lengths and angle measures.

Table 2-9. Measurement Standard Excerpt: One of Two Standards in Content Area of Measurement (PSSM, 2000)

Measurement Standard	Pre-K-2 Expectations	Grades 3-5 Expectations	Grades 6-8 Expectations	Grades 9-12 Expectations
	Instructional programs from prekindergarten through grade 12 should enable all students to—	Instructional programs from prekindergarten through grade 12 should enable all students to—	Instructional programs from prekindergarten through grade 12 should enable all students to—	Instructional programs from prekindergarten through grade 12 should enable all students to—
Understand measurable attributes of objects and the units, systems, and process of measurement	*Recognize the attributes of length, volume, weight, area, and time; *Compare and order objects according to these attributes; *Understand how to measure using nonstandard and standard units; *Select an appropriate unit and tool for the attribute being measured.	*Understand such attributes as length, area, weight, volume, and size of angle and select the appropriate type of unit for measuring each attribute; *Understand the need for measuring with standard units and become familiar with standard units in the customary and metric systems; *Carry out simple unit conversions, such as from centimeters to meters, within a system of measurement; *Understand that measurements are approximations and understand how differences in units affect precision; *Explore what happens to measurement of a two-dimensional shape such as perimeter and area when the shape is changed in some way.	*Understand both metric and customary systems of measurement; *Understand relationships among units and convert from one unit to another within the same system; *Understand, select, and use units of appropriate size and type to measure angles, perimeter, area, surface area, and volume.	*Make decisions about units and scales that are appropriate for problem situations involving measurement.

<u>Principles and Standards for School Mathematics *Related to* Standards for Technological Literacy</u>

The *Principles and Standards for School Mathematics* and *Standards for Technological Literacy* complement each other. As one reads from the *Principles and Standards for School Mathematics* such verbiage as, "In some activities, models allow a view of a real-world phenomenon, such as the flow of traffic, through an analytic structure imposed on it" (NCTM, 2000, p. 70), may make one feel as if he or she is reading from *Standards for Technological Literacy.* "Systematic reasoning is a defining feature of mathematics" (NCTM, 2000, p. 57) as systematic thinking is a defining feature of technology.

Not only do Tables 2-7, 2-8, and 2-9 illustrate the width of all grades Pre-kindergarten-12, as well as the specific grade band expectations within each standard, they also illustrate common connections that mathematics and technology share. Technology and mathematics educators can find value in reading and referencing both documents to produce students who can globally compete in tomorrow's world. "Change is an ubiquitous feature of contemporary life, so learning with understanding is essential to enable students to use what they learn to solve the new kinds of problems they will inevitably face in the future" (NCTM, 2000, pp. 20-21).

COMPARISON OF *NATIONAL SCIENCE EDUCATION STANDARDS, BENCHMARKS FOR SCIENCE LITERACY, PRINCIPLES AND STAN-DARDS FOR SCHOOL MATHEMATICS,* AND *STANDARDS FOR TECHNOLOGICAL LITERACY*

Technology has many interdependent relationships with science and mathematics. These points are made clear when studying the four documents: *National Science Education Standards, Benchmarks for Science Literacy, Principles and Standards for School Mathematics*, and *Standards for Technological Literacy.* Helping students become informed about the history of technology, apart from that of science and mathematics, yet rich in interrelationships, is necessary for complete understanding.

With the ideas and concepts identified that correlate and support each subject matter, there are clear distinctions in the format and layout of each document. In addition to specifying the standards that every student needs to know and be able to do in order to understand science in the *National Science Education Standards* or mathematics in the *Principles and Standards for School Mathematics,* each document serves as a guide to help teachers in their classroom roles and to provide assessment to determine student learning and understanding. In contrast, *Benchmarks for Science Literacy* does not provide additional guidance for a teacher, however, this is clarified in companion documents titled, *Designs for Science Literacy* (AAAS, 2000) and *Blueprints for Reform, Science, Mathematics, and Technology Education* (AAAS, 1999).

A major concept, system thinking, is common across all four documents. System thinking is the ability to analyze parts, subsystems, interactions, and matching of parts beyond just calling them a system.

> The main goal of having students learn about systems is not to have them talk about systems in abstract terms, but to enhance their ability (and inclination) to attend to various aspects of particular systems in attempting to understand or deal with the whole system (AAAS, 1993, p. 262).

In addition, the documents recommend offering opportunities to learn about systems in a variety of approaches to enable students the opportunity to understand a system and how its components interact. Research has shown that students develop misconceptions about systems and their properties, as well as develop misunderstandings about systems when viewed in limited situations.

OTHER SUBJECT MATTERS STANDARDS RELATED TO *STANDARDS FOR TECHNOLOGI-CAL LITERACY*

Geography for Life *Standards*

Geography for Life (GESP, 1994, p. 243) states that the guidelines for geographic education, K-12, established the five themes of geography: location, place, region, human environment and interaction, and movement. The five themes led to the development of five skills: asking geographic questions, acquiring geographic information, organizing geographic information, analyzing geographic information, and answering geographic questions. The results of this initial work led to the development of the Geography Education National Implementation Project in 1985, which developed guidelines for grades K-12 from 1987 to 1989. Following the Education Summit in 1989, which focused on five subject areas: geography, science, mathematics, English, and history, work began on the geography standards. The standards document titled, *Geography for Life* (GESP, 1994), has a mission, which is geographic competency. "To achieve geographic understanding on a national scale requires a concerted effort by the educational system to ensure that all students receive a basic education in geography" (GESP, 1994, p. 26). The standards are intended for life. A geographically informed person "allows [one] to see, understand, and appreciate the web of relationships between [among] people, places, and environments" (GESP, 1994, p. 29).

Geography for Life is divided into eight chapters: The Geographic View of Our World, The Components of Geography Education, Geographic Skills and Perspectives, The Subject Matter of Geography, National Geography Standards—Grades K-4, National Geography Standards—Grades 5-8, National Geography Standards—Grades 9-12, and Student Achievement in Geography. Technology is covered in various areas in the document, but it can be found explicitly in Standard 10: Human Systems Grades 9-12 and Standard 16: The Changes that Occur in the Meaning, Use, Distribution, and Importance of Resources (GESP, 1994).

The results of the efforts to develop geography standards have been mixed. Most states are not rising to the recommendation as noted in *State Curriculum Standards* (Munroe & Smith, 1998). A select few have adopted the recommendations and one state, Colorado, has developed a strong program that emulates the ideas as set forth in the standards. "Unfortunately, some states have rejected the ideas suggested by the *Geography for Life*. For example, the Commonwealth of Virginia made the decision to do their own work stating they could do better on their own during the development of the Standards of Learning. The result is very little geography reflected in the state mandated guidelines" (R. Morrill, personal communication, September 27, 2000).

National Standards for History

The National Endowment for the Humanities and the United States Department of Education co-funded the National History Standards Project in 1992. A broad-based consensus building process was used to develop understanding about the purpose for history in schools and to identify what students need to know. The resulting publication by the National Council for History Standards (NCHS) was the *National Standards for History*. It took four years to complete and was published in 1996.

The mission of *National Standards for History* is to set the stage for helping students begin to develop "...a comprehensive understanding of the history of the world, and of the peoples of many cultures and civilizations who have developed ideas, institutions, and ways of life different from students' own" (NCHS, 1996, p. 1). The idea that people are doomed to repeat the history they are not aware of is apparent in the opening pages of the document. The significance of history and its relationship to society and the study of technology are also captured in the ideas put forth in Chapter 1. Through the study of history "[s]tudents may acquire the habit of seeing matters through others' eyes and come to realize that by studying others, they can also better understand themselves" (NCHS, 1996, p. 1).

The initial reception of preliminary documents released in 1994 was negative at best. The developers of the history standards after much debate agreed to revise the document resulting in the 1996 publication. The early criticisms were directed primarily at the teaching examples provided and not the standards themselves. The revised publication of *National Standards for History* resulted in clear, concise statements of what students should understand.

> The revised standards call attention to the rise of individualism, the development of representative government, and the importance of the European Enlightenment in shaping America, as well as the growth of the middle class. An entirely new standard calls for study of science and technology and their role in revolutionizing American life (Ravitch & Schlesinger, Jr., 1996, paragraph 9).

The document is divided into two main parts: National Standards for History (K-4) and National Standards for United States and World History. Technology is covered throughout the document, but it can be found explicitly in K-4 Topic 4: The History of Peoples of Many Cultures Around the World—Standard 8: Major Discoveries in Science and Technology, Their Social and Economic Effects, and the Scientists and Inventors Responsible for Them, and grade cluster 5-12 Era 1: The Beginnings of Human Society—Standard 1: The Biological and Cultural Processes that Gave Rise to the Earliest Human Communities, and Standard 2: The Processes that Led to the Emergence of Agricultural Societies Around the World.

Since the release of *National Standards for History*, many states have adopted versions of the recommendations and developed related state standards. In the past two years there has been a strong improvement in establishing what students should know in history as reported by David Warren Saxe in the report of the *State of the State Standards 2000* prepared by The Thomas B. Fordham Foundation. "For the vast majority of the states, history is now part of the educational infrastructure" (Saxe, 2000, paragraph 1).

Standards for the English Language Arts

The International Reading Association (IRA) and the National Council of Teachers of English (NCTE) prepared *Standards for the English Language Arts* through the English Language Arts Standards Project. The project began in 1991 and *Standards for the English Language Arts* was published in 1996. The document is organized based on two guiding principles:

> There is not one best way to organize subject matter in a given field of study, rigorous national standards should not be restricted to one set of standards per subject area and content standards should embody a coherent, professionally defensible conception of how a field can be framed for purposes of instruction (NCTE, 1996, pp. vii-viii).

The mission of *Standards for the English Language Arts* is to:

> define what students should know about language and be able to do with language. Our goal is to define, as clearly and specifically as possible, the current consensus among literacy teachers and researchers about what students should learn in the English language arts—reading, writing, listening, speaking, viewing, and visually representing (NCTE, 1996, p. 1).

The document is divided into four chapters: Setting Standards in the English Language Arts, Perspectives Informing the English Language Arts Standards, The English Language Arts Standards, and Standards in the Classroom. A glossary and appendices with suggestions and background follow each chapter on the development of the standards. The concept of technology is covered in the characteristic style of information and communication as multi-media relates to the delivery and presentation of ideas.

Since the release of *Standards for the English Language Arts*, many states have risen to the call for strong standards in English and language arts and several states met the "common core criterion" as established by the American Federation of Teachers. In the report, *The State of State Standards 2000*, Stotsky states, "Altogether, these grades (and the ratings on which they are based) suggest that the current documents, whether final drafts or under revision, are generally stronger than those I examined [in 1997]" (p. 14, paragraph 3). The general reception of *Standards for the English Language Arts* has been well received and overall very positive.

READER REFLECTION

Prior to the release of the *National Science Education Standards, Benchmarks for Science Literacy, Principles and Standards for School Mathematics,* and *Standards for Technological Literacy,* "…in the United States, unlike in most developed countries in the world, technology as a subject has largely been ignored in the schools. It is not tied to graduation requirements, has no fixed place in elementary education, is absent altogether in the college preparatory curriculum, and does not constitute part of the content in science courses at any level (*Benchmarks for Science Literacy,* 1993, p. 41)

The description above is slowly changing in some school districts around the country, but not in significant numbers. It is clear that the use of the documents mentioned will help in laying the foundation for building "…technology education into the curriculum, as well as use technology to promote learning, so that all students become well informed about the nature, powers, and limitations of technology" (*Benchmarks for Science*

Literacy, 1993, p. 41). However, teachers and teacher educators need to be aware of the need to understand the standards and benchmarks described in the *National Science Education Standards, Benchmarks for Science Literacy,* and *Principles and Standards for School Mathematics* and their relationship to each other and to *Standards for Technological Literacy*. This understanding would result in the study of technology giving reason for studying of other subject matter fields and integrating the subject matter fields together. Hence, learning would become interdisciplinary and reflect the real world.

SUMMARY

A review of standards in different subject matter fields makes the reader aware that their development has existed since the late 1980s and they have had a profound effect on education. Standards have established desired outcomes in given subject matter fields, which results in the subject matter educational systems being revamped to achieve the desired outcomes. Most of the subject matter fields included technology.

The more knowledgeable educators are about other subject matter standards and their relationship to the study of technology, the more effective they will be in using time and resources to the full benefit of students at all grade levels. The territorial barriers that have long been a part of the education system must be removed and collaborative efforts employed in order to minimize redundancy and enhance relevancy for why students need to know and be able to understand the various fields of learning. Time is an enemy. It takes time to understand the ideas conveyed in the separate documents. Yet, it is apparent, even on a small scale that technology is a common thread that may be used to help integrate and motivate the knowledge necessary for students. All documents cited in some way referred to a technological artifact or process and relied on current technological systems and processes to enable the transfer of ideas. Helping students to recognize the validity and necessity to develop an understanding of interrelated knowledge will empower them to develop deeper thinking, and enable them to make sense about the world in which they live. This is the ultimate mission of all learning.

REFERENCES

American Association for the Advancement of Science (AAAS). (1989). *Science for all Americans.* New York: Oxford University Press.

American Association for the Advancement of Science (AAAS). (1993). *Benchmarks for science literacy.* New York: Oxford University Press.

American Association for the Advancement of Science (AAAS). (1999). *Blueprints for reform, science, mathematics, and technology education.* New York: Oxford University Press.

American Association for the Advancement of Science (AAAS). (2000). *Designs for science literacy.* New York: Oxford University Press.

Geography Education Standards Project (GESP). (1994). *Geography for life: National geography standards.* Washington, D.C.: National Geographic Research and Exploration.

International Technology Education Association (ITEA). (2000). *Standards for technological literacy: Content for the study of technology.* Reston, VA: Author.

Munroe, S. & Smith, T. (February, 1998). State geography standards: An appraisal of geography standards in 38 states and the District of Columbia. [On-line].

National Council for History Standards (NCHS). (1996). *National standards for history.* Los Angeles, CA: National Center for History in the Schools.

National Council of Teacher of English (NCTE). (1996). *Standards for the English language arts.* Urbana, IL: International Reading Association and the National Council of Teachers of English.

National Council of Teachers of Mathematics (NCTM). (2000). *Principles and standards for school mathematics.* Reston, VA: Author.

National Research Council (NRC). (1996). *National science education standards.* Washington, D.C.: National Academy Press.

Saxe, D.W. (January, 2000). The state of state standards in history in the report *The state of state standards 2000.* [On-line]. http://www.edexcellence.net/library/soss2000/2000soss.html#history

Stotsky, S. (January, 2000). The state of state standards in English language arts/reading in the report *The state of state standards 2000.* [On-line].http://www.edexcellence.net/library/soss2000/2000soss.html#English

Rationale and Structure for *Standards for Technological Literacy*

Chapter 3

G. Eugene Martin
Southwest Texas State University

Every major organized endeavor has a point of beginning—a genesis, but not necessarily an ending point. Such has been the case to date with the development of the content standards for technology education.

The International Technology Education Association (ITEA) first presented the technology content standards to the profession in the publication, *Standards for Technological Literacy: Content for the Study of Technology* (*Standards for Technological Literacy*), at the beginning of the new millennium. Leaders in the profession had worked tirelessly for six long years to develop first a *Rationale and Structure* for the study of technology and then the technology content standards.

In 1996 the ITEA published a *Rationale and Structure* document and in April 2000, the technology content standards became public. Content standards informed the profession and the general public what "should be," and the *Rationale and Structure* told them the reason "why." It was only logical that a *Rationale and Structure* be developed first as the profession and general public had to know the reason "why" before it could even possibly know what "should be." A *Rationale and Structure* document would be the profession's first definitive and public argument for the development of technological literacy for all Americans.

The development of what ultimately resulted in the publication, *A Rationale and Structure for the Study of Technology* (*Rationale and Structure*), had its beginnings in the early 1990s when it became evident to technology education leaders that the field lacked a specific and organized direction as might be provided in a comprehensive set of standards. Other subject areas had already commenced the development of a set of standards for their disciplines. Technology education standards—content, student assessment, teacher enhancement and preparation, and program—would provide a general framework from which state and local school systems' personnel could develop curricula and ultimately programs.

As a result of successfully securing two major grants, one each from the National Science Foundation (NSF) and the National Aeronautics and Space Administration (NASA), the ITEA formed three major groups in 1994 to address the development of a *Rationale and Structure* document. The first group was the Project Staff. The second group was The National Commission for Technology Education, a commission consisting of eminent scholars and leaders from the fields of engineering, science, mathematics, the humanities, education, government, professional associations, and industry. The third group was the Writing Consultants (a subgroup of the National Commission) who had the unenviable task, with the assistance of the Project Staff, of writing the many early drafts of the *Rationale and Structure*. Without the collective and collaborative energies of all three groups, and the talents of hundreds of practitioners of technology, science, mathematics, engineering, and other areas at all levels who served as reviewers and evaluators, the answer to the reason "why" of technology studies would never have come to fruition, particularly in the form of a publication.

Why was a *Rationale and Structure* document so important to the profession at this time in its history? What could possibly be accomplished by publishing such a document? Who was its intended audience? What was the desired action of the reader once the *Rationale and Structure* had been read? These questions, and hundreds of others just like them, simply helped to underscore the profession's need for a formal document that would provide a definitive argument calling for and implementing major educational reform on a grand scale. Never before had the power and promise of technology been so eloquently and so thoroughly addressed and never before had the need for technological literacy been so substantiated as was found in the words, photographs, and even the wisdoms of the *Rationale and Structure*. Technological literacy, people's ability to use, manage, and understand technology, became the profession's 'calling card' since no other discipline was claiming the study of technology solely as its body of knowledge like what was being done by the technology education profession. When asked, "What is the product of your program?, classroom teachers, teacher educators, and supervisors could honestly, justifiably, and proudly say, "a technologically literate person." Technology, human innovation in action, gave the profession a common definition from which to operate. The *Rationale and Structure* helped the reader understand why technology is the result of human innovation in action and that technologically literate people, for example, possess the ability to understand the nature, power, and consequences of technology.

PREPARING STUDENTS FOR A TECHNOLOGICAL WORLD

The Great Integrator

The power of technology resides with the people who develop it, while the promise of technology rests with the people's ability to use, manage, and understand it. In the final analysis, however, power and promise are inseparable in a democratic society. Without technology, the world as we know it today would not exist; as a result of technology, people and societies have learned how to adapt by modifying their local, regional, national, and international environments. For example, people developed products, processes, and systems to construct the United States interstate highway system, a complex network of roadways that connects all parts of America into one giant transportation system. In turn, the interstate system has an effect on every one's life. People are closer together due to this transportation system. People also die as a result of automobile accidents.

As this example shows, technology has created a complex world but with one common denominator – constant change. Some people embrace technology and its potential for rapid acceleration of change, while others are threatened by it; some people welcome it and all of its complexities, while others view it as impersonal and even try to ignore it; some people see technology as solving major societal problems, while others view it as creating major problems. The fact remains that regardless of one's personal views about technology, we as educators have a challenge to create a subject that encompasses and embraces what might be the total universe of all possible personal views, nurture these views, and then allow them to flourish in a teaching and learning environment.

One of the *Rationale and Structure*'s purposes is to call attention to all these possibilities because in the final analysis, technology is created, managed, and used by societies and individuals, according to their goals and values. Goals and values thus become the determining factor as to which technologies will be developed, which technologies will be ignored, and which technologies will be eliminated. As each decision is made, there are consequences – short and long term. The consequences come about as a result of the interrelatedness of technologies and technological systems. Ultimately, however, people who possess the ability to use, manage, and understand technology have better positioned themselves to make judgments about the nature, power, and consequences of technology.

Technological Literacy

Great differences exist throughout the world in individuals' and societies' technological ability and understanding, and maybe it is nowhere more self-evident than when one examines the economic prosperity of nations. At any given point in time, nations that exhibit high economic prosperity are nations that also exhibit high technological activity. A nation's people decide what technology should be developed, how it should be developed, and when it should be developed. The what, how, and when decisions are based upon their goals and are a reflection of their values. Their comfort zone in making what, how, and when decisions is based upon their ability to use, manage, and understand technology. Differences in technological ability and understanding will exist within a nation and among nations; that is, there will be differences in technological literacy.

The challenge to technology educators is to recognize and accept that there will be differences in technological ability and understanding of their students and then develop a "measure of technological literacy within each graduate so that every American can understand the nature of technology, appropriately use technological devices and processes, and participate in society's decisions on technological issues" (ITEA, 1996, p. 1).

DIMENSIONS OF TECHNOLOGY

The *Rationale and Structure* sets forth a framework for implementing the educational reform necessary to ensure technological literacy for all. Foremost and at center stage, it defines technology as "human innovation in action" involving the "generation of knowledge and processes to develop systems that solve problems and extend human capabilities" (ITEA, 1996, p. 16). People develop technological knowledge, for example, to gain a better understanding of the nature and evolution of technology and to better comprehend and appreciate the linkages between how technology influences and is affected by society and the environment. Through human innovation, people also create, invent, design, transform, produce, control, maintain, and use products or systems. These are technological processes. People use technological knowledge to create, invent, design, etc., new technological processes and sometimes in creating, inventing, designing, etc., these technological processes, new technological knowledge is also created. There would not be a need for technological knowledge and processes unless we also fully understood the context in which they will be developed, applied, and studied. "People develop technological processes and knowledge for a reason – they want to develop and use systems that solve problems and extend their capabilities" (ITEA, 1996, p. 16). It is this individual or societal desire to solve problems and to extend capabilities that provides the foundation for developing technological literacy for all Americans.

Technology is not science, mathematics, social studies, language arts, the humanities, art, music, or any other field of study. Yet, it has close linkages to all of them. In fact, some people would argue rather strongly that you cannot "know" and "do" technology in isolation from these other fields of study. When people study science, for example, they are studying the natural world. Technology, you will recall, is human innovation in action and when people alter the natural world, they are making an impact on science. Science depends on technology "to develop, test, experiment, verify, and apply many of its natural laws" and technology depends on science for its "understanding of how the natural world is structured and how it functions" (ITEA, 1996, p. 28). Mathematics, unlike science and technology, provides both with their exact language. Technology has also helped revolutionize the fields of music and visual arts. A technologically literate person exhibits functional levels of understanding and appreciation of the interdisciplinary connectedness of these different fields. The technologically literate person's comfort zone includes the ability to communicate and interact with peers from these different disciplines.

The *Rationale and Structure* defines technological literacy as the "ability to use, manage, and understand technology" (ITEA, 1996, p. 6), while recognizing that each individual and society possesses varying levels of technological knowledge, capability, and confidence, at any given moment in time. To clearly differentiate between use, manage, and understand technology, the *Rationale and Structure* provides the following descriptions:

- The ability to **use** technology involves the successful operation of the key systems of the time. This includes knowing the components of existing macro systems, or human adaptive systems, and how the systems behave.

- The ability to **manage** technology involves ensuring that all technological activities are efficient and appropriate.

- Understanding technology **involves** more than facts and information, but also the ability to synthesize the information into new insights. (ITEA, 1996, p. 6)

It is interesting to note that when the technology content standards were developed, "assess" was inserted into the definition of technological literacy.

In a democratic society, technological literacy has individual, societal, and environmental implications. As individuals, for example, people need (a) to develop technological abilities so they will better know how to use products; (b) to assess the impacts of technological actions; and (c) to develop better decision making abilities in order to determine which technological system or process to use or not use. As a society, technological literacy provides a basis for people (a) to make conscious decisions about technological issues confronting that society; (b) to engage in technological activities to improve the country's economy; and (c) to participate responsibly and make contributions in the technological decision making process. Finally, technological literacy is critical to the Earth's ability to sustain life. Technologically literate people, for example, understand the consequences to their environment of any decisions they make about the use and development of different technological processes. They also understand that their decisions can help solve environmental problems and maybe even create them.

What is a technologically literate person? How would you best describe a technologically literate person? Is the level of technological literacy that one achieves influenced by a country's goals and values? Listed below are a few statements from the *Rationale and Structure* that describe the characteristics of a technologically literate person. The list is not exhaustive and the reader should add to it.

- They are capable problem solvers who consider technological issues from different points of view and in relationship to a variety of contexts.
- They acknowledge that the solution to one problem often creates other issues and problems.
- They appreciate the interrelationships between technology, individuals, society, and the environment.
- [They] understand that technology involves systems, which are groups of interrelated components designed to collectively achieve a desired goal or goals.
- [They] can identify appropriate solutions, and assess and forecast the results of implementing the chosen solution.
- [They] understand the major technological concepts behind the current issues.
- They are skilled in the safe use of the technological processes that are lifelong prerequisites for their careers, health, and enjoyment.
- [They] understand and appreciate the importance of fundamental technological developments.
- Most importantly, they understand that technology is the result of human activity. It is the result of combining ingenuity and resources to meet human needs and wants. (ITEA, 1996, p. 11)

Should every American possess the same level of technological understanding and capability? How influential are one's background, education, interests, attitudes, and abilities in his or her level of technological literacy? Why do most Americans not even begin to comprehend the basic concepts of today's technological society? Why can only a few Americans comprehend technological issues in the daily news, perform routine technological activities, or appreciate a technological breakthrough? While these questions beg for answers, it is clear that if our society is to achieve technological literacy on a grand scale, a major effort is needed. The *Rationale and Structure* underscores the role of our nation's educational system in assisting every child to become technologically literate. The *Rationale and Structure* also calls for an "articulated, comprehensive technology education program" (ITEA, 1996, p. 13) that guarantees participation by every child. This program will provide students an opportunity to further develop technological knowledge and learn technological processes needed to solve problems and extend human capabilities. The program referred to in the *Rationale and Structure* is called technology education or technological studies. It is a school subject specifically designed to develop technological literacy skills in every child.

Never before in our lifetime has there been such a sense of urgency for effective technology studies programs from elementary through high school and beyond; a sense of urgency for a school subject that provides experiences that instill insight and problem solving capabilities; and, a sense of urgency to include technological studies in the core curriculum. While technology education has an extremely important role to play in addressing this sense of urgency, it cannot do it alone. It will take the combined energies of stakeholders in all subject areas if the goal of a technologically literate society is to be realized. Tantamount to this effort is total and unequivocal collaboration among all subject areas, including teachers, curriculum designers, and administrators. While technology education must take the lead role in bringing about this major yet fundamental change in the school curriculum, other subjects such as science, mathematics, social studies, art, the humanities, etc., must also come to the realization that they have an equally important role in developing technological literacy skills and knowledge in children. Technology education teachers are at the threshold of an opportunity to perform a key leadership role in this total school collaborative effort.

Technological studies also have a critical role to perform in helping children learn content in other subjects within the school environment. That is, it has a strong and powerful role as an integrator of knowledge by reinforcing and complementing material students learn in other school subjects. This role is no more evident than in technology laboratory-classrooms as these facilities provide a teaching and learning environment for people of different subjects to come together to develop solutions to practical problems. Students just don't use technological knowledge in isolation. They must synthesize and apply knowledge from other subjects to solve practical problems. Subject matter integration helps not only to develop connections among different subject areas but also to appreciate that all knowledge is interconnected. This interconnectedness once again underscores that all subjects have a role to play in the development of a technologically literate society.

EVOLUTION OF TAXONOMIC ORGANIZERS FOR THE STUDY OF TECHNOLOGY

In the *Rationale and Structure*, the study of technology is provided in a taxonomic structure in the universals of technology (ITEA, 1996, pp. 16-17). This structure is presented by three universals which represent the processes, knowledge, and context for the study of technology. The processes are those actions that people undertake to create, invent, design, transform, produce, control, maintain, and use products or systems. The processes include the human activities of designing and developing technological systems, determining and controlling the behavior of technological systems, utilizing technological systems, and assessing the impacts and consequences of technological systems. Technological knowledge includes the nature and evolution of technology; linkages based on impacts, consequences, resources, and other fields, and technological concepts and principles. This includes much of the knowledge of how the technological processes are developed, applied, and used. The contexts of technology involve the many practical reasons why technology is developed, applied, and studied. People develop technological processes and knowledge for a reason – they want to develop and use systems that solve problems and extend their capabilities. The systems that are developed can easily be categorized as informational systems, physical systems, and biological systems (ITEA, 1996, p. 16).

In *Standards for Technological Literacy*, the 20 standards provide an evolution of the universals from the *Rationale and Structure*. Some of the universals were elevated to a higher taxonomic level while others were given a lower taxonomic status in the standards. Refer to Figure 3-1 for a visual representation of how the universals in the *Rationale and Structure* evolved to the 20 standards in *Standards for Technological Literacy*.

It is important to recognize that the universals in the *Rationale and Structure* were instrumental in providing the philosophical and content foundation for what led to the creation of the 20 standards in *Standards for*

Figure 3-1. Evolution of Taxonomic Organizers

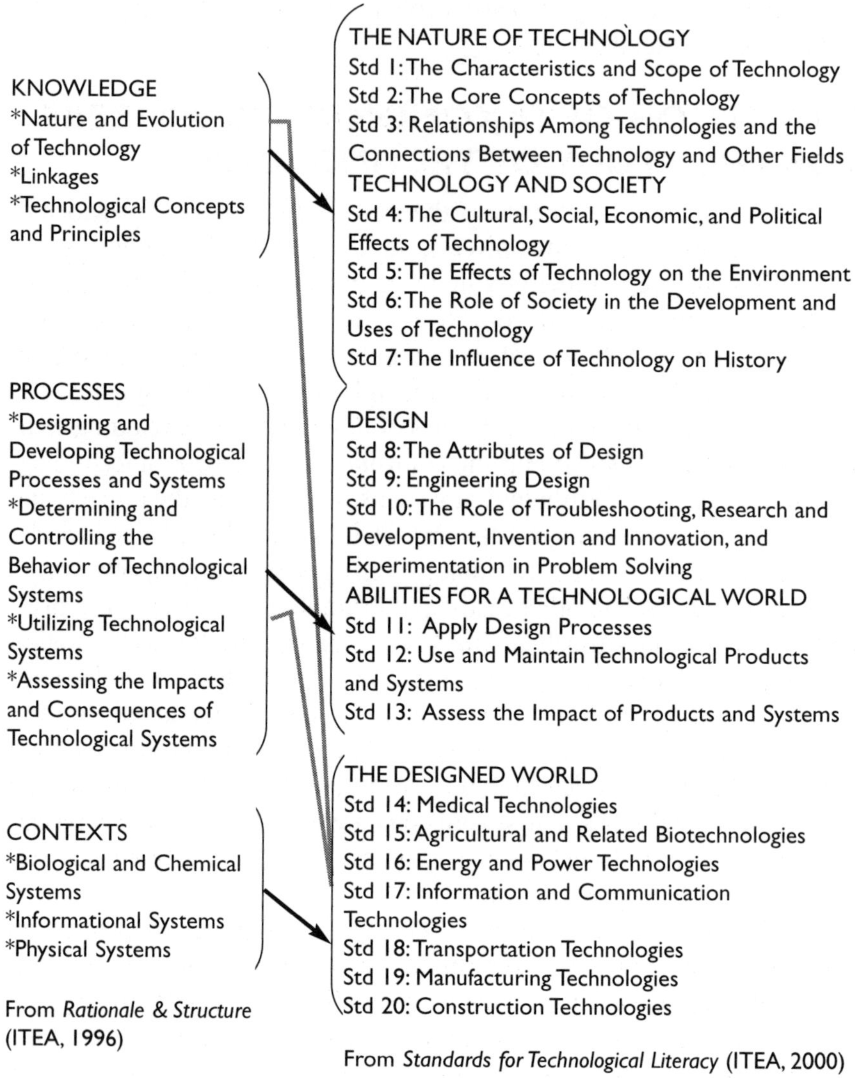

KNOWLEDGE
*Nature and Evolution
of Technology
*Linkages
*Technological Concepts
and Principles

THE NATURE OF TECHNOLOGY
Std 1: The Characteristics and Scope of Technology
Std 2: The Core Concepts of Technology
Std 3: Relationships Among Technologies and the
Connections Between Technology and Other Fields
TECHNOLOGY AND SOCIETY
Std 4: The Cultural, Social, Economic, and Political
Effects of Technology
Std 5: The Effects of Technology on the Environment
Std 6: The Role of Society in the Development and
Uses of Technology
Std 7: The Influence of Technology on History

PROCESSES
*Designing and
Developing Technological
Processes and Systems
*Determining and
Controlling the
Behavior of Technological
Systems
*Utilizing Technological
Systems
*Assessing the Impacts
and Consequences of
Technological Systems

DESIGN
Std 8: The Attributes of Design
Std 9: Engineering Design
Std 10: The Role of Troubleshooting, Research and
Development, Invention and Innovation, and
Experimentation in Problem Solving
ABILITIES FOR A TECHNOLOGICAL WORLD
Std 11: Apply Design Processes
Std 12: Use and Maintain Technological Products
and Systems
Std 13: Assess the Impact of Products and Systems

CONTEXTS
*Biological and Chemical
Systems
*Informational Systems
*Physical Systems

THE DESIGNED WORLD
Std 14: Medical Technologies
Std 15: Agricultural and Related Biotechnologies
Std 16: Energy and Power Technologies
Std 17: Information and Communication
Technologies
Std 18: Transportation Technologies
Std 19: Manufacturing Technologies
Std 20: Construction Technologies

From *Rationale & Structure*
(ITEA, 1996)

From *Standards for Technological Literacy* (ITEA, 2000)

Technological Literacy. Without the research and work that was grounded
in the universals, the profession could not have produced the breadth and
depth of content, which was refined in the reviews of the final *Standards
for Technological Literacy.*

REFLECTIONS

In many ways, the ITEA's *Rationale and Structure* is a landmark publication for the technology education profession. Its true significance, however, may be found in the collective and collaborative talents, energies, and imaginations of people who came together to create it and through the consensus building process that brought it to fruition.

Through the demonstrated leadership of the ITEA's office staff and its officers and the Technology for All Americans Project staff, the profession came together to develop a definitive statement on the *Rationale and Structure* for the study of technology. While some people may wish to take argument with the specifics of the *Rationale and Structure* publication, no one can question the sincerity of the intent and the integrity of the key individuals who caused it all to happen. Questions will always be raised about the publication, and they should be raised—but they should be raised, discussed, and debated in professional meetings where all have an opportunity to participate and engage in the discourse.

There are many topics identified in the *Rationale and Structure* publication and no topic is more significant or more important than the argument made for developing a functional level of technological literacy in all Americans. The argument put forth is clear, concise, and convincing and now it is up to those who teach technological studies to bring life to the term technological literacy. Just as the publication was the result of a collaborative process, so must the implementation of technology studies be a collaborative process. If technology teachers try to do it alone, they will surely fail. They must learn to integrate and connect technology studies with other subject matter areas, as that may just well be where its true strength lies as a school subject.

The *Rationale and Structure* is a professional publication, but it must be more than that if it is to have any significant impact at the K-12 level. Classroom teachers, teacher educators, and supervisors have a very critical role to perform when implementing technology studies. For some individuals, this may require in-service training and for others, pre-service training will be required. Whatever the requirements, now is the time for action.

The *Rationale and Structure* is a point of beginning, not an ending. It is the genesis for a new way of offering a technological studies program. Successful implementation of this program depends on the knowledge and creativity of people who call themselves technology teachers.

REFERENCES

International Technology Education Association (ITEA). (1996). *A rationale and structure for the study of technology.* Reston, VA: Author.

International Technology Education Association (ITEA). (2000). *Standards for technological literacy: Content for the study of technology.* Reston, VA: Author.

Standards for Technological Literacy: Content for the Study of Technology

4

William E. Dugger, Jr.
International Technology Education Association
Technology for All Americans

What is the importance of standards on public education in the United States? In an article in *Education Week* (October 21, 1998), Christopher T. Cross, president of the Council for Basic Education, stated, "I am often asked in forums across the country whether standards are here to stay or simply a passing fad that will soon be replaced by another fad. My answer remains firm and consistent: Standards are here to stay. The effort has survived almost a decade of attempts to sabotage it and, in fact, public support is stronger than ever." He also stated that most policymakers in education have yet to understand that content standards are only the first step in the process which involves curriculum revision, assessment standards, program standards, teacher in-service standards, and teacher pre-service standards. There must be close collaboration between all of these components to assure that the standards will act as a positive catalyst for reform across the educational spectrum. The bottom line is whether student learning is improving.

The International Technology Education Association (ITEA) released *Standards for Technological Literacy: Content for the Study of Technology* (*Standards for Technological Literacy*) on April 6, 2000, at its conference in Salt Lake City. This publication was the culminating effort of over 4,000 educators, administrators, engineers, scientists, parents, and others over a four-year time period (1996-2000). These standards, in the later versions, went through a rigorous review by the technology community, the National Research Council (NRC), and the National Academy of Engineering (NAE). It is significant to note that this marks the first time that the NAE supported a publication that it did not write.

Broadly speaking, standards are written statements about what is valued in education that can be used for making a judgment of quality. More specifically, content standards specify what students should know and be able to do in technology. They indicate the knowledge and processes that are essential in the study of technology that should be taught and learned in school in grades K-12. *Standards for Technological Literacy* is <u>not</u> a curriculum. A curriculum specifies how the content is delivered day-in and day-out by the teacher(s) which includes the structure, organization, balance, sequencing, and presentation of the content in the laboratory-classroom from the learner's point of view. Curriculum developers, teachers, and others should use *Standards for Technological Literacy* as a guide for developing curriculum. The standards do <u>not</u> specify what should go on in the laboratory-classroom. Similarly, *Standards for Technological Literacy* does <u>not</u> prescribe courses or programs (groups of courses) at grade levels. Qualified education personnel at the local or state level should develop the curriculum, courses, and programs. *Standards for Technological Literacy* is voluntary and does <u>not</u> represent a federal policy or mandate. Finally, *Standards for Technological Literacy* does <u>not</u> prescribe an assessment process that deals with how well students learn the content in technology.

Standards for Technological Literacy provides a vision for what a technologically literate person should be. If a student goes through an articulated standards-based technology education program from grades K-12, he or she will be technologically literate at graduation from high school. *Standards for Technological Literacy* was created with the following guiding principles:

- They offer a common set of expectations for what students should learn in the study of technology.

- They are developmentally appropriate for students.

- They provide a basis for developing meaningful, relevant, and articulated curricula at the local, state, and provincial levels.

- They promote content connections with other fields of study in grades K-12.

- They encourage active and experiential learning.

What is included in *Standards for Technological Literacy*? How is it formatted and organized? What are the benchmarks that follow each Standard? What information in the publication prepares a person philosophically for technological literacy as interpreted through the standards? Are there examples of classroom activities provided that will help in interpreting the standards into everyday teaching and learning? The answers to these and other questions are found next in this chapter.

A BRIEF TOUR OF *STANDARDS FOR TECHNOLOGICAL LITERACY*

Standards for Technological Literacy is designed to help a person easily find information that is needed. It is laid out to be user-friendly, and the table of contents at the front of the book coupled with the index at the end of the book help the reader to locate what is available. There is plenty of "white space" on the pages to allow for notes to be written by the user.

Standards for Technological Literacy begins with an impressive foreword (2000, p. v) by William A. Wulf, President of the NAE. He documents a need for technological literacy in this country. Moreover, Wulf calls for support for *Standards for Technological Literacy* as a dynamic document, which can enhance the technological literacy of the nation.

Standards for Technological Literacy includes the following parts:

- Chapter 1 (Preparing Students for a Technological World) establishes the need for technological literacy for everyone through a standards-based study of technology.

- Chapter 2 (Overview of *Standards for Technological Literacy*) describes the format of the standards and their enabling benchmarks. Also presented in this chapter is a discussion of the primary users of the standards.

The following five chapters discuss the standards and benchmarks in five major categories:

- Chapter 3 (The Nature of Technology) presents what students should understand about the nature of technology in order to become technologically literate. It includes standards, which address what technology is, the common core of concepts, which permeate all technologies, and the relationships among various technologies and among technology and other fields of study.

- Chapter 4 (Technology and Society) deals with how technology affects society and the environment, as well as how society influences the development of technology, and how technology has changed and evolved over the course of human history.

- Chapter 5 (Design) discusses what the attributes of design are, and specifically how students will develop an understanding of engineering design. Also in this chapter is a standard that presents what students should know about some other problem solving approaches, such as troubleshooting, research and development, invention and innovation, and experimentation.

- Chapter 6 (Abilities for a Technological World) presents the development of important abilities by students for a technological world, which include applying the design process, using and maintaining technological products and systems, and assessing products and systems.

- Chapter 7 (The Designed World) is the product of a design process, which provides ways to turn resources—materials, tools and machines, people, information, energy, capital, and time—into products and systems. It includes standards in major organizational areas of technology, including medical technologies, agricultural and bio-related technologies, energy and power technologies, information and communication technologies, transportation technologies, manufacturing technologies, and construction technologies.

- Chapter 8 (Call to Action) presents the challenges which need to be overcome in achieving the vision of *Standards for Technological Literacy* by various individuals and groups including teachers, curriculum developers, publishers, equipment designers and manufacturers, students, the overall educational community, parents, the engineering profession, researchers, and other technology professionals.

- Appendices include a brief history of the ITEA's Technology for All Americans Project, a listing of all the 20 standards, a compendium of all the benchmark topics under the standards, and an articulated curriculum vignette for grades K-12. Additionally, in the appendix is a list of references, an acknowledgements section recognizing the contributions of many individuals and groups who assisted in the development and review of *Standards for Technological Literacy*, a glossary of most used terms in the book, and an index.

STRUCTURE OF *STANDARDS FOR TECHNOLOGICAL LITERACY*

<u>Standards</u>

The standards specify what every student should know and be able to do in order to be technological literate. They offer criteria to judge progress toward a vision of technological literacy for all students. All standards should be met for a student to obtain the optimal level of standards technological literacy at graduation from high school. There are 20 standards in the book, which are expressed in sentence form. *Standards for Technological Literacy* should be applied in conjunction with other national, state, and locally developed standards in technological studies and for other fields of study. The standards should be integrated with one another rather than being presented as separate parts (e.g., *Standard* 1 with *Standard* 8 or *Standard* 19 with 17 and 20).

The individual standards fall into two types: what students should know and understand about technology, and what they should be able to do. The first type, which could be termed "cognitive" standards, sets out basic knowledge about technology – how it works, and its place in the world – that students should have in order to be technologically literate. The second type, the "process" standards, describes the abilities that students should have. The two types of standards are complementary. For example, a student can be taught in a lecture about a design process, but the ability to actually use a design process and to apply it for finding a solution to a technological problem comes only with hands-on experience. Likewise, it is difficult to perform a design process effectively without having some theoretical knowledge of how it is usually done. See Table 4-1 for a comprehensive listing of the standards under each of the categories in Chapters 3-7.

After each standard, a brief (one to two page) narrative follows which explains the intent of the standard. Grade level material is presented next for grades K-2, 3-5, 6-8, and 9-12. Under each grade level, a narrative follows that further explains the standard specifically at the grade level under discussion and provides suggestions on how the standard can be implemented in the laboratory-classroom by the teacher.

References that were used in the development of *Standards for Technological Literacy* include the following standards in other subject areas: *National Science Education Standards* (National Research Council, 1996), *Benchmarks for Science Literacy* (American Association for the Advancement of Science, 1993), *Curriculum and Evaluation Standards for School Mathematics* (National Council of Teachers of Mathematics, 1989), *Principles and Standards for School Mathematics* (National Council of Teachers of Mathematics, 2000), and others. It is important to keep in mind that the standards are the target and these should be kept as ultimate goals for achieving technological literacy by all students.

Table 4-1. The Standards for Technological Literacy

The Nature of Technology (Chapter 3)

Standard 1. Students will develop an understanding of the characteristics and scope of technology.

Standard 2. Students will develop an understanding of the core concepts of technology.

Standard 3. Students will develop an understanding of the relationships among technologies and the connections between technology and other fields of study.

Technology and Society (Chapter 4)

Standard 4. Students will develop an understanding of the cultural, social, economic, and political effects of technology.

Standard 5. Students will develop an understanding of the effects of technology on the environment.

Standard 6. Students will develop an understanding of the role of society in the development and use of technology.

Standard 7. Students will develop an understanding of the influence of technology on history.

Design (Chapter 5)

Standard 8. Students will develop an understanding of the attributes of design.

Standard 9 Students will develop an understanding of engineering design.

Standard 10. Students will develop an understanding of the role of troubleshooting, research and development, invention and innovation, and experimentation in problem solving.

Abilities for a Technological World (Chapter 6)

Standard 11. Students will develop the abilities to apply the design process.

Standard 12. Students will develop the abilities to use and maintain technological products and systems.

Standard 13. Students will develop the abilities to assess the impact of products and systems.

The Designed World (Chapter 7)

Standard 14. Students will develop an understanding of and be able to select and use medical technologies.

Standard 15. Students will develop an understanding of and be able to select and use agricultural and related biotechnologies.

Standard 16. Students will develop an understanding of and be able to select and use energy and power technologies.

Standard 17. Students will develop an understanding of and be able to select and use information and communication technologies.

Standard 18. Students will develop an understanding of and be able to select and use transportation technologies.

Standard 19. Students will develop an understanding of and be able to select and use manufacturing technologies.

Standard 20. Students will develop an understanding of and be able to select and use construction technologies.

Benchmarks

Each grade level discussion is followed by a series of benchmarks, which provide the fundamental content elements under the broadly stated standards (See Table 4-2). Benchmarks, which are statements that provide the specific knowledge and abilities that enable students to meet a given standard, are provided for each of the 20 standards at the K-2, 3-5, 6-8, and 9-12 grade levels. The benchmarks are identified by an alphabetical listing (e.g., A, B, C) and are highlighted in bold type. They are followed by supporting sentences (not in bold) that provide further detail, clarity, and examples. An example of a standard and its enabling benchmarks (C and D) for grades 3-5 is shown in Table 4-2.

The standards and benchmarks were established for guiding a student's progress toward technological literacy. To better understand the conceptual organizational structure between the standards, the categories, and benchmarks, please refer to Figure 4-1. The benchmarks, which are not listed in Figure 4-3 for each grade level for each standard, are required in order for students to meet the standards. Teachers may create additional benchmarks if they think that these will help students to meet a specific standard.

Table 4-2. A Representative Standard and Benchmarks

Standard 8 – Students will develop an understanding of the attributes of design.

In order to realize the attributes of design, students in grades 3-5 should learn that

C. The design process is a purposeful method of planning practical solutions to problems. The design process helps convert ideas into products and systems. The process is intuitive and includes such things as creating ideas, putting the ideas on paper, using words and sketches, building models of the design, testing out the design, and evaluating the solution.

D. Requirements for a design include such factors as the desired elements and features of a product or system or the limits that are placed on the design. Technological designs typically have to meet requirements to be successful. These requirements usually relate to the purpose or function of the product or system. Other requirements, such as size and cost, describe the limits of a design.

Figure 4-1. Structure of the Standards

	Standards	Benchmark K-2	Benchmark 3-5	Benchmark 6-8	Benchmark 9-12
The Nature of Technology →	*The characteristics and scope of technology				
	*The core concepts of technology				
	*The relationships among technologies and the connections between technology and other fields of study				
Technology and Society →	*The cultural, social, economic, and political efffects of technology				
	*The effects of technology on the environment				
	*The role of society in the development and use of technology				
	*The influence of technology on history				
Design →	*The attributes of design				
	*Engineering design				
	*The role of troubleshooting, research and development, invention and innovation, and experimentation in problem solving				
Abilities for a Technological World →	*Apply the design process				
	*Use and maintain technological products and systems				
	*Assess the impact of products and systems				
The Designed World →	*Medical technologies				
	*Agricultural and related biotechnologies				
	*Energy and power technologies				
	*Information and communication technologies				
	*Transportation technologies				
	*Manufacturing technologies				
	*Construction technologies				

The benchmarks are articulated from grades K-2 through 9-12 to progress from very basic ideas at the early elementary school level to more complex and comprehensive ideas at the high school level. Certain content "concepts" are found in the benchmarks, which extend across various levels to ensure continual learning of an important topic related to a standard.

Vignettes

A selection of vignettes is included in *Standards for Technological Literacy* to provide snapshots of laboratory-classroom experiences. They offer detailed examples of how the standards can be implemented by a teacher. A large majority of the vignettes were authentic in that they have been successfully used in an actual laboratory-classroom with students. A few of the vignettes were generated especially for these standards and are fictional—they were not tried and tested. Readers should be cautioned that any vignette is presented as a possible example and should not be interpreted as a curriculum.

A COMPENDIUM OF STANDARDS AND BENCHMARKS FOR *STANDARDS FOR TECHNOLOGICAL LITERACY*

A compendium is provided in *Standards for Technological Literacy*, which provides a summary of the content included in the 20 standards and their enabling benchmarks by grade levels of K-2, 3-5, 6-8, and 9-12. While the compendium provides an abbreviated overview of the standards and benchmarks, it is recommended that the reader use the full text in the actual standards and benchmarks to comprehend the accurate meaning intended by the developers of this document. A compendium of technology standards is presented in Table 4-3.

Table 4-3. Compendium of Major Topics for Technology Content Standards

Standard	Benchmark Topics Grades K-2	Benchmark Topics Grades 3-5	Benchmark Topics Grades 6-8	Benchmark Topics Grades 9-12
Nature of Technology **Standard 1:** The Characteristics and Scope of Technology	• Natural world and human-made world • People and technology	• Things found in nature and in the human-made world • Tools, materials, and skills • Creative thinking	• Usefulness of technology • Development of technology • Human creativity and motivation • Product demand	• Nature of technology • Rate of technological diffusion • Goal-directed research • Commercialization of technology
Standard 2: The Core Concepts of Technology	• Systems • Resources • Processes	• Systems • Resources • Requirements • Processes	• Systems • Resources • Requirements • Trade-offs • Processes • Controls	• Systems • Resources • Requirements • Optimization and Trade-offs • Processes • Controls
Standard 3: The Relationships Among Technologies and the Connections Between Technology and Other Fields	• Connections between technology and other subjects	• Technologies integrated • Relationships between technology and other fields of study	• Interaction of systems • Interrelation of technological environments • Knowledge from other fields of study and technology	• Technology transfer • Innovation and Invention • Knowledge protection and patents • Technological knowledge and advances of science and mathematics and vice versa
Technology and Society **Standard 4:** The Cultural, Social, Economic, and Political Effects of Technology	• Helpful or harmful	• Good and bad effects • Unintended consequences	• Attitudes toward development and use • Impacts and consequences • Ethical issues • Influences on economy, politics, and culture	• Rapid or gradual changes • Trade-offs and effects • Ethical implications • Cultural, social, economic, and political changes

Table 4-3. Compendium of Major Topics for Technology Content Standards (continued)

Standard	Benchmark Topics Grades K-2	Benchmark Topics Grades 3-5	Benchmark Topics Grades 6-8	Benchmark Topics Grades 9-12
Standard 5: The Effects of Technology on the Environment	• Reuse and/or recycling of materials	• Recycling and disposal of waste • Affects environment in good and bad ways	• Management of waste • Technologies repair damage • Environmental vs. economic concerns	• Conservation • Reduce resource use • Monitor environment • Alignment of natural and technological processes • Reduce negative consequences of technology • Decisions and trade-offs
Standard 6: The Role of Society in the Development and Use of Technology	• Needs and wants of individuals	• Changing needs and wants • Expansion or limitation of development	• Development driven by demands, values, and interests • Inventions and innovations • Social and cultural priorities • Acceptance and use of products and systems	• Different cultures and technologies • Development decisions • Factors affecting designs and demands of technologies
Standard 7: The Influence of Technology on History	• Ways people have lived and worked	• Tools for food, clothing, and protection	• Processes of inventions and innovations • Specialization of labor • Evolution of techniques, measurement, and resources • Technological and scientific knowledge	• Evolutionary development of technology • Dramatic changes in society • History of technology • Early technological history • The Iron Age • The Middle Ages • The Renaissance • The Industrial Revolution • The Information Age

Table 4-3. Compendium of Major Topics for Technology Content Standards (continued)

Standard	Benchmark Topics Grades K-2	Benchmark Topics Grades 3-5	Benchmark Topics Grades 6-8	Benchmark Topics Grades 9-12
Design **Standard 8:** The Attributes of Design	• Everyone can design • Design is a creative process	• Definitions of design • Requirements of design	• Design leads to useful products and systems • There is no perfect design • Requirements	• The design process • Design problems are usually not clear • Designs need to be refined • Requirements
Standard 9: Engineering Design	• Engineering design process • Expressing design ideas to others	• Engineering design process • Creativity and considering all ideas • Models	• Iteration • Brainstorming • Modeling, testing, evaluating, and modifying	• Design principles • Influence of personal characteristics • Prototypes • Factors in engineering design
Standard 10: The Role of Troubleshooting, Research and Development, Invention and Innovation, and Experimentation in Problem Solving	• Asking questions and making observations • All products need to be maintained	• Troubleshooting • Invention and innovation • Experimentation	• Troubleshooting • Invention and innovation • Experimentation	• Research and development • Researching technological problems • Not all problems are technological or can be solved • Multidisciplinary approach
Abilities for a Technological World **Standard 11:** Apply the Design Process	• Solve problems through design • Build something • Investigate how things are made	• Collecting information • Visualize a solution • Test and evaluate solutions • Improve a design	• Apply design process • Identify criteria and constraints • Model a solution to a problem • Test and evaluate • Make a product or system	• Identify a design problem • Identify criteria and constraints • Refine the design • Evaluate the design • Develop a product or system using quality control • Reevaluate final solution(s)

Table 4-3. Compendium of Major Topics for *Technology Content Standards* (continued)

Standard	Benchmark Topics Grades K-2	Benchmark Topics Grades 3-5	Benchmark Topics Grades 6-8	Benchmark Topics Grades 9-12
Standard 12: Use and Maintain Technological Products and Systems	• Discover how things work • Use tools correctly and safely • Recognize and use everyday symbols	• Follow step-by-step instructions • Select and safely use tools • Use computers to access and organize information • Use common symbols	• Use information to see how things work • Safely use tools to diagnose, adjust, and repair • Use computers and calculators • Operate systems	• Document and communicate processes and procedures • Diagnose a malfunctioning system • Troubleshoot and maintain systems • Operate and maintain systems • Use computers to communicate
Standard 13: Assess the Impact of Products and Systems	• Collect information about everyday products • Determine the qualities of a product	• Use information to identify patterns • Assess the influence of technology • Examine trade-offs	• Design and use instruments to collect data • Use collected data to find trends • Identify trends • Interpret and evaluate accuracy of information	• Collect information and judge its quality • Synthesize data to draw conclusions • Employ assessment techniques • Design forecasting techniques
<u>**The Designed World**</u> **Standard 14:** Medical Technologies	• Vaccinations • Medicine • Products to take care of people and their belongings	• Vaccines and medicine • Development of devices to repair or replace certain parts of the body • Use of products and systems to inform	• Advances and innovations in medical technologies • Sanitation processes • Immunology • Awareness about genetic engineering	• Medical technologies for prevention and rehabilitation • Telemedicine • Genetic therapeutics • Biochemistry

Table 4-3. Compendium of Major Topics for Technology Content Standards (continued)

Standard	Benchmark Topics Grades K-2	Benchmark Topics Grades 3-5	Benchmark Topics Grades 6-8	Benchmark Topics Grades 9-12
Standard 15: Agricultural and Related Biotechnologies	• Technologies in agriculture • Tools and materials for use in ecosystems	• Artificial ecosystems • Agriculture wastes • Processes in agriculture	• Technological advances in agriculture • Specialized equipment and practices • Biotechnology and agriculture • Artificial ecosystems and management • Development of refrigeration, freezing, dehydration, preservation, and irradiation	• Agricultural products and systems • Biotechnology • Conservation • Engineering design and management of ecosystems
Standard 16: Energy and Power Technologies	• Energy comes in many forms • Energy should not be wasted	• Energy comes in different forms • Tools, machines, products, and systems use energy to do work	• Energy is the capacity to do work • Energy can be used to do work using many processes • Power is the rate at which energy is converted from one form to another • Power systems • Efficiency and conservation	• Law of Conservation of Energy • Energy sources • Second Law of Thermodynamics • Renewable and non renewable forms of energy • Power systems are a source, a process, and a load

Table 4-3. Compendium of Major Topics for Technology Content Standards (continued)

Standard	Benchmark Topics Grades K-2	Benchmark Topics Grades 3-5	Benchmark Topics Grades 6-8	Benchmark Topics Grades 9-12
Standard 17: Information and Communication Technologies	• Information • Communication • Symbols	• Processing information • Many sources of information • Communication • Symbols	• Information and communication systems • Communication systems encode, transmit, and receive information • Factors influencing the design of a message • Language of technology	• Parts of information and communication systems • Information and communication systems • The purpose of information and communication technology • Communication systems and sub-systems • Many ways of communicating • Communication through symbols
Standard 18: Transportation Technologies	• Transportation system • Individuals and goods • Care of transportation products and systems	• Transportation system use • Transportation systems and subsystems	• Design and operation of transportation systems • Subsystems of transportation system • Governmental regulations • Transportation processes	• Relationship of transportation and other technologies • Intermodalism • Transportation services and methods • Positive and negative impacts of transportation systems • Transportation processes and efficiency

Table 4-3. Compendium of Major Topics for Technology Content Standards (continued)

Standard	Benchmark Topics Grades K-2	Benchmark Topics Grades 3-5	Benchmark Topics Grades 6-8	Benchmark Topics Grades 9-12
Standard 19: Manufacturing Technologies	• Manufacturing systems • Design of products	• Natural materials • Manufacturing processes • Consumption of goods • Chemical technologies	• Manufacturing systems • Manufacturing goods • Manufacturing processes • Chemical technologies • Materials use • Marketing products	• Servicing and obsolescence • Materials • Durable or non-durable goods • Manufacturing systems • Interchangeability of parts • Chemical technologies • Marketing products
Standard 20: Construction Technologies	• Different types of buildings • How parts of buildings fit	• Modern communities • Structures • Systems used	• Construction designs • Foundations • Purpose of structures • Buildings systems and sub-systems	• Infrastructure • Construction processes and procedures • Requirements • Maintenance, alterations, and renovation • Prefabricated materials

WHAT IMPACTS WILL THE STANDARDS HAVE ON TECHNOLOGY TEACHER EDUCATION PROGRAMS?

College and University Teacher Education Programs

    Standards for Technological Literacy will have a major impact on college and university technology teacher education programs throughout the country. The colleges and universities preparing the teachers for the future will need to put the standards into practice. Since the study of technology is a vital field of education, those in charge of teacher education programs need to revise their curricula and teaching methodologies to reflect the vision of *Standards for Technological Literacy*. Faculty members in technology teacher education programs should address *Standards for Technological Literacy* and what they mean for enhancing the technological literacy of future students. Becoming an effective technology teacher is an on-going process that begins in the earliest days of pre-service preparation in the undergraduate years and continues throughout one's professional career. Since the study of technology is a continuously changing field of study, teachers must be well prepared and have the ability and desire to stay informed and current on technological and educational advances throughout their careers.

    The preparation of teachers should assume that all pre-service students are prepared in the content areas as specified in *Standards for Technological Literacy*. It is imperative that the 20 standards be infused into the technology courses, the technological laboratory courses, professional courses, the clinical experiences, and the university core courses, which are taken by each pre-service student.

    The preparation of teachers requires that the knowledge and processes of technology be integrated within pedagogical courses. This will provide a connection between the study of technology and technology education. Teachers need to be lifelong learners themselves to inspire in others the desire to continue learning as an integral part of life. Colleges and universities can provide excellent examples here through their professors. Professors can set examples by being scholars, researchers, and professionals keenly interested in and involved in the study of technology.

    As previously stated, those who prepare technology teachers should review and revise undergraduate and graduate degree programs by using *Standards for Technological Literacy* as the basis for teaching technology.

Furthermore, strategies can be designed and implemented for recruiting and preparing a sufficient number of newly trained and credentialed technology education teachers.

Alternative Teacher Education Programs and Certification/Licensure

Alternate certification/licensure programs may be established in states and provinces with serious shortages of technology teachers. If alternate certification/licensure programs are established, they should comply with *Standards for Technological Literacy*. The institutions and agencies providing alternate certification/licensure should become very familiar with the content listed in *Standards for Technological Literacy* so that the students enrolled in the alternate certification/licensure program will become knowledgeable about and know how to use *Standards for Technological Literacy*. The teacher being prepared under alternate certification/licensure programs should be qualified both philosophically as well as in the content dealing with the teaching of technology.

Other Leadership Roles for Technology Teacher Education Faculty

It is also necessary to develop in-service programs to teach technology educators how to implement *Standards for Technological Literacy*. Supervisors are encouraged to provide support and philosophical leadership for reform in the field because they are in an ideal position to implement long-range plans for improving the delivery of technology education subject matter at the local, district, state, and province levels. It is vital to gain the support of the technology education profession in the acceptance and implementation of *Standards for Technological Literacy*. By using this document as a basis for modifying their instruction, teachers will demonstrate the importance of technological studies, the value of technological literacy, and their own abilities to teach about technology.

Other leadership roles for technology teacher education faculty include serving as ITEA/CTTE/NCATE program reviewers. This is a very important role that the faculty member can play in assessing other teacher education programs in the United States. Also, faculty members can work on committees when their undergraduate degree program comes up for NCATE approval. This will give them valuable experience in planning to assure that they are in compliance with the *ITEA/CTTE/NCATE Curriculum Guidelines* (ITEA/CTTE/NCATE, 1997). Additionally, technology teacher education faculty can work with committees within their program to assure that they meet certification/licensure requirements which are based on *Standards for Technological Literacy*.

Teacher education programs can provide valuable in-service to technology teachers. This can be done through regular graduate courses or conducting special workshops for teachers within the state or at certain school districts or regions. Historically, teacher education programs in the United States have provided valuable in-service to technology teachers who are becoming re-certified or being certified under temporary license or requirements.

Another leadership role for technology teacher education faculty is to provide service to other agencies in education. These include working with state departments of education and state supervisors of technology education in enhancing the teaching of technology within a given state. Also, it is very important that faculty in technology teacher program work with faculty from other university disciplines to develop interdisciplinary technology-based courses that contribute to the education of future technology education teachers.

PHASE III OF THE TECHNOLOGY FOR ALL AMERICANS PROJECT

The ITEA's Technology for All Americans Project is currently developing additional standards to complement and support *Standards for Technological Literacy*. This is made possible because of continued support and funding from the NSF and the NASA. These additional standards include:

- Assessment Standards for Technological Literacy
- Professional Development Standards for Technological Literacy
- Program Standards for Technological Literacy

All of these standards will impact teacher education programs. Additionally, the Council on Technology Teacher Education (CTTE) is using *Standards for Technological Literacy* to revise the *ITEA/CTTE/NCATE Curriculum Guidelines* (ITEA/CTTE/NCATE, 1997), accreditation guidelines for technology education.

CONCLUSIONS

For the first time in history, the technology education profession has a set of nationally developed and reviewed standards that prescribes what the content for the study of technology should be. The ultimate vision of these standards is that every student should and can become technologically literate. The difficult task is what lies ahead in implementing *Standards for Technological Literacy* in classrooms in school districts across the nation, in state departments of education, and in teacher preparation programs at colleges and universities. The seeds of progress have been sown, now the profession will have to nurture and cultivate them to create a new level of technology understanding and literacy for the generations to come.

REFERENCES

American Association for the Advancement of Science (AAAS). (1993). *Benchmarks for science literacy.* New York: Oxford University Press.

Cross, C. (October 21, 1998). The standards wars: Some lessons learned. *Education Week,* 32-35.

International Technology Education Association (ITEA). (1996). *A rationale and structure for the study of technology.* Reston, VA: Author.

International Technology Education Association (ITEA). (2000). *Standards for technological literacy: Content for the study of technology.* Reston, VA: Author.

International Technology Education Association/Council on Technology Teacher Education/National Council for Accreditation of Teacher Education (ITEA/CTTE/NCATE). (1997). *ITEA/CTTE/NCATE Curriculum guidelines.* Reston, VA: International Technology Education Association.

National Council of Teacher of Mathematics (NCTM). (1989). *Curriculum and Evaluation Standards for School Mathematics.* Reston, VA: Author.

National Council of Teachers of Mathematics (NCTM). (2000). *Principles and standards for school mathematics.* Reston, VA: Author.

National Research Council (NRC). (1996). *National science education standards.* Washington, D.C.: National Academy Press.

Future Technology Teacher Education Programs Based on *Standards for Technological Literacy*

Anthony F. Gilberti
Indiana State University

G. Eugene Martin
Southwest Texas State University

Throughout the history of humankind, civilizations have struggled to find better ways to coexist. Some have been more successful than others and the reasons are many, and sometimes varied and complex. Today's global society demands that people develop their knowledge and abilities to their fullest potential. A significant part of this process and one measure of success is the development of a literate society and literate individuals. Raising literacy levels and lowering illiteracy levels are challenges in every society.

A LITERATE CITIZENRY

A literate person is commonly referred to as being an educated person who understands the culture in which one lives. As might be expected, functional levels of literacy vary from one society to another and from one individual to another. When the phrase is spoken, "he or she is a literate person," it commonly refers to an educated and cultured person. Thus, to the layperson, literacy is often associated with reading and writing, and sometimes even speaking and mathematics. But there are many other forms of literacy including music literacy, art literacy, history literacy, social studies literacy, etc., that also deserve equal attention. Today, a new form of literacy is gaining the attention and respect of all the inhabitants of our global society. It is called technological literacy. A person cannot attain a functional level of technological literacy unless a functional level of basic literacy has first been achieved. Gardner (2000) recognizes the important role that literacy plays in education today. He believes that training students in the basic literacies and then introducing them to the major families of subject matter areas is fundamental to helping them understand the world around them.

World leaders have recognized for decades that technology is the one
discriminating factor that separates industrialized from non-industrial-
ized nations, developed from underdeveloped nations, and powerful from
non-powerful nations. Yet, while its importance is recognized and accepted by leaders, globally very little is being done in formal school settings to
create laboratory-classroom environments that foster the study of technology. For example, the study of technology is not widely practiced in any
form on a grand scale at the elementary, middle, and secondary school levels, at least not in the United States and in most other countries of the
world. At a time when business and community leaders and other key and
influential members of our society are promulgating the need for a school
subject in the study of technology, there has been a significant decline both
in the number of technology teacher training programs and in new
licensed technology teachers entering the field. Unfortunately, both situations, may, in the future, cause the closing of many technology studies or
technology education programs in elementary, middle, and secondary
schools.

The United States educational system has simply not kept pace with
what's happening in the technological world, resulting in its inability to
respond quickly and decisively to meet the changing technological needs
of society. There has also been a lack of technology education standards—
content, student assessment, professional development, and program—to
provide a general framework from which state and local school systems'
personnel could develop curricula and ultimately programs. Factors such
as these have placed schools and their personnel and curricula, and teacher
training institutions in a precarious situation. How do school personnel
provide a program for the study of technology when teacher-training
institutions are not licensing a sufficient number of teachers to meet the
demand for new and existing technology education teaching positions?
How do school personnel add a new curricular area to an already crowd-
ed school curriculum? Does the study of technology make a contribution
to the learning of other subject matter content areas? These questions and
many others continue to beg for answers. With the release of ITEA's
Standards for Technological Literacy: Content for the Study of Technology
(*Standards for Technological Literacy*) in 2000, these questions can be provided with many of the answers.

Technology is human innovation in action and since we as people create technology, technology helps to shape our lives and our society, and in

turn, our society helps to shape technology. Since technological change is driven by the purposeful actions of people, it is of paramount importance that when people make decisions as to which technology is to be developed, which technology is used, which technology is to be modified, and even which technology is to be eliminated, the people making those decisions must be technologically informed, or, in other words, they must be technologically literate. Since all people are part of the decision making process in a democratic society, this means that they must have a functional level of technological literacy. All people must be able to use, manage, assess, and understand technology in order to be contributing members of their society. In fact, possessing the ability to use, manage, assess, and understand technology clearly defines the nature of a technologically literate person, and when people attain this ability, neither will they be threatened by technology nor necessarily obsessed by it. Finally, technologically literate people possess the capability of making educated decisions about which technological process to use and the what, how, and when to develop or use various technological systems.

While technological literacy and technical literacy are often used interchangeably, they are definitely not the same. Technologically literate people possess the ability to use, manage, assess, and understand technology, while technically literate people place greater importance on their ability to perform with tools (psychomotor skill development, e.g., automotive repair person) and to communicate using technical terms. In the process of becoming technologically literate, people learn <u>about</u> technology and they learn to <u>do</u> technology. In the process of becoming technically literate, people learn to <u>do</u> technology with less or little emphasis on learning <u>about</u> technology.

Now more than ever before the global society needs to become more technologically literate. In the United States, this need can be addressed by implementing the study of technology in elementary, middle, and secondary schools. The outcome of this program is a technologically literate person. When the development of technological literacy becomes one of the primary goals and is central to the mission of our schools, then there will be direct measurable benefits to our students and society. Examples of these benefits are people understanding the role of technology in society and culture, making technology decisions including the ability to differentiate which technology to use to solve an individual or societal problem, and technology career awareness.

The publication, *Standards for Technological Literacy*, clearly underscores the need for technological literacy development at all levels of education. Furthermore, it argues rather convincingly that if the United States is to remain the most technologically advanced country in the world, an improved program of study in technology needs to be implemented immediately. It calls for developing functional levels of technological literacy in all school-age children so they will be able to use, manage, assess, and understand technology in the world around them. Finally, it calls for children to learn about technology and learn to do technology.

The immediate challenge to teacher education program personnel is to develop quality curricula and modes of instruction that prepare future teachers to teach in this new laboratory-classroom environment. This may require some teacher educators to redefine the role and scope of their teacher education programs and to collaborate with school personnel throughout the process, and that they do it continuously without interruption. While teacher educators must not teach to the new content standards, it is important that they use the standards to set the framework for preparing new technology education teachers.

DIMENSIONS OF TECHNOLOGY

In *A Rationale and Structure for the Study of Technology* (1996), the ITEA takes the position that "Technology is human innovation in action. It involves the generation of knowledge and processes to develop systems that solve problems and extend human capabilities" (p. 16). Therefore, with human innovation in action as the focal point of technology, it must have a process, knowledge, and contextual base (p. 16). One cannot exist in isolation of the others, as they are mutually dependent on one another. For example, people must have technological knowledge to create a technological product and at the same time, the creation of the product and the knowledge used to create it must be done within a technological context or as used in this example, there must be a reason for the development of the product. As existing technological knowledge is used to create a new product, new technological knowledge may also be created and new technological contexts in which the product might be developed may also be generated. It is a never-ending life cycle of generating new technological knowledge, new technological processes, and new technological contexts, with the creating of new technology being at the heart of the life cycle.

IMPLEMENTING TECHNOLOGY EDUCATION PROGRAMS

The publication, *ROAD MAPS: Perspectives for Excellence in Technology Education Programs* (*Road Maps*) (Balistreri, Daugherty, Gray, & Valesey, 1998), provides four authoritative perspectives on "...what should be addressed by administrators and professional educators in their quest for excellence" (p. 1) in technology education programs. Their perspectives are based on an array of professional experiences at the local administration, state/provincial administration, higher education, and state/provincial association levels. Their message is very clear and direct. If technology education is ever to be successfully implemented on a grand scale throughout all the educational systems in the United States, then teachers and administrators of elementary, middle, secondary, and post-secondary school technology programs must become more "...active educators, prove the value of their programs, set high expectations, teach effective courses, put goals into action, verify quality, and market the technology education experience" (p. 1). The challenge to the technology profession is immense and immediate, and it requires that all its members work constructively and collaboratively to bring about purposeful change and then sustain the change process. *Road Maps* was published before *Standards for Technological Literacy* was released. They contain information that should be helpful in implementing *Standards for Technological Literacy*.

Road Maps provide a framework to initiate substantial change. As it relates to teacher education programs and the potential positive impact of the content standards, the process should include but not be limited to the following:

- Frame a teaching and learning environment that promotes the value of research by first establishing a research agenda for all faculty and undergraduate and graduate students. Integrate research activities throughout the teacher preparation curriculum. Emphasize the value of research by making it an integral part of the life cycle of the teacher preparation experience.

- Emphasize the importance of recruitment of the highest order. Recruit individuals to become technology teachers who are good people-persons and who are committed to making a difference in the lives of others. Make yourself (teacher educators) visible at meetings where potential new teachers are in attendance and interact with them. Identify successful recruitment strategies used in other subject matter areas and emulate and incorporate them when developing and implementing a recruitment plan. Learn from others so as not to repeat their mistakes in your efforts.

- Be a proactive proponent for technology education at all meetings where standards for teacher preparation or enhancement, such as the Professional Development Standards for Technological Literacy which will be released in 2003, are an agenda topic. As content standards are developed in other subject matter areas, form alliances with these areas, particularly those whose standards might have an impact on technology education.

- Remember that professional development is a lifelong process and every technology teacher education program should have a professional development program for teachers in its service area. Include program topics (e.g., selected content standards) that are most germane to the immediate needs of teachers. Form a professional development council that includes classroom teachers as part of its membership to help identify these topics.

- Set and maintain high expectations and content standards beginning at the initial teacher preparation experience (pre-service) and continuing through all in-service activities. Lead by example and attend and participate in professional meetings, serve on committees, volunteer in the community, present professional papers, expose students to outstanding practicing teachers in the community, and reward students with excellent student teaching and clinical experiences.

- Develop and maintain a technology teacher preparation program that is recognized in the university community for its relevancy and quality. Form technology program advisory groups or councils that include membership from representatives of the university community and from industries in the community. Actively seek grants and other forms of financial support to initiate new endeavors such as implementing content standards, curricular revision, and professional development of technology teachers.

- Serve and be recognized as the leader in bringing about change in the technology education community. Promote your teacher education program by being the "hub" of activity in *Standards for Technological Literacy* implementation, regardless of the implementation level. Host workshops, and in-service and professional development activities that focus on the standards implementation. Appoint one faculty member in your department to be the first point of contact to the public on implementing *Standards for Technological Literacy* implementation.

- Serve and be recognized as the leader in your geographical area for developing and implementing quality assessment measures including assessment tools and programs. Ensure that measures of quality teaching and learning are recognized as vital functions of the teacher preparation experience and that they continue throughout the life cycle of being a classroom teacher.

- Perform the lead role in collecting data on the teaching and learning experience. Analyze, interpret, and distribute results to the technology education community in order to bring about purposeful improvements in student learning, content, programs, and teaching methodologies. Host in-service workshops for classroom teachers to interpret and disseminate the data and share the results of the data collection and interpretation processes with leaders in other subject matter areas.

- Most importantly, market the value of technology education to individuals and groups who make decisions about the worthiness of a program of study in technology. In consultation with marketing experts, develop strategies that will change public perceptions, increase student enrollments, and increase financial support for your technology program. Serve as the lead institution in your geographical area and coordinate the marketing of technology education programs at all levels in the area.

While the preceding statements provide ideas to initiate the process of establishing excellence in technology teacher education programs, including the implementation of *Standards for Technological Literacy*, the key to success lies in the people who will ultimately bear the responsibility to implement and maintain these programs at a high level of quality. Technology teacher educators must share in this responsibility both personally and professionally. Personally, they must commit their time and talent and make a concerted effort to improve the overall teaching and learning environment. Professionally, they must be dedicated to preparing quality technology teachers, through both in-service and pre-service activities, that will be fully qualified to engage students in a contemporary technology studies program. Also, they must be leaders in establishing alternative teacher preparation programs, determining licensure criteria, getting technology teacher education programs approved by *International Technology Education Association, Council on Technology Teacher Education, and National Council for Accreditation of Teacher Education Approved Curriculum Guidelines (ITEA/CTTE/NCATE Curriculum Guidelines)* (ITEA, 1997), establishing state curriculum guides for technology education, and participating in national professional organizations.

WHAT SHOULD TECHNOLOGY TEACHERS DO DIFFERENTLY?

Fostering Technological Literacy

A contemporary and effective technology education program that fosters *Standards for Technological Literacy* requires that educators have a sound philosophical basis of the study of technology. This philosophical foundation should provide pre-service teachers with the reasons why the study of technology is important, major tenets of the technology, historical foundations, and future directions. This knowledge is necessary in order for the pre-service student to make connections from the content of technology education to the broader educational goals established by society. Further, this knowledge will serve future educators well as they articulate the need for the study of technology as a core subject and its relevance to society. Teacher educators at the postsecondary level must help pre-service teachers to:

- Understand the nature and significance of technology in human affairs.
- Use technological devices and processes and manage their appropriate use.
- Assess technology in terms of its social, cultural, and environmental consequences.
- Recognize the limitations of science and technology in solving problems.

- Apply technology-based problem solving as a method to foster creativity and verify conclusions.
- Utilize value-clarification skills and processes for making informed decisions and considering alternative modes of behavior with regard to technological endeavors.
- Develop and implement curriculum that is in alignment with state and national standards.
- Assess student outcomes and curriculum in light of the best practices of teaching and learning.

The above items should not be considered a laundry list that teacher educators can select from at will. If technology education is to be successful in fostering the development of a technologically literate individual, then we can expect no less from our future educators. Thus, our future educators must be technologically literate prior to graduating from a postsecondary institution. Graduates who operate at high functional levels of technological literacy will be better prepared to implement *Standards for Technological Literacy.*

Curriculum Development

To successfully foster technological literacy at the K-12 levels, technology teacher educators must move beyond the traditional approaches used in the past to develop curriculum. *Standards for Technological Literacy* is more inclusive than the study of industries around the thematic areas of communication, construction, manufacturing, transportation, and power and energy. While these content areas served the profession well in the past, today they represent only a portion of the technologies used in society. For example, agricultural, biotechnologies, and medical technologies are influencing society at an ever-increasing rate, and technology teacher educators need to be prepared to teach in these areas. Additionally, many technology educators have treated these content areas as distinct technical units of instruction. They have failed to include how the nature of technology influences society, illustrated the interdependencies that exist among these technical units, nor explained how scientists, engineers, and technologists who work in these technical endeavors make decisions.

The *Standards for Technological Literacy* calls for an in-depth study of technology in order to develop technological literacy. This social application of technology requires future teachers to develop knowledge and skills in the following areas:

- Nature of Technology
- The Role of Technology in Society
- Design
- Abilities for a Technological World, and
- The Designed World

It is the authors' perspective that an in-depth knowledge of technology can only be achieved when a radical departure from the traditional tool, material, and skill development approaches used in some technology teacher education programs has occurred. The future technology teacher education program must be restructured to include the study of technology from a holistic perspective. This coherent curriculum should hold together and make sense as a whole. It should be logically integrated, have a sense of purpose, be relevant, and provide a series of unforgettable experiences for pre-service teachers. A dynamic and coherent technology education curriculum includes a study of the following:

- The roles of engineering, design, and product development.
- Sustainable development of technological endeavors.
- Resource management and integrated planning.
- Bio-related technologies and environmental ethics in all systems.
- Technology assessment and forecasting.
- The role of innovation and invention to solve technological problems.
- The connections between technology, science, mathematics, and other subjects.
- System integration and interdependencies.
- The history and trends of technology.

To bring about this curriculum, technology teacher educators will have to foster new instructional strategies. These strategies and curriculum will likely require the interdisciplinary efforts of technologists, scientists, mathematicians, engineers, environmentalists, political scientists, philosophers, and others who can illustrate the connections of technology with the humanities and the social sciences. Fortunately, these educators already have a prominent role at colleges and universities. By developing partnerships with these professionals and with conceptually designed programs that use team teaching, multisensory learning, and student-centered activities, teacher educators would have the ability to enhance the technological capabilities of their students. More importantly, our future educators would be positioned to implement *Standards for Technological Literacy* upon leaving the university with the knowledge acquired from the above partnerships.

Delivering technology education programs will involve making decisions about delivery strategies, teaching approaches, facilities, and assessment (both curriculum and student assessment) to enhance the skills of pre-service teachers. The curriculum developed at postsecondary teacher education programs must be connected to each of the above elements in order to be successful.

Delivery Strategies and Teaching Approaches

Technology teacher educators will have to link the appropriate delivery strategy with its content and activities to enhance the teaching-learning process. As Beane (1995) noted, students benefit from a delivery system that is structured to meet their needs, interests, and individual abilities. Delivery strategies and teaching approaches most appropriate to technology pre-service education may include any one or more of the following: Applied Science Approach, Design Education Approach, Integrated Subject Approach, Science/Technology/Society Approach, or a Technology Concepts Approach. Each of these different approaches is presented briefly below.

The Applied Science Approach

The Applied Science Approach has typically used science teachers to demonstrate the application of scientific concepts and theories. Examples of this approach can be seen in CORD's Applications in Biology/Chemistry (2001) courses. Technology teacher educators could use this approach to explore the design of new technologies. While science teachers emphasized only the theoretical understanding of scientific ideas, the technology teacher educator could emphasize the practical applications of science and engineering concepts.

The Design Education Approach

The Design Education Approach allows students individually or in teams to identify a problem and develop one or more solutions to test and redesign a project or product to meet its intended purpose. While technology educators utilize this approach, some of the design problems or materials used to solve problems may have no social or cultural relevance. The problems provided to students are merely problem solving activities. This approach, however, could be used to allow students to investigate and solve social and/or environmental problems that are relevant at the local or regional level (Wright, 1995).

The Integrated Subject Approach

The Integrated Subject Approach uses the integration of several curriculum areas into one unified curriculum endeavor. Thus, the teaching can range from the use of a single instructor integrating subject matter areas, to teams of teachers using multidisciplinary instruction in a single or integrated laboratory environment. This approach can also have a topical or thematic base. As previously noted, this approach can be used in teacher preparation programs to bring about a greater understanding to the significance of technology in human affairs. While science, mathematics, engineering, and environmental studies might seem to have the most logical connections to the study of technology, other curricular areas should also be considered when technology content and activities are integrated across the K-12 curriculum (American Association for the Advancement of Science, 1989; Zuga, 1988).

The Science/Technology/Society Approach

The Science/Technology/Society Approach has been used in liberal arts and science courses. Science/Technology/Society courses are usually organized around science issues that are occurring at the local level (e.g., students explore scientific concepts and attempt to solve the problem at hand in view of current economic and social considerations). These courses often explore the interactions between science, technology, and society. Technology teacher education programs can successfully use this approach by focusing on the technology element of these types of investigations. Technology teacher educators have a unique opportunity with the use of Science/Technology/Society (STS) approach due to the laboratory-based nature of these studies. When team-taught with educators from a variety of subject matter areas, this approach can provide a powerful stimulus in the teaching-learning process (Gilberti, 1992; Hurd, 1995).

The Technology Concepts Approach

The Technology Concepts Approach focuses on learning about the processes of technological development. This approach also focuses on system concepts and models. A teacher education program can expand upon this approach by including how technologists solve problems via design and innovation processes. With such an approach, the use of models and simulations can be used more effectively (Schwaller, 1995).

When implementing these teaching approaches and delivery strategies, teacher educators will have to design laboratories to meet the needs of students and the curriculum under study. Currently, some technology educators have used industrial technology laboratories to provide for a skilled workforce (e.g., computer-aided design, electronics, robotics, etc.). These laboratories, by their nature, emphasize the production of objects rather than design, research and experimentation, or the interactions of technology on society, culture, or the environment.

Facilities for the Future

The future laboratories in technology teacher preparation programs must become more versatile and, therefore, serve as an aid in student learning. For example, laboratories need to be equipped in a way to allow students to 'design' the laboratory environment for the problem, activity, or content being investigated. Laboratories should include the full range of machine tools for students to prototype new devices, manufacture products, and explore system operations. Further, laboratories should provide the necessary equipment to allow students to conduct research, experiment with materials and processes, and develop simulations.

While the temptation may be to outfit laboratories with state-of-the-art machines used by contemporary business and industry, this may not always be the best approach. Tabletop equipment can often be used to demonstrate the key concepts to be learned, and these are viable alternatives to industrial-based equipment. Moreover, these tools are more likely what pre-service teachers will be able to afford in their own technology education programs when they leave the university. These types of machines also allow for the quick setup, breakdown, and storage needed when designing and constructing technology activities.

Perhaps more importantly, the technology teacher educator of the future must move beyond the traditional approaches to teaching and learning. While most technology teacher educators have relied on state-assisted funding to secure laboratory equipment, there are numerous teaching and learning laboratories that exist within the local community. For example, technology teacher educators could develop partnerships with local industries to allow students to have access to technologies not available to them at the postsecondary institution. Additionally, by using the full range of opportunities to study technology, as it exists at the local or regional level, pre-service teachers will see a greater relevance to their studies. Pre-service educators will also be more likely to use these same approaches when they graduate.

EVALUATION OF TECHNOLOGY TEACHER EDUCATION PROGRAMS

Assessment

To assess the effectiveness of standards-based technology teacher education programs, all levels of the teaching-learning environment will need to be evaluated. This assessment will need to focus on the appropriateness of the curricula being used, the instructional and delivery processes, and the knowledge and skills obtained by pre-service teachers as they move through the teacher preparation program. The overall purpose of these assessments should be to provide information that improves the teaching and learning environment. These assessments should also provide evidence to determine whether the intended learning outcomes have been achieved in relation to pre-established performance standards.

To perform these assessments, both formative and summative assessments will have to be used. Formative assessments are ongoing and provide data that can help to improve teaching and learning during a regular cycle of activities. Examples of formative assessments include tests, oral reports, and exams at the end of a unit of study.

Summative assessments occur periodically and provide data about student achievement at the conclusion of a specific time period (e.g., at the end of the first year of studies). These assessments can include the use of benchmark assessments like national standardized tests. Additionally, summative assessments can take the form of senior projects or student portfolios. These types of assessments may also be used to examine the effectiveness of curriculum, teaching strategies, or instructor competency.

Regardless of the type of assessment being used, the overall assessment should provide useable data to what students know and can do as a result of instruction and laboratory experiences. The assessments used in technology education teacher preparation programs must be authentic and challenging. Assessments should also be based on the accepted practices established for the profession. Thus, the assessments should be performance based.

Performance based assessments should allow pre-service teachers to perform the following:

- Demonstrate an understanding that shows what students know and can do in meaningful contexts.
- Generate in-depth responses rather than produce pre-provided brief responses.
- Demonstrate their knowledge base according to a set of criteria or standards.

It is important to note that performance assessments should be based on actual student demonstrations or student observations. These assessments have the potential to redirect learning so that pre-service teachers take a more active role in their learning process. They can be used to assess the lifelong learning outcomes of critical thinking, communication skills, teamwork, and integrating content from multidisciplinary activities.

ITEA/CTTE/NCATE CURRICULUM GUIDELINES

In order to bring about a quality technology teacher education program, more effort needs to be directed to helping institutions meet the *ITEA/CTTE/NCATE Curriculum Guidelines* (ITEA, 1997). These guidelines have been put into place to assure that pre-service teachers are acquiring the knowledge and skills necessary to become effective technology teachers. To assure the overall quality of these programs, the *ITEA/CTTE/NCATE Curriculum Guidelines* will be rewritten to reflect *Standards for Technological Literacy* (See Chapter 9).

Further, all technology teacher education programs that have met the *ITEA/CTTE/NCATE Curriculum Guidelines* should have in place a procedure for in-service education. The technology education profession has a tremendous need for continual in-service education to implement the content standards and to make the teaching-learning environment a continual lifelong commitment for educators. As more educational research impacts the profession of teaching and as technology is constantly changing, educators will require continual in-service to be effective and skilled resource managers of their curriculum area.

REFLECTION

Technology teacher educators are focusing their energies to better prepare students to enter the vibrant and dynamic world of teaching. They are positioning their programs to cause significant change in the role and scope of elementary, middle, and secondary school programs through the integration of a technology curriculum.

Teachers in the 21st century need to possess many traits. Technology teachers, for example, need to understand technology, have a thirst for new knowledge and skills, a strong commitment to the growth and development of children, and an awareness of the importance of being professionally active throughout their teaching careers.

Technology teacher educators have a responsibility to make a significant contribution to the development of these traits. They need to place greater emphasis on the importance of preparing quality teachers who possess the desire and ability to work collaboratively with colleagues in other subject matter areas in order that technology studies be integrated throughout the K-12 curriculum. They need to ensure that their graduates are well educated and trained in delivery strategies and teaching approaches that promote the development of technological literacy. They need to prepare their graduates to be able to successfully work and communicate with elementary and secondary school teachers and administrators, while providing them convincing arguments why technological literacy should be an equal partner with all other forms of literacy. They need to prepare technology studies teachers in ways to design and implement assessment measures that ensure the continued development of technological literacy in K-12 students. And, in the final analysis, they need to prepare future teachers who accept that the product of every technology studies program is a person who possesses a functional level of technological literacy "…a person who understands—with increasing sophistication—what technology is, how it is created, how it shapes society, and in turn is shaped by society is technologically literate" (ITEA, 2000, p. vi).

A challenge now before every technology teacher educator is to identify methods of preparing future teachers through pre-service education and practicing teachers through in-service education to implement *Standards for Technological Literacy*. The challenge may cause some educators to restructure their curriculum in order to make it more coherent, cohesive, and in tune with the development of the new content standards. While the challenge may be great, it cannot be ignored if technology education is to be widely accepted as an integral part of the K-12 curriculum.

THOUGHT-PROVOKING ACTIVITIES

1. What are the characteristics of a literate citizenry? What does it mean to say that a person has a functional level of literacy? Is it possible to be literate in one area (e.g., mathematics) and illiterate in another area (e.g., technology)?

2. Some countries are implementing technology studies in their school systems at a rate faster than what is being done in the United States. Identify some of these countries and illustrate what they are doing that the United States may not be undertaking.

3. Technology is an integral part of every person's life in the 21st century. People who make decisions about what is included in the K-12 curriculum and who ignore the importance of including technology studies are depriving students the opportunity to study in an enriched and dynamic program. Develop a list of convincing arguments that underscore the importance of incorporating technology studies in the K-12 curriculum. Which items on your list would you present to your peers? A school principal? A group of parents? Members of the local chamber of commerce? The state board of education?

4. Undertaking a research project provides the investigator valuable data to solve a problem that is being researched. University faculty, undergraduate and graduate students, and classroom teachers in elementary and secondary schools all conduct research. Identify one problem area that you believe needs to be researched in technology

education and describe how you would go about investigating the problem.

5. Currently, an insufficient number of people are entering the teaching profession, and this shortage is at a critical point in technology education. Identify some strategies to attract more students to become technology teachers. What techniques could be used to market these strategies? Develop a recruitment plan that includes the identified strategies and marketing techniques. What should be the main ingredients of a recruitment plan? How would a recruitment plan for technology education be different from a plan for another subject matter area?

6. Education is a lifelong process. Most technology studies teachers will need to participate in professional development activities to keep their endorsements current and to be better prepared as teachers. What are some in-service activities that technology educators will need in order to be a successful teacher during the first 10 years of employment? What have been your most rewarding in-service activities?

7. Identify the knowledge, skills, and attitudes that are important to becoming a technologically literate person. Compare the knowledge, skills, and attitudes identified with those of your peers. How are they the same? How are they different?

8. What needs to be done at the postsecondary level to better prepare students to implement the content standards for technology education? Compare the list developed with those of your peers. What are the similarities and dissimilarities?

9. This chapter identified five delivery strategies and teaching approaches for technology pre-service education. Select one of the five approaches and illustrate how to incorporate it in a classroom-laboratory environment. Be specific with your response and illustrate at least four laboratory activities that can be used with middle or high school students.

10. Explain the difference(s) between formative and summative assessments. Identify specific examples when a teacher would use each type of assessment in a technology education program.

11. Portfolio based assessments provide physical evidence of students' ability to meet desired program standards and lifelong learning skills. How should pre-service teacher portfolios be developed to represent transition points in their education? Illustrate how multiple validations and portfolios could be weighted in a technology teacher education program.

REFERENCES

American Association for the Advancement of Science (AAAS). (1989). *Project 2061: Science for all Americans.* Washington, D.C.: Author.

Balistreri, J., Daugherty, M., Gray, R., & Valesey, B. (1998). *ROAD MAPS: Perspectives for excellence in technology education programs.* Reston, VA: International Technology Education Association.

Beane, J. A. (1995). Introduction: What is a coherent curriculum? In J. A. Beane (Ed.). *Toward a coherent curriculum: 1995 ASCD yearbook,* (pp. 1-14). Alexandria, VA: Association for Supervision and Curriculum Development.

CORD. (2001). CORD applications in biology/chemistry. Waco, TX: CCI Publications.

Gardner, H. (2000, May). *An education for the future: The foundation of science and values.* Paper presented at the symposium of the Tsuzuki International Scholarship Fund, Tokyo, Japan.

Gilberti, A.F. (1992). The science/technology/society approach. In A.F. Gilberti (Ed.). *Integrating technology, people and the environment.* Reston, VA: International Technology Education Association.

Hurd, P.D. (1985). A rationale for a science, technology, and society theme in science education. In R. W. Bybee (Ed.). *Science technology society: 1985 yearbook of the National Science Teachers Association.* Washington, D.C.: National Science Teachers Association.

International Technology Education Association (ITEA). (2000). *Standards for technological literacy: Content for the study of technology.* Reston, VA: Author.

International Technology Education Association (ITEA). (1996). *Technology for all Americans: A rationale and structure for the study of technology.* Reston, VA: Author.

International Technology Education Association/Council on Technology Teacher Education/National Council on Accreditation of Teacher Education. (ITEA/CTTE/NCATE) (1997). *ITEA/CTTE/NCATE Curriculum guidelines.* Reston, VA: International Technology Teacher Association.

International Technology Education Association (ITEA). (2000). *Teaching technology: Middle school strategies for standards-based instruction.* Reston, VA: Author.

Schwaller, A.E. (1995) Instructional strategies for technology education. In G.E. Martin (Ed.). *Foundations of technology education: 44th yearbook of the council on technology teacher education,* (pp. 247-285). New York: Glencoe McGraw-Hill.

Wright, R.T. (1995). Technology education curriculum development efforts. In G.E. Martin (Ed.). *Foundations of technology education: 44th yearbook of the council on technology teacher education,* (pp. 247-285). New York: Glencoe McGraw-Hill.

Zuga, K.F. (1988). Interdisciplinary approach. In W.H. Kemp and A.E. Schwaller (Eds.). *Instructional strategies for technology education: 37th yearbook of the council on technology teacher education,* (pp. 56-71). New York: Glencoe McGraw-Hill

Restructuring the Technology Teacher Education Curriculum

Rodney L. Custer
Illinois State University

R. Thomas Wright
Ball State University

In a recent report on the role of standards as a catalyst for educational reform issued by the National Research Council (NRC), the assertion is made that significant improvement in student learning is "unlikely until teachers are educated in ways that enable them to implement and teach curricula that are consistent with the vision, goals, and content of the national standards" (NRC, 2000, p. 18). Viewed from this perspective, standards assume a more critical role than simply identifying, clarifying, and structuring the content knowledge of a discipline, as if that were a simple matter. Rather, before meaningful change can occur at the K-12 level of implementation, teacher education programs must engage in critical and honest reflection about how well they are addressing national standards.

Over the next few years, technology teacher educators will decide the extent they agree or disagree with this assertion—that educational reform at the K-12 level is fundamentally grounded in seriously addressing *Standards for Technological Literacy: Content for the Study of Technology (Standards for Technological Literacy)* (ITEA, 2000). At one level, the issue is curricular (i.e., configuring courses and student activities to align with standards). Viewed more broadly, serious engagement with the standards has the potential of triggering fundamental reform of how technology teacher education is configured and delivered. As indicated in previous chapters, implementing the standards will include changing the teacher education curriculum, but it is only one component for implementing a technology based education system. From this perspective, the stakes are much higher and the risks associated with significant change are very real.

The National Commission on Teaching and America's Future (NCTAF), in a report critical of teacher education in America, reported that the view persists that anyone can teach, especially if they have adequate content knowledge (NCTAF, 1996). The report goes on to voice the view, shared by many, that "teacher preparation programs contribute little to the production of qualified teachers and high-quality teaching" (NCTAF, 1996). Some of these same perceptions, and misperceptions, are also apparent in technology education. Within technology education, the perception (and perhaps the reality) persists that the profession is strong on activities and limited in terms of content knowledge. The profession is in an exciting, and perhaps even terrifying, period of time when many teachers are uncertain of their grasp of content knowledge as well as their ability to employ the kinds of new teaching methods required to meet the standards. Given this situation, it is very important that technology teacher education programs be equipped to have a major effect on students who are preparing to become technology education teachers.

Thus, the challenge for technology teacher educators and the purpose of this chapter extends beyond how to teach pre-service educators how to teach the content contained in *Standards for Technological Literacy* in their K-12 classrooms. Rather, it is important that the field think more broadly about curricular reform, including such thorny challenges as integrating technology content across disciplines, stimulating students to engage in meaningful reflection on technological activities, and equipping students to cope with the inherently dynamic and expansive nature of technology.

It is important to note at the outset that the authors' purpose throughout this chapter is to raise, frame, and clarify curricular issues that, in our judgment, must be addressed as a function of <u>what</u> *Standards for Technological Literacy* contains. The authors have attempted to refrain from prescribing <u>how</u> our colleagues at various teacher education programs should respond in making their curricular decisions. Those are local decisions and the profession stands to benefit by the development of a variety of creative implementation strategies and models. The authors' charge is to raise the issues and stimulate dialog.

COMPETENCE FOR TECHNOLOGY TEACHERS

At a basic level, the preparation of technology education teachers involves three primary dimensions: knowing, doing, and valuing. These are not new and a strong element of each is woven throughout the standards. Throughout the history of the field, the profession has in various ways concentrated on all three, with arguably a primary emphasis on the "doing" component. If successful, *Standards for Technological Literacy* will cause the profession to rethink these dimensions in several important ways. First, these standards contain material that redefines and expands what it is that technology educators have traditionally <u>known</u>, <u>done</u>, and <u>valued</u>. All three dimensions have been dramatically expanded to include content that may be relatively new to many teachers and teacher educators. It will take time, hard choices, and considerable professional development to conceptualize and craft new curriculum materials capable of delivering this expanded body of content.

A second shift has to do with an increased emphasis on the <u>knowing</u> (content) dimension. It is important to recognize that *Standards for Technological Literacy* is inherently designed to define the essential content knowledge of technology education. *The National Science Education Standards* by NRC (1996) and American Association for the Advancement of Science (AAAS) *Benchmarks for Science Literacy* (1993) and *Principles and Standards for School Mathematics* (2000) by National Council of Teachers of Mathematics (NCTM) were specifically intended to identify, clarify, and structure the content knowledge of their respective fields. They both raised and attempted to address the question, "What, in this modern world, do students need to know about science and mathematics?" To a lesser extent, both subject matter areas addressed broader learning and pedagogical issues. But the primary focus was on content. *Standards for Technological Literacy* also contains a strong emphasis on content. What is the base content knowledge of technology? What do all citizens in a technological culture need to know about technology? What does it mean to be a technologically literate person? The profession has and will continue to ask, "What do students need to be able to do with and value about technology?" But, the standards were developed on the premise that there is such a thing as a body of technological knowledge and that technology is more than the application of knowledge from other subject matter areas (e.g., mathematics and science).

As such, technology teacher education must continue to concentrate on the knowing, doing, and valuing aspects of technology. What must now be addressed is how to best equip new teachers to deliver an expanded (and perhaps unfamiliar), standards-based body of content and activity. A significant part of this challenge is to do so in a way that maintains an appropriate balance among the three. It simply will not do to recast the study of technology into a passive, intellectual exercise devoid of active engagement with a variety of technologies. At the same time, *Standards for Technological Literacy* will force the profession to confront a tendency to engage in activities apart from meaningful and focused learning. Also, it is quite likely that this will force us to engage in increased levels of collaboration with other academic disciplines in ways that may be threatening and challenging.

FUNDAMENTAL KNOWLEDGE BASE FOR THE STUDY OF TECHNOLOGY

The first ten technology standards deal generally on defining the base content knowledge for the study of technology. More specifically, three general areas of concentration (Chapters 3-5) are identified and developed in detail. These include a fundamental understanding of The Nature of Technology, Technology and Society or its role and function in society, and Design or the elements and essence of design and problem solving. The authors will address each of these three categories. In each case, the authors will attempt to pinpoint key curricular issues that in our judgment need to be addressed in order to implement the standards.

The Nature of Technology

The first three initial standards focus on The Nature of Technology. Technology teacher education curricula must include components that cause students to think in depth about what is meant by technology. There are at least three challenges associated with this aspect of the content. First, considerable confusion persists, and will almost certainly continue to persist, about the meaning of the term, technology. The vast majority of Americans think of technology as having something to do with computers. Simply, technology is how we as humans change our natural world. The evening news reports on the technology (computer-related) stocks. Politicians strike a positive chord when they promote the increased use of technology in the schools. Curriculum materials need to be designed that increase the awareness of the complexity of the term to include artifacts (things), processes (ways of doing), and technological knowledge. Students need to think about technology as tools, as a mechanism for extending human capability, and about how technology is distinct from the study of science and the study of the natural world. So, an initial curricular challenge is to conceive of ways to expand students' awareness of the complexity of what is meant by technology.

A second challenge follows directly from the first. As with many other content areas, it is one thing to reflect and think about the complexities of technology within the walls of the university. It is quite another to configure university level curriculum in ways that will enable future teachers to engage K-12 students in thinking about technology in engaging and developmentally appropriate ways.

A third challenge has to do with program and curriculum marketing. The release of *Standards for Technological Literacy* certainly will not lead to automatic and immediate acceptance in the school curriculum. The schedule is already full. Future teachers must know that it is one thing to possess basic understanding of the nature of technology. It is quite another matter to be able to communicate these understandings in clear and compelling ways to educational decision-makers. It is essential that university level curricula be developed to cause students to wrestle with these issues in depth and to learn and practice techniques needed to quickly and effectively capture the imagination of a variety of audiences (e.g., students, other teachers, administrators, and parents). Technology education teachers must market the study of technology for all Americans.

One unique and interesting aspect of The Nature of Technology that has been embedded in *Standards for Technological Literacy* has to do with "core concepts" of technology (Standard 2). The framers of the standards attempted to address the question, "What are the core concepts that collectively make technology distinct from other areas of study?" As conceptualized in this standard, these include systems, resources, requirements, optimization and trade-offs, processes, and controls. While other elements could be (and have been) identified, this section presents an interesting and potentially useful conceptual framework for curriculum and program developers. It also represents a substantial departure from the structures used historically to frame curriculum in technology education, which among others have included materials (woods, metals, plastics, etc.), systems (transportation, manufacturing, production, communication, etc.), processes (printing, welding, finishing, etc.), and more. A key issue here is how to incorporate and infuse these core elements into the curriculum. Can they be used as major organizers or do they more appropriately serve the curriculum as persistent threads of emphasis within other curriculum organizational structures? These questions remain to be addressed. But the challenge remains to consider these core concepts seriously as essential to the study of technology.

Technology and Society

Another aspect contributing to a fundamental understanding of technology has to do with its interaction with social and cultural structures identified in the four standards classified as Technology and Society. Since technology is fundamentally a human activity, students must reflect about the ways in which the two, technology and society, interact and exert influence on one another. In some respects, this emphasis on Technology and Society is not new to the technology education curriculum. *Jackson's Mill Industrial Arts Curriculum Theory* (Snyder & Hales, 1981) used the term "human adaptive systems" and many university level technology education programs have been offering courses in technology and society on a campus-wide, general education basis.

What is new in *Standards for Technological Literacy* is an emphasis on the bi-directional nature of the interaction between technology and society. The technology education profession has had much to say about the "impact of technology" on society. This is appropriate and true, but it is simplistic and ignores the complexities of the relationship. Technology has affected virtually every aspect of culture and social institutions in powerful ways including patterns and modes of travel, mechanisms used to communicate with others around the world, forensic analysis of crime scenes, altering natural biological processes, and much more. Society and culture have been fundamentally and profoundly changed by the dramatic and pervasive growth of technology. *Standards for Technological Literacy* quite appropriately acknowledges and elaborates on this important point.

But *Standards for Technological Literacy* also contributes another important understanding to this discussion. Not only does technology impact and influence society, the reverse is also true. Cultural values and social institutions have a powerful shaping influence on technology. Technologies are selected, shaped, marketed, and used, not because they are inherently valuable or even needed. Rather, technology is shaped by powerful cultural and social influences, including factors such as status, competition, efficiency, comfort, and much more.

Technology teacher educators need to understand and help their students understand that this is more than just an interesting academic nuance. Rather, it moves students beyond a simplistic and deterministic view of the role that technology plays in society by causing them to think in more sophisticated ways about the complex, two-way interactions among multiple technologies and complex social systems. Engineering, at its best, is much more involved than designing efficient, functional devices that will somehow impact society, hopefully in positive ways. Rather, most engineering activity is embedded within a rich social context that contains a complex mix of social, cultural, political, and economic constraints, which collectively interact to force engineers to make tradeoffs and compromises.

Technologically literate citizens are aware of how technology influences their lives and communities, both in positive and negative ways. Conversely, they are also equipped and empowered to participate in the process of selecting and shaping the technologies that ultimately gain acceptance and help to decide what will be rejected. Technologically literate citizens are full, participating partners and decision makers, capable of reflecting intelligently about decisions that affect their communities, others, and the environment. To simply observe that technology "impacts" society is to relegate its citizenry to a helpless and passive position. When viewed as a complex interaction among technological and social systems, citizens become active and engaged participants and decision-makers. This is technological literacy and is as it should be in a participative democracy.

Problem Solving, Design, and Technology

The three design standards in Chapter 5 of *Standards for Technological Literacy* identify the elements and essences of design and problem solving. The technology education profession has a rich history of activity-based and applied learning. At best, laboratory activities have involved complex problem solving and sophisticated procedures. At times, technology activities have involved rather low level, uncritical repetition of demonstrated procedures. "Do it this way because it's the best way." Further, some activities have been developed to enhance and reinforce clearly established education goals and objectives. Unfortunately, many technology education activities are selected primarily because they are fun and engaging, instead of their inherent educational value.

If taken seriously, *Standards for Technological Literacy* will challenge and enable teacher educators to develop action-based curricula that clearly are designed to facilitate student learning and enhance technological literacy. This will not be an easy task. As noted earlier, *Standards for Technological Literacy* is designed to clarify the content base of technology, which means that the emphasis will, to some extent, shift away from doing and activities and move toward knowing, reflecting, and thinking. A significant challenge for curriculum developers will be to find ways to facilitate student learning of concepts in active and engaging ways.

Another challenge for teacher educators will be to understand the multidimensional nature of technological problem solving. While *Standards for Technological Literacy* places considerable emphasis on design, a careful reading will reveal that range of technological activity is actually much broader. This is an important point. *Standards for Technological Literacy* presents design and problem solving as a continuum of related, but different processes, which are accomplished in a variety of ways. *Standards for Technological Literacy* resists the tendency to reduce design and problem solving to a series of generic steps that can be applied universally to all situations. They instead realize that different situations and problems may trigger a variety of different strategies and approaches, depending on factors such as expertise, knowledge base, and preferred problem-solving style. In short, most problems can be and are solved in a variety of different ways. One important implication of this for technology teacher education, beyond accounting for the complexity of technological activity, has to do with research. Much remains to be learned about how a variety of factors influence how students learn how to solve a variety of technological problems. This represents fertile ground for research in technology education.

The discussion will now turn to a description of the broad framework used in the standards for understanding technological problem solving and design. As stated in *Standards for Technological Literacy* (ITEA, 2000), "...problem-solving is basic to technology. Design is one type of problem solving, but not all technological problems are design problems. Technology includes many other types of problems and different approaches to solving them..." (p. 90). This is an important point, for more than conceptual reasons. The purpose of technology education and technological literacy extends well beyond teaching students how to be good designers. Rather, engagement with a variety of design and problem-solving situations provides a rich context for learning and can trigger a variety of positive outcomes including learning transfer, critical thinking, active inquiry, and more.

Technological problem solving is a broad category that contains many different types of activity. Students also need to know that not all problems are technological problems. Some problems are social, for example, when two individuals are embroiled in conflict. Other problems may be political, economic, or psychological. As important as these problems are, the focus of technology educators is primarily on solving problems that are technological.

Technology teacher education programs should attempt to configure curricula to engage students across the entire spectrum of technological problems. These include primarily design, troubleshooting, research and development, invention and innovation, and experimentation in problem solving (ITEA, 2000, p. 106). Design involves goal directed activity within a set of constraints. The design process is inherently open-ended, with often, endless solution possibilities as various individuals and teams approach the design task in different ways. Often, design solutions reflect the knowledge base and interests of individual designers. Also, counter to what is sometimes taught, there is no single, generic design process that works in all situations.

Troubleshooting is a distinctly different form of technological problem solving. Whereas multiple solutions are possible with design problems, troubleshooting situations typically concentrate on identifying and isolating a single fault in a system. Also, successful troubleshooting will not occur in the absence of specific technical knowledge. More complex technological systems require increasingly more specialized knowledge. For example, specialized knowledge is required to diagnose and repair a malfunctioning computer network. Good troubleshooting typically involves a systematic and deliberate set of procedures designed to test and to isolate a specific fault. Usually, this involves a set of experiments where a variety of tests are applied on various systems configurations. Research and development involves a wide range of activities designed to move products from design concepts to the market. Most initial designs represent "proofs of concept," where the primary focus is on a design's functionality. Will it work? Research and development addresses a set of larger and typically more complex issues including those that are both technical (how can design be best refined and optimized?) and social (is there sufficient demand for a product or service of this type?). Research and development efforts often engage collaborative teams of engineers, technicians, designers, and scientists.

Invention involves developing creative new technological solutions to address a wide range of needs or possibilities. Typically, invention is a creative enterprise where individuals "think outside of the box" to transform abstract ideas into new objects, devices, or systems. Thought processes are typically divergent, where knowledge is drawn from diverse fields in ways that are often ingenious and sometimes surprising.

Innovation is another key element of technological problem solving. In many cases, innovation represents a "mindset" or corporate philosophy rather than an isolated activity or step in a process. For example, the 3M Corporation, as part of its corporate culture, promotes and awards innovation. Employees are encouraged to come up with new ideas for products as well as new applications for existing products. Innovation involves "thinking outside of the box." Many industries and companies have found that innovation can be stimulated when it is rewarded as part of the corporate culture and teams of employees from diverse departments and varied backgrounds are encouraged to collaborate on finding new solutions to difficult problems.

Experimentation is a form of technological problem solving that is closely associated with science and the scientific method. It is important to note that experimentation is not the same thing as trial and error. Trial and error tends to involve uninformed and even random activity, where the hope is that something will eventually work – that a workable solution will emerge. In contrast, experimentation is much more deliberate and intentional. At its best, it is much more closely associated with the systematic procedures of the scientific method, where steps are planned and tested based on data and experience. Given the need for data and expertise, experimentation is typically conducted collaboratively with scientists, engineers, and technicians.

Procedural development ranges from implementing procedures and plans that have been developed by others to developing the procedures based on knowledge of technological processes. Examples of the first type include assembling a bicycle, exercise machine, or sound system following a set of directions that was included with the packaging materials. An illustration of the second is when an individual uses experience and knowledge of procedures to develop a process plan (step-by-step) from a set of drawings. Similar to the design process, procedural development often involves multiple possibilities.

In sum, the challenge of *Standards for Technological Literacy* is to develop curricula that encompass the breadth of technological problem solving experiences. One serious danger is that technology education programs will concentrate on only one or two forms of technological problem solving to the exclusion of a broader range of experiences and activities.

Given the prominence of design in *Standards for Technological Literacy*, the tendency may exist to focus exclusively on design. As important as design is to technology, the focus is unnecessarily restrictive.

Another tendency that should be resisted is the impulse to reduce various types of technological problem solving and design to simplistic formulas or steps. Real problems are typically quite complex and draw on a range of knowledge from a variety of disciplines. Different people and groups solve many of these problems in different ways. As the profession develops the curriculum needed to implement the standards, it is important that pre-service students be engaged in a rich variety of authentic, creative, and integrative experiences. As with other components of the curriculum, this must be done in ways that are developmentally appropriate and within the reasonable grasp of students' ability. This said, it is important that the profession resist the tendency to oversimplify complex technological activities.

FUNDAMENTAL PROCESSES FOR THE STUDY OF TECHNOLOGY

As noted in Chapter 4 of this Yearbook, there are two major types of standards in *Standards for Technological Literacy*: What students should know and understand about technology, and What they should be able to do. The first ten standards could be termed as "cognitive" standards. The second ten standards could be classified as "process" standards, which describes the abilities they should have. The process standards are classified as Abilities for a Technological World (*Standards for Technological Literacy*, Chapter 6) and The Designed World (Chapter 7).

Abilities for a Technological World

Humans must balance their daily activities in three distinct worlds. Surrounding all inhabitants of the globe is the <u>natural world</u> with its laws and principles that are described by science. People interact with other people through their <u>social world</u> with its cultures, mores, political and legal systems, religions and beliefs, and economic activities. Finally, humans have created the <u>designed world</u> with its technological systems and artificial environments to enable them to adapt to and partially control the natural world.

A comprehensive knowledge of technological actions and activities is essential for an understanding of the designed world. This requires individuals to know how people develop, produce, use, and assess technological products, systems, and environments in a number of different contexts.

Design Abilities

The designed world is a product of human creativity and volition. There are numerous ways that the products and structures that make up the designed or human-built world come into being. These activities are often described using terms such as troubleshooting, research and development, innovation, invention, experimentation, and engineering. All of these techniques involve creativity, problem solving, critical thinking, and decision-making. Commonly these approaches are grouped under a term called design, which should be a fundamental focus for any contemporary technology teacher education program. In these programs, students should engage in activities that develop both the knowledge of design and the ability to design artifacts and systems. The students should be prepared to describe and apply the principles of design to a technological problem or opportunity that has appropriate requirements and constraints. This would involve conducting research into consumer and technical issues related to the problem, using divergent thinking to identify or create numerous solutions that solve the problem, using convergent thinking to select an appropriate solution, communicating the solution through appropriate graphic and verbal techniques, and constructing, testing, and evaluating the solution.

Producing Abilities

Designs become useful to people only when they are used to make the things we need or want. A design for a more fuel-efficient automobile is of little value until the design is materialized through production activities. Technology teacher education students should have experiences that allow them to develop fundamental understandings of and abilities to use tools, materials, and technical means to transform materials into products, structures, and environments. They also need to have experiences with organizing, communicating, and storing data, information, and ideas as well as with converting and applying various forms of energy to do appropriate tasks, growing and processing food crops and animals, moving people and cargo, and improving the health and well-being of people.

Using Abilities

Humans use technological products and systems daily and, in many cases, without much thought or understanding. However, a technologically literate person should be able to select, use, and manage appropriate technological products and systems. Therefore, technology teacher education students should develop the ability to identify a range of products and systems that will fulfill needs, select appropriate products or systems for various applications, properly and safely use technological devices and systems, diagnose operational malfunctions, and identify maintenance that is required to restore the product or system to its intended use.

Assessing Abilities

People have serious differences of opinion on the appropriateness of various technologies. A cursory review of any major newspaper will highlight these differences. Technology education students should learn how to assess technology on its merits including, identifying intended and unintended outcomes, and measuring negative and positive impacts, suggesting courses of action to emphasize the intended positive impacts while reducing negative impacts on people and the environment.

The Designed World

Technology is as old as humankind. Its development is one important aspect that differentiates humans from other living beings. Early technology was crude and limited in scope while today's technology is extremely complex and varied. Technology teacher education students should be able to understand how technology is developed, produced, and used in various technological contexts. One list of contexts appears in *Standards for Technological Literacy* (ITEA, 2000, p. 139). It is important to note that this list was intended to represent current and major arenas of technological activity. Given the rapid pace of technological change, other contexts will emerge over time. Given this, the standards document suggests that it is easier to study and understand technology using a classification system that divides the technology into smaller parts or contexts of activity. The activity contexts listed in the document are medical, agricultural and related biotechnologies, energy and power, information and communication, transportation, manufacturing, and construction technologies. The importance of such a list of contexts for technology teacher education students is that they need to understand how technology is embedded in a variety of contexts as they study how technological products and systems are developed, produced, used, and assessed.

TEACHING TECHNOLOGY

Being an effective technology teacher requires more than knowing technological information and possessing certain capabilities. Technology teachers must be able to teach others about technology.

Developing and Using a Philosophy

Early in the educational experience, technology teacher education students should develop a contemporary philosophy that is built upon an understanding of the role of schools in meeting the needs of students and the needs of society. They should understand the challenges involved with balancing the needs of society and the need of individuals in a democratic society. This philosophy should focus on developing technological literacy in all students at all grade levels. The philosophy should also help students articulate the social, cultural, and economic benefits for studying technology.

They should use this philosophy to develop educational goals for technology education programs and individual courses. These goals should focus on helping students learn to understand, use, and manage technological products, systems, and environments.

Determining Program and Course Content

In addition to developing a sound philosophy and appropriate educational goals, technology teacher education students should develop the ability to identify the body of knowledge called technology. This body of knowledge includes events and people that have contributed to the formation of the discipline (e.g., inventions and leaders), techniques that are used to develop new knowledge and practices within the discipline (e.g., design process, invention, and innovation), communication avenues unique to the discipline (e.g., technical vocabulary and technical drawing), and processes used by people in the discipline (e.g., material processes, communication processes, and energy conversion processes).

Students also need to learn how to use their philosophies and goals to select appropriate program and course content from the body of knowledge. This content should define the scope of the course and be sequenced so that students can see logic in the way it is presented. In essence, this is what *Standards for Technological Literacy* was intended to define and clarify.

Developing and Presenting Courses

The essence of the teacher education program is to prepare teachers to present technology to students in an interesting and exciting way. To do this, technology teacher education students must learn how to use numerous teaching methods and strategies. These strategies should range from content-centered to process-centered, individual to group activities, and teacher-led to student-directed experiences.

Assessing Achievement

Finally, technology teacher education students should be challenged with experiences that prepare them to assess at least three different factors. They should be able to assess program adequacies using approved local, state, and national standards. They should also be able to identify strengths of these programs and develop remedial methods to address deficiencies and gauge teacher effectiveness using self, peer, and student evaluation. Third, they should assess student progress using performance measures, examinations, and portfolios.

TECHNOLOGY TEACHER EDUCATION MODELS

No single model can be developed for a technology teacher education program. Since there is considerable diversity among the states and countries and even teacher education institutions within a state, this chapter will present two representative models. One model will be for a technology teacher education program, which is a "stand-alone" program where the majority of the technology education technological, technical, and pedagogical courses are delivered by technology education faculty. The other is an "imbedded" program in which the majority of the technical content is delivered by industrial technology or engineering faculty with the technological and pedagogical instruction controlled by technology education faculty members.

Regardless of the type of program, most university teacher education programs contain four components. First, there is a general education component that is required of all students in the university or the college of education regardless of the subject matter specialty the student is pursuing. Generally, this component has a strong liberal arts focus. Second, there is a general pedagogical component that is required of all students in the college of education regardless of the major being pursued. Third, the subject-specific pedagogical component addresses the teaching concerns and abilities unique for a specific major. Finally, there is the department technical component that addresses the knowledge and skills needed to teach a specific subject in elementary and secondary schools.

This discussion will address the components that are generally under the control of the faculty that delivers technology teacher education; namely, the unique pedagogical and technical content needed by the technology teacher education student.

Stand-Alone Program Model

The stand-alone program allows the university to deliver courses that are focused directly on developing the knowledge and abilities needed to be an effective technology teacher. The students in the program take courses designed to develop broad understanding and general proficiencies needed by technology teachers rather than completing in-depth technical courses from other majors that tend to develop narrower understandings and more specific skills. The representative course titles and descriptions for one example of a stand-alone program are teaching technology courses, design courses, producing courses, using and assessing courses, and capstone courses.

Teaching Technology Courses

Introduction to Technology. Presents an overview of technology and how it interacts with individuals, society, and the environment.

Exploring Technology Education. Introduces teaching technology in elementary and secondary schools.

Teaching Technology. Studies the development and implementation strategies for teaching technology education.

Curriculum Development and Implementation. Studies the design and evaluation of technology-based curriculum and instruction.

Design Courses

Design Techniques. Introduces techniques for developing and communicating technological designs with experiences in sketching, rendering, mechanical and computer-aided drawing, modeling, and presentation skills.

Product Design. Explores a variety of design models and techniques with a focus on elements and principles of design; design processes; and developing, evaluating, modeling, and presenting solutions.

Designing Technological Systems. Explores the design of technological systems and their interrelationship with individuals, society, and the environment.

Producing Courses

Processing Techniques. Presents the tools and machines used for materials, energy, and information processing.

Medical Technology. Studies how medical technology has improved and extended human life.

Agricultural and Medical Technology. Studies how technology is used to improve life through agriculture, biotechnology, and medical applications.

Communication and Information Technology. Studies communication and data processing techniques and systems with emphasis on electronic and graphic media and computer systems.

Construction Technology. Studies construction systems, materials, and processes as they apply to producing buildings and structures.

Energy and Power Technology. Studies how energy is converted and applied to do work.

Manufacturing Technology. Studies technological systems that are used to produce products.

Transportation Technology. Studies technology as it is applied to vehicular and support systems for moving people and cargo in various environments.

Using and Assessing Course

Using and Assessing Technology. Explores the appropriate use and assessment of technology.

Capstone Courses

Technological Enterprise. Presents the relationship between technology and the corporate sector with emphasis on the organization, management, operation, and impacts of a technological enterprise.

Capstone Experience in Technology. A technological product, process, or system is studied through an in-depth research on an approved topic related to technology.

Stand-Alone Program Model Variations

In addition to the typical stand-alone program model (described above), emerging trends in education and the thrust of *Standards for Technological Literacy* suggests two possible variations. These are (a) an integrated, multidisciplinary model and (b) a core concept model.

(a) **Integrated, Multidisciplinary Model.** One important aspect of education reform has focused on the desirability and importance of multidisciplinary connections, integrated content, and learning transfer. As a result, related disciplines (particularly science and mathematics) have included technology components in their content standards and are actively pursuing collaborative opportunities with technology education. Indicators of this interest include the active support of technology education in recent years such as involvement with organizations such as the National Science Foundation and the National Academy of Sciences and Engineering.

An innovative integrated, multidisciplinary model could be developed where large blocks of time could be dedicated to integrated modules, team taught by faculty from different disciplines (e.g., technology and science education faculty). These courses could focus on such topics as the shared content between disciplines, the challenges associated with promoting interdisciplinary teaching in the public schools, shared activity ideas, etc. These integrated modules could serve as "plug-ins" in lieu of (or in addition to) more typical stand alone model courses or topics (i.e., construction, design, etc.). These could be conducted on a seminar or short course basis, which would facilitate flexibility. Alternatively, these courses could be processed through the formal curriculum process and become regularly offered and required by participating departments.

While the development of this type collaborative model usually presents difficult challenges for academic administrators and faculty, the thrust of multiple sets of standards and the demand for and interest in cross-disciplinary collaboration suggest interesting and exciting possibilities.

(b) **Core Concept Model.** A second variation on the stand-alone model
focuses on core concepts. One of the historical problems that have
confronted technology education has been a tendency to emphasize
activities and processes over content and conceptual development.
The development of the *Standards on Technological Literacy* represents a major step forward by shifting the emphasis toward what it is
that students should be learning through activity-rich technology
classes.

Similar to the multidisciplinary "plug-in" model described above,
a course could be designed to explore core technological concepts in
depth. This would focus on the concepts identified in *Standard* 2 of
Standards for Technological Literacy (i.e., optimization, trade-offs,
systems, etc.), but it could also be expanded to focus on topics such
as outcomes, technological assessment, technology transfer, etc.
Again, as with the integrated, multidisciplinary model variation, this
core concept model represents an alternative conceptual framework
for program and curriculum development.

Imbedded Program Model

The primary difference between the stand-alone and imbedded program models for technology teacher education has to do with the method
used to deliver technical content and experiences. The general education
and pedagogical components of the two program models are typically very
similar. The discussion in this section will concentrate on the technical
component of the program.

In many universities around the United States, technology teacher
education is housed in departments of industrial or engineering technology where a comprehensive range of technical and managerial courses are
being delivered by industrial or engineering technology faculty to non-
teaching and teaching majors. Within these programs, typical concentra-
tions include manufacturing, electronics, computer-aided drawing/design,
printing, graphic design, construction management, computer network
systems, telecommunication systems, industrial safety and maintenance,
aviation technology, and automotive systems.

The primary rationale for delivering technical courses in these programs is to provide students with a general base of experience and knowledge with the types of equipment and processes that are used by technicians. In many cases, the equipment is similar to that used in industry and the focus is on preparing technically-oriented managerial professionals. These arrangements pose some difficulty for technology education students, who need to be prepared to use smaller table-top equipment, modules, and other more generally applicable tools and equipment. Among the significant challenges for technology teacher education faculty in institutions using the imbedded model is to assist students in thinking through how to appropriately translate their learning obtained in industrially-based laboratories into the kinds of laboratories and classrooms that they will encounter in the public schools. The old adage that "we teach how we were taught" still applies. It is important that university technology teacher education faculty discuss these distinctions rather than assuming that students will be able to figure it out when they enter their public school classrooms and laboratories.

With regard to content, technology teacher education students in imbedded programs typically enroll in the same courses as their fellow industrial or engineering technology students. In most cases, however, teacher education programs specify a broad selection of courses spanning a range of technological systems (e.g., transportation, production, construction, communication). This is in contrast to industrial and engineering technology programs where technical courses are categorized in a particular industrial area (e.g., electronics, printing, computer-aided manufacturing, construction management). Conceptually, the difference is that teacher education programs are designed to focus on general technological literacy for all students (breadth), whereas industry-based programs concentrate on preparing students for middle management roles in industry (depth).

Consistent with the comments previously made about laboratory differences, it is important that university technology teacher education faculty assist students with connecting and "translating" technical content into activities and curricula that are appropriate for technology education at the K-12 level. This must be an intentional process for the faculty. Since many teachers teach the way they have been taught, technology teacher educators must show students how to take highly technical content, such as that learned in university industrial technology laboratories, and translate it into curriculum and activities appropriated for K-12 technology education classes.

Strategies for helping students grapple with the differences between technical experiences obtained in industry-based courses and what they must be prepared to deliver in K-12 classrooms include:

- Have teacher education assignments in technical courses as alternatives to those focused on industrial applications (i.e., developing a unit of instruction or a lesson plan).

- Engage teacher education students in focused discussion of how to translate their laboratory experiences into their classrooms. Most teacher education programs using the imbedded model conduct this type of discussion as part of advanced level teaching methods courses.

- Form ties between technical courses and methods courses.

- Constantly work with technical course faculty, encouraging them to provide teaching major alternatives and opportunities.

- Encourage students to utilize electronic portfolios or other techniques to keep a catalog of technical experiences for use in the classroom.

CONCLUSION

Standards for Technological Literacy represents a significant opportunity and challenge for the technology education field. This is particularly true for technology teacher educators, who are charged with the critically important task of reconceptualizing pre- and in-service education to align with *Standards for Technological Literacy*. Taken seriously, this could represent one of the most significant and demanding challenges to be confronted in the history of technology teacher education.

THOUGHT-PROVOKING ACTIVITIES

1. What components of *Standards for Technological Literacy* are not yet being incorporated into your technology teacher education program? What would you need to change in order to incorporate these components?

2. Given the strong emphasis of design and problem solving in *Standards for Technological Literacy*, what changes are needed in your

program to prepare pre-service teachers to teach this content and ability in their classrooms?

3. In the curriculum and program development components of your teacher education program, and in light of *Standards for Technological Literacy*, what suggestions will you make to pre-service teachers about how to structure courses and curriculum? Should curriculum be organized around the Designed World contexts (*Standards* 14-20) or around topics such as design, technology and society (*Standards* 4-7), core concepts (*Standard* 2), etc.?

4. This chapter outlines two models for technology teacher education programs, the Stand-Alone Program Model and the Imbedded Program Model. Which most closely describes your program and what aspects of the alternative model could be incorporated to improve your program?

REFERENCES

American Association for the Advancement of Science (AAAS). (1993). *Benchmarks for science literacy*. New York: Oxford University Press.

International Technology Education Association (ITEA). (2000). *Standards for technological literacy: Content for the study of technology*. Reston, VA: Author.

National Commission on Teaching and America's Future (NCTAF). (September 1996). *What matters most: Teaching for America's future*. New York: Author.

National Council of Teachers of Mathematics (NCTM). (2000). *Principles and standards for school mathematics*. Reston, VA: Author.

National Research Council (NRC). (2000). *Inquiry and the national science education standards: A guide for teaching and learning*. Washington, DC: National Academy Press.

National Research Council (NRC). (1996). *National science education standards*. Washington, DC: National Academy Press.

Snyder, J. & Hales, J. (1981). *Jackson's mill industrial arts curriculum theory*. Charleston: WV, West Virginia Department of Education.

Alternative Programs for Technology Teacher Preparation

Chapter

7

John M. Ritz
Old Dominion University

Leon Copeland, Sr.
University of Maryland, Eastern Shore

Alternative teacher preparation is abuzz in the educational community. Teacher preparation institutions and state agencies for education are concerned how they will meet the demand for qualified teachers. State accrediting groups are being pressured. There are those who believe that higher education, state education agencies, and accreditation associations such as the National Council on the Accreditation of Teacher Education (NCATE) have a monopoly on how teachers are prepared and judged to qualify to enter the teaching profession.

As the 21st century begins, there is a shortage of qualified technology education teachers. School systems are being forced to hire under-qualified individuals to carry out the responsibilities of teachers. Lobbying groups are backing individuals who are content experts in teaching disciplines and seeking to teach. This has caused politicians to ask state boards of education for waivers or alternative licensure plans. Some refer to these populations as career changers or switchers. They are individuals who have a wealth of experience in the subjects they wish to teach, but they have been rejected by educational systems because they do not qualify for a teaching license. Some believe these individuals should be hired to teach because of their content knowledge. However, they have been judged as not qualified for the classroom, because they have not completed the necessary teacher preparation courses or had the practical field experiences obtained through student teaching.

Some have sought to develop and gain approval for alternative licensing programs. Through alternative technology teacher preparation programs, the delivery of courses and their competencies are varied to meet the needs of the teaching candidates and employing school systems. Through alternative programs, faculties can continue to maintain the same licensure content standards as required in their state approved teacher preparation program. However, they may vary the class meeting schedules for technical courses (weekends or evenings), grant credit for work experience, integrate professional course content into single name courses, provide alternative course delivery methods (distance learning), and vary the way and time that field experiences are gained. State agencies that license teachers usually consider these to be "variations" of the university approved program. These changes are similar to the professional development schools that are being implemented by colleges of education. These programs provide alternatives that seek the same outcome, qualified teaching candidates with the content and pedagogical skills learned through slightly altered means.

Examples of alternative models for technology teacher preparation will be discussed in this chapter. In addition, content for alternative programs will be proposed that will lead to technology teaching licenses and the knowledge and skill needed to implement *Standards for Technological Literacy: Content for the Study of Technology* (*Standards for Technological Literacy*) (ITEA, 2000) will be discussed. Finally, a virtual program will be presented that would prepare teachers to educate learners to become the technologically literate citizens of the 21st century.

NEED FOR QUALIFIED TECHNOLOGY TEACHERS

As the 21st century begins, too few candidates are being prepared for technology teaching positions through the traditional pathways of undergraduate study. Studies by Weston (1997) and Ritz (1999) indicate the United States will be short by 4000 qualified technology teachers through the 2001 school year. Weston predicted the number of vacancies; Ritz projected the number of graduates that would be qualified through teacher education programs. The *1999 Executive Summary, Teacher Supply and Demand in the United States* (2000), indicates technology education is one of the most demanded subject areas for teacher need following the severe shortages for special education. In the Northwest and Great Plains/Midwest regions of the United States, considerable shortages of technology education teachers are reported. In the West, South Central, Southeast, Great Lakes, Middle Atlantic, and Northeast, some shortages exist (American Association for Employment in Education, Inc., 2000).

These statistics and the need for the preparation of additional technology education teachers are the prime reasons for the development of alternative technology teacher preparation programs. Currently, many universities are unable to recruit sufficient numbers of traditional students into their teacher preparation programs. While the supply of qualified teachers is low, technology education programs continue to expand in both elementary and secondary schools. Besides being a practical subject that can contribute to student's technological literacy and capabilities, block scheduling has afforded students additional elective courses to enroll, and technology education seems to be the subject of student choice in many schools. Increasing numbers of technology education teachers will be needed.

EXAMPLES OF ALTERNATIVE TECHNOLOGY TEACHER EDUCATION PROGRAMS

Some universities have seen the shortages of teachers in their service areas and have created alternative programs to reduce the problem. Following are descriptions of alternative technology teacher preparation programs that have developed in our field.

Old Dominion University

At Old Dominion University, technology teacher education faculty became interested in alternative teacher preparation when they saw the results that other campus teacher preparation programs had in recruiting active duty military personnel to become teachers. During the 1990s, the military was downsizing its ranks. The campus unit that worked closely with the military was known as the Military Career Transition Program. Old Dominion University is located in Southeastern Virginia. It is the East Coast homeport for the United States Navy. In addition there are Army, Marine, Air Force, and Coast Guard bases throughout the region.

Faculties felt that senior enlisted personnel and officers had a wealth of real world applications that they could use to enhance teaching, and most senior military personnel had instructor experience while in service. The government, through its Troops to Teachers Program, supported these types of transition programs. The program assisted retiring military members with tuition payment and also paid qualifying school systems a percent of the teacher's salary for the first five years of employment. Also, the state education agency allowed this program to reduce student teaching time, from ten to six weeks, for those who were seeking a teaching license through the Master of Science (MS) degree and who also served as an instructor in the military. The university offered classes on the military bases after duty hours for student convenience.

In technology teacher preparation, the university initially was granted permission by the Virginia Department of Education to offer a special license for middle school technology teachers. This was a variation from the state licensure regulations. Later, faculty revised the program using a variation from its standard licensure program, grades 6-12, and used military schooling to replace up to half of the technical courses required for licensing, 18 semester credit hours. Old Dominion University uses military courses that have been reviewed by American Council on Education (ACE) and recommended as university credits. Old Dominion will use technical credits such as those earned by the candidates who attended military schools for aviation electronics, electronics, airframe maintenance, machinist, ship and aircraft power systems, construction trades, etc. Although these credits are more closely aligned with industrial technology, faculty structure the remainder of the licensing program so it allows teaching candidates to understand the technology education curriculum and differentiate it from trade or occupational education and industrial technology. If teaching candidates are in the Bachelor of Science (BS) degree program, they continue to undertake two seven-week student teaching placements. MS degree candidates complete one secondary teaching placement. A number of professional teaching courses are required. Students must complete or have equivalent courses to drafting and design with Computer-Aided Drawing/Design (CAD), materials processing, manufacturing/construction, graphic communication processes, and communication technology. In addition, students complete a course on the social and cultural impacts of technology and a course on laboratory management, including modular laboratories and program renewal. Other pedagogy courses that meet state licensing requirements are designed into the program.

Florida Model, 2 Plus 2 Program

The Florida 2 plus 2 program was designed at the University of South Florida. Technology education in Florida receives significant support for laboratory installations and renovations from the Florida State Government. However, like so many areas, Florida has a severe shortage of technology education teachers.

Students who enter the University of South Florida alternative "…program are expected to have successfully completed, at a community college, most of the technical laboratory courses required for Florida Teacher" (http://www.coedu.usf.edu/adltvoct/technoled/bsteched.htm) licensure. Florida licensure requires students to have completed 30 technical hours of credit, with three hours in four of the following areas: materials and processes, drafting and design with CAD, energy, graphics, electronics, construction, or industrial systems (Smith, 1998).

University of South Florida technology education students must complete a professional education core of 40-41 semester hours including a teaching internship, in addition to 23 semester hours in pedagogy in the technology education teaching specialty. These 23 semester hours are composed of courses in technology and society, program management, curriculum construction, technology education methods, and facility design and management.

This 2 plus 2 model builds upon a technical major that a student may complete at a technical or junior college. With Florida's shortage of licensed technology education teachers, their state government has created an additional incentive to attract students to teaching areas where a shortage of qualified teachers exists. It is a loan forgiveness program and is based on the Florida Teacher Critical Needs List. Graduates of programs on this list, such as technology education, can borrow $4,000 their junior year and $4,000 their senior year and the loans will be forgiven if the graduates teach in Florida for two years. This loan program also applies to graduates of other states who move to Florida to teach technology education.

Interdisciplinary Model

The interdisciplinary alternative technology teacher preparation model was adopted by Texas A&M University. It provides candidates with technical content preparation from engineering and other technical departments outside the professional education unit. "The Bachelor of Science in Interdisciplinary Technology program utilizes courses in mathematics, science, and computer science as well as technical courses that are intended for students in engineering and other technical majors" (Householder, 1992, p. 7). Technical course work is taken in four areas: contemporary technological systems, communication systems, energy systems, and production systems. Table 7-1 lists the required technical courses in the Texas A&M program.

Table 7-1. Technical Courses for the Texas A&M Interdisciplinary Program

Agricultural Engineering
Farm Tractor and Power Units
Fundamentals of Farm Building
    Construction
Agri-Industrial Applications of
    Electricity
 	
Construction Science
Construction Materials and
    Methods I
 	
Environmental Design
Environmental Design I
Course Making
 	
Health and Physical Education
Introduction to Safety
    Education
 	
Civil Engineering
Plane Surveying
Transportation Engineering
 	
Computer Science
Introduction to Computing
 	
Engineering Design Graphics
Engineering Graphics
 	
Physics
Mechanics
Electricity
	Engineering Technology
	Manufacturing and
	    Assembly Processes I
	Manufacturing and Assembly
	    Processes II
	A Study of Modern Industry
	Numerical Control and
	    Computer-Aided
	    Manufacturing
	Electronic Systems I
	Electronic Systems II
	Robotic Applications
	
	English
	Technical Writing
	Technical Writing and Editing
	
	History
	Technology and
	    Engineering in Western
	    Civilization
	
	Journalism
	Graphics
	Photojournalism I
	
	Philosophy
	Technology and Human Values
	
	Mathematics
	Engineering Mathematics I
	Engineering Mathematics II

Texas A&M students must complete an 18 semester hour sequence of professional education courses. This includes student teaching and an early field experience. While meeting Texas licensure requirements, this program is a practical alternative for technology teacher preparation. It could become more prevalent as universities eliminate technical laboratories because of the costs involved in updating and maintenance.

Maryland Model

Maryland is one of only a few states that require a technology education credit for graduation for high school students. Changes in the high school graduation requirements, along with upgrading of program offerings to reflect current technology and growing school populations, have resulted in program expansions and increased enrollment in technology education programs in Maryland. The University of Maryland, Eastern Shore is the only institution in Maryland offering an approved undergraduate technology teacher education program. A graduate program was recently established to provide advanced professional development and licensure opportunities statewide. The university offers courses to assist with the growing need for technology education teachers at the Maryland Center for Career and Technology Education Studies in metropolitan Baltimore, in the western region of the state at an area technical center, and at Frostburg State University. Several courses have been delivered through distance learning and others are planned and being developed using various virtual formats. Eighty to 100 pre-service and in-service teachers pursue study part-time at these locations. The majority is enrolled in Baltimore pursuing licensure through traditional routes approved by the Department of Education.

In Maryland, it became clear that the traditional routes of access to licensure of technology education teachers were not adequate to meet the need. To address this problem, an emergency licensure program was developed. This program provides an alternative route for licensed teachers from selected disciplines to become technology teachers in an accelerated schedule. The emergency program is based on existing state guidelines, but it is performance based and delivered using "best practices" that reflect the integration of mathematics and science, design and problem solving, and authentic assessment. The program allows local school systems to recruit Maryland public school licensed teachers from several disciplines including computer science, general science, physics, chemistry, social studies, agriculture, media technology, biotechnology, biology, and mathematics. Degreed career and occupational (vocational) teachers can also be recruited from the areas of electronics, communications, graphic arts, drafting, heating/ventilation/air conditioning and refrigeration, automotives, construction, industrial maintenance, and business education. Teachers cannot be recruited from critical shortage subject matter areas.

Five, 3 semester hour in-service, courses are required in this program including foundations of technology education, technology education instructional management and delivery, core technologies I & II (including mechanical, structural, optical, electrical, electronic, fluid, thermal, biological, and materials technology), and information systems. These course experiences are designed to provide specific technical content knowledge for teachers who possess pedagogical skills and teaching experience but wish to change disciplines and teach technology education. Course content covers the mission and goals of technology education, laboratory management and safety, nature of technology and society, and knowledge and skills related to the core technologies. Technical graphics, communication systems, and computer applications are also topics taught in relation to design and problem solving and technological literacy. Teaching and learning strategies that have proven successful in the delivery of technology education content are emphasized and demonstrated throughout the licensure experience. When the candidate has completed the program, his or her name is submitted to the designated specialist in the Division of Certification and Accreditation at the Maryland State Department of Education with a recommendation for certification.

United Kingdom Open University Model

In 1994, the Center for Research and Development in Teacher Education at the Open University in the United Kingdom (UK) launched the largest pre-service distance learning teacher education program in Europe. Using a mixture of audio-visual and text materials, combined with an on-line computer conferencing system, each year 1500 potential teachers are educated and trained part-time at home with a series of full-time school placements. The program is intended to provide a new point of access for graduates from any university who wish to train to teach through a part-time route at home. The government, which had a problem of teacher supply in some areas of the UK and some subjects, was particularly interested in the Open University model. They agreed to fund a new part-time program for primary teachers, and secondary teachers in the six subjects of English, mathematics, science, technology, history, and modern languages, e.g., French.

Progressively, students move from the position of observer and helper of experienced practitioners towards solo teaching. Students work in a school close to their home, which has agreed to enter into a partnership with the university to jointly train the beginning teacher. The schools are resourced to enable them to appoint an experienced member of the staff to serve as a "mentor" while the student is on placement at the school. To avoid a theory and practice separation, experiences from school placements are used to contribute to and support study with the distance learning materials used at home. This program works as a three term continuous practicum, where students apply the knowledge learned through distance learning course work directly into the classroom as they learn it.

The program lasts eighteen months. Students are then ready to begin their first employment when the school year starts in September. Although this is part-time study, students are required to carry out three blocks of full-time school experience. The program is in three stages. Stage One: the induction phase is where students become familiar with the life of a school and mainly observe and assist with the teaching of an experienced class teacher who serve as their mentor (three week block practice). Stage Two: the collaborative teaching phase is where students work with their school mentor to develop and analyze their beginning teacher skills (four week block practice). Stage Three: the solo teaching phase is where students have responsibility for planning and teaching lessons on their own but still working in close cooperation with their school mentor (eight week block practice).

The distance learning materials used are "multi-media" in the sense that they exploit the strengths of different traditional means of communication as well as using more modern devices such as video and computers. The program is directed from a text-based study guide which links together the different components – resource boxes, video and audio-cassettes, school experience activities, and computer-based resources.

Each student is loaned a computer during the eighteen months of the course, after which time it is given to the school as part of the resource allocation for its involvement in the program. Each student is able to develop his or her own instructional technology skills, to produce high quality classroom materials, and to word-process assignments. The computer enables communication between students on the same subject who might be geographically remote, with their personal tutor, and with members of the course team. As the program develops, students are encouraged to access central databases to download curriculum materials and to update elements of the course. The program is based on a set of competencies and professional qualities and students are required to provide evidence of mastery of each element by the end of the course. The competency model was developed to be vigorous enough to give a valid judgment of the classroom expertise of the student, but also to be manageable by all mentors in any type of school. The Open University describes the teaching process in terms of five areas of teaching competence: (1) Curriculum/subject planning and evaluation; (2) Classroom/subject methods; (3) Classroom management; (4) Assessment, recording and reporting; and (5) The wider role of the teacher (Banks, 1998).

The Engineering Model

The Department of Technology and Society at the State University of New York at Stony Brook has proposed an alternative technology teacher preparation program based on *Standards for Technological Literacy*. It uses engineering as the base discipline for this alternative model. The faculty's belief is that *Standards for Technological Literacy* is closely aligned with engineering studies and that engineering graduates possess the technological knowledge needed for teaching technology education.

The engineering model will enable engineering and engineering technology graduates to pursue further study that leads to licensure as a technology education teacher. This model is a 21 semester credit graduate licensure program that provides the theory and practice needed to teach in New York. The program's focus is on instructional methods, adolescent growth and development, and supervised student teaching. The developers of this model believe students entering the program will have mastery of mathematics, science, and technology knowledge and skills. The technology content has been attained through the students' preparation to become engineers and engineering technologists. The engineering model emphasizes developing skills for the delivery of *Standards for Technological Literacy* to K-12 learners (Liao, 2000).

CONTENT TO BE ADDRESSED THROUGH ALTERNATIVE TEACHER EDUCATION MODELS

In the development of alternative technology teacher education programs, it is important to base curriculum and program development decisions on *Standards for Technological Literacy*. This section will make suggestions of curriculum content and literacy standards that should be included in alternative technology teacher education programs.

Elementary Grades

Technology has been taught to elementary students for many years. Usually it has been used as an activity method to increase the interest of learners. Technology education professionals might remember working on social studies or history projects at night with parents. Technology was also used to reinforce core academic content. In the study of the core academic areas, technological developments were introduced as major events that changed society. Students learned of the covered wagon, steamboat, and railroad as technologies that opened up nations so populations could be more mobile. They learned of air and space travel in science. Reading and literature taught the changes that technology had on the lives of individuals and communities. Although addressed as new knowledge, often testable, these subjects were usually not taught from a technological education prospective, as our profession would like.

With the recent development of technological standards and benchmarks for learners K-5, a need arises for integrating *Standards for Technological Literacy* into the elementary teacher preparation curriculum. As a minimum, elementary teachers need to know the nature of technology, so they can assist learners in understanding that the world is full of human-made products, that people create and use technology, and that technological systems and products are designed by humans using resources and processes. They also need to learn of the interrelatedness of technology and other subject areas. Technology uses other academic subjects in solving problems, and it also provides knowledge and tools to help with the understanding of other subject matter areas. Teachers and students need to realize that technology is a thinking process and the results of technology affect individuals, societies, culture, and the environment. Both elementary teachers and students need to understand that the technological world is a human-made, designed world. They should experiment with creative designs to visualize various types of products and systems that have resulted from technological innovation, i.e., medical, agricultural, energy, information, etc. Specific standards information that focuses on the nature of technology, technology and society, design, etc., can be found in *Standards for Technological Literacy*. These are the outcomes that need to be integrated into the elementary teacher preparation curriculum. Technology professionals must be involved in leadership roles to have this occur. School leaders must be convinced of the need to study technology at the elementary level and shown that it can make a difference in student performance and achievement of academic standards established in their states.

Middle Grades

At the middle school level, grades 6-8, alternative programs for technology teacher preparation must also expand their outlook toward the content and processes of technology, so teaching candidates can deliver appropriate technological literacy content standards to these grade levels. Some alternative technology teacher preparation programs may focus only on the licensing of middle education teachers. With this option, candidates should be required to master basic technical knowledge while in teacher preparation. However, with the adoption of *Standards for Technological Literacy*, there is a new need for the development of a teaching philosophy in those teachers who complete the licensing program. New content and processes must be learned so *Standards for Technological Literacy* can be integrated into the programs for grades 6-8.

Teachers of the middle grades will need preparation that will enable their students to achieve specific standards. Important in the redesign of alternative teacher preparation programs is to provide courses that study the nature of technology and its relationship with society. Specifically, teacher education programs should include courses in technology as a cultural experience, engineering design, and application of the design processes to the study of technology. Technical courses are also needed which will develop abilities to use technological tools and apply these to the systems that transform technology into meaningful outcomes. Teacher educators must analyze the level of technical sophistication that teachers need for teaching technology at the middle grades. What technical capabilities will they need to teach about the systems of medical technologies, agricultural and related bio-technologies, energy and power technologies, information and communication technologies, transportation technologies, manufacturing technologies, and construction technologies?

It is not suggested that middle school teaching candidates should have separate courses in each of the technological systems, but broader content experiences. Alternative teacher preparation courses could be designed that would allow middle grade teachers to efficiently teach a sixth grade course such as Exploring Technology (broad conceptual-based course to introduce the study of technology), a seventh grade course titled Innovation and Engineering Design (where students would be involved in design work, problem-solving, and the creation of innovative products), and an eighth grade course titled Technological Systems (where they would explore the systems of technology that have resulted from the design work of people working with technology). (Note: these are recommended ITEA Center to Advance the Teaching of Technology & Science (CATTS) courses for the middle school.)

To teach these courses, what knowledge and skills would the teacher need? The authors believe that the alternative teacher preparation courses should include technology and culture, design principles and processes, planning and designing effective instruction, and courses to develop basic technical capabilities and skills (i.e., sketching, CAD, materials processing, and system control). It is suggested that the middle school teacher should complete courses that explore the various technological systems and use these to solve contextual problems related to technology. This is where technology teacher educators need to be creative. The authors do not believe that future teachers need to develop in depth technical skills for the seven systems found in *Standards for Technological Literacy*. They only need technical capabilities to assist them in the design of curriculum, instruction, and activities that will excite students about the various applications of technology. The focus should be on the nature of technology, its design applications, and its impact on people, societies, culture, and the environment.

In the pedagogy area, future teachers of middle school learners need to be able to analyze the technology content standards. Suggested courses for teacher preparation are those that prepare teachers to plan, deliver, and evaluate instruction. These could include:

- Practicum (early field experience(s) to observe how students learn, teachers work, technology education is taught, and schools are operated)
- Instructional Strategies (the planning and preparation of lessons; approaches to teaching; individual and group learning; providing lectures, demonstrations, projects, modules; instructional materials and media; assessment of learners; etc.)

- Curriculum for Technology Education (what to teach by grade level; approved curriculum frameworks for the state in which the teacher will teach; international and national curriculum trends; establishing and managing student organizations; course, unit and lesson planning; linkages with academic standards; etc.)
- Planning and Designing Effective Instruction (program renewal; laboratory organization; classroom management including modular settings; assessment; human development and its relationships to technological potentials, etc.)
- Student Teaching or Mentored Internship (development and application of teaching talents)

After completing alternative course work and developing these skills, the middle school technology teacher should be able to deliver the grades 6-8 standards.

Secondary Grades

Secondary program teachers (those who may be certified/licensed to teach grades 6-12 or 9-12) will need to implement those standards and benchmarks related to the upper grade levels. What is the minimum that teachers need to know and be able to do, so they feel comfortable teaching technological literacy to advanced students? To answer this question, an additional review of the standards is needed. This discussion will suggest what would be required to design the curriculum for an alternative teacher preparation program to deliver this knowledge.

Candidates will need similar course work as those preparing for the middle grades, i.e., nature of technology, technology and society, and design. However, their depth of knowledge and skill should be developed to a higher level. Examples of high school courses that technology teachers should teach include ITEA/CATTS recommended general courses such as the Foundations of Technology (a course that looks at the nature of technology and the resources and systems of technology) and Technology Assessment (an investigation of the impacts of technology and trends of future developments). Additionally, some advanced courses such as Issues in Technology and Engineering Design Fundamentals might be developed. These should be determined by consulting with the various technology groups in the state/region, since the state education agency plays a major role in what is approved to be taught in schools.

"How much depth is needed?" will always be a question that will concern technology teacher educators? If too much depth in technical courses is provided, it could be confusing to the formation of future teacher's philosophical development. Distinguishing between technology education and industrial technology could become a problem. Should technical competence or technological literacy become their instructional aim?

It would be a recommended route to direct the teacher education program toward technological literacy by developing a compromise in using courses that develop abilities for a technological world. In addition to the same pedagogy courses used for the preparation of the middle grade technology education teacher, the secondary technology education teacher should study with some depth the systems covered in the designed world section of *Standards for Technological Literacy*. These courses could include combinations of content matter and skill such as combining medical, agricultural and biotechnologies studies all within one course. Combining energy and power with transportation technology could do the same. Manufacturing and construction could serve as another combined alternative content teacher preparation course. Information and communication technologies could become another specific course. A key for appropriately teaching such courses is to establish course requirements that use the design processes and problem solving and, at the same time, develop technological abilities. Within these courses, basic technological principles and impacts should be integrated. This integration will lead to the development of more comprehensive teaching practices by the teaching candidate.

This study of technological abilities course content should always be discussed with the teacher education candidate and set into the context of technological literacy. Tomorrow's teachers should develop a philosophy of how programs should be designed so students become technologically literate. Secondary technology teacher education courses should remain general and investigate the nature of technology, its many systems applications, and the interrelationship between technology and society.

A VIRTUAL MODEL PROGRAM

Alternative teacher preparation models are making a difference by providing an additional supply of technology education teachers. A potential alternative that the profession might explore is a virtual technology teacher preparation program. This idea has developed because of the current capabilities of electronic transmission of instruction. Various universities are delivering classes via the web and television transmission. They have found that theory-based courses such as human growth and development and the inclusion of special needs learners are deliverable using distance learning formats. Also, methods and curriculum development courses can be properly taught through television or other distance learning delivery. Email has been found to be an exceptional method of keeping watch and exchanging knowledge during courses and field experiences such as practicum and student teaching.

However, can universities deliver technical laboratory courses through a virtual means? Safety and liability issues and access to equipment and materials continue to be factors that keep most universities away from teaching these courses in a virtual environment. For years, the health professions have used internships to enable their students to leave the confines of universities to practice their newly learned skills with patients under the watchful eyes of mentors at health care facilities. Is this a possibility for technology education? Could learners receive lectures and demonstrations via electronic means, i.e., web, live satellite television, videotape, or CD? Could mentors be instructed and used to oversee the university student learning and mastering of technical skills? Could future teachers be placed in an internship situation to practice their teaching skills during the regular school day and the teacher/mentor oversee their learning of technical skills after school in technology education laboratories? Could teaching candidates complete their assignments and laboratory experiences after school hours to ensure they can properly perform technical processes and refining the technical skills they need to instruct and creatively solve technical design problems?

With virtual programs and courses, mentors would need to be trained. Practicing technology education teachers already possess the training and skills to teach technology education. Many are members of professional associations and keep up with the changes in the profession, including *Standards for Technological Literacy*. They currently instruct students in a safe and productive manner. Using mentors with ties to virtual programs could cause us to plan for new logistical problems. The logistics involve training the mentor teachers and gaining permission to use public environments, schools, or community college laboratories. Who would be responsible? Who would pay for access to the technical facilities? How would the mentor teachers be selected? What criteria would be used and how much would mentor teachers be paid for their services?

The profession is challenged to identify answers to the problems associated with the implementation of an alternative, virtual delivery of technology teacher preparation. Could cohorts of future technology teachers be identified and be trained at the same time that their mentors would be trained, perhaps during the summer before the program would begin? The profession currently trains mentors to supervise student teachers, and most do a quality job. Would community leaders and school superintendents be willing to accept the liability for the training of the new teacher? If the candidates were employed as interns and pledged to teach for the school system after they earned licenses, the school system might be willing to assist. These questions and possible solutions to the virtual preparation of technology education teachers need further study.

One technology that is emerging for this potential type of instructional delivery is called video streaming. It can be used to telecast courses from university studios to desktop computers. The format allows the learner to view video, live or at any time, and see instructor media such as computer-generated slides or other graphics. It allows for on-line chats and question and answer sessions with the instructor. Technical demonstrations could be given and captured on video and incorporated into courses. Development costs, along with instructor's time, are challenges that would need to be resolved.

If courses of this nature could be prepared by a number of teacher preparation institutions, one institution would not be required to undertake the entire developmental burden. Learners could enroll in courses from various institutions, usually paying in-state tuition costs, since the courses can be delivered to the student's home. This would enable more learners to have access to the curriculum when their schedules permit.

Distance or virtual learning is in its electronic and logistical infancy but has a great deal of promise. Will technology teacher educators be willing to use this technology to provide alternative means for their preparation of technology teachers?

SUMMARY

Due to our continued shortage of qualified teachers and the increased demand for student's study of technology in our schools, K-12, alternative technology teacher preparation programs will continue to be needed. This chapter has reviewed alternative technology education programs that have been successful and has shown how alternative teacher preparation programs could be altered so new teachers could be prepared to deliver *Standards for Technological Literacy*. The authors have identified the standard that will need to be addressed in alternative programs for preparing quality elementary, middle school, and high school technology education teachers. The authors have also challenged the profession to develop a virtual alternative technology teacher preparation program to meet the shortage of technology teachers. The virtual model could reach a larger population of potential teachers and focus on preparing them to deliver *Standards for Technological Literacy*.

THOUGHT-PROVOKING ACTIVITIES

1. With the possibility of only seven, three-credit courses, what courses and content would you offer to prepare middle school teachers who can deliver the concepts needed for students to become technological literate?

2. Your technology faculty has an opportunity to develop a course for elementary teacher preparation. Outline what should be taught in this course.

3. You have one month, 9-5 daily, to prepare career switchers who have bachelor's degrees to become technology teachers. What would you teach them during the month-long training? What would you do as follow-up during their first year of teaching?

REFERENCES

American Association for Employment in Education, Inc. (2000). 1999 *Executive summary, teacher supply and demand in the United States.* Columbus, OH: Author.

Banks, F. R. J. (1998). *Developing new open and distance teacher education programmes for the millennium: The OU (UK) experience.* Presented to the World Council for Curriculum and Instruction Ninth Triennial World Conference on Educating for balance: integrating technology and the human spirit on a global scale, Bangkok, Thailand.

Gray, R.C. (1998). *Emergency certification program.* Proposal presented to the Maryland State Department of Education, Division of Certification and Accreditation, Baltimore, MD.

Householder, D.L. (1992). Redesign of technology teacher education: Model programs for the future. *Critical Issues in Technology Education*, (pp. 4-9). Reston, VA: International Technology Education Association.

International Technology Education Association (ITEA). (2000). *Standards for technological literacy: Content for the study of technology.* Reston, VA: Author.

Liao, T.T. (Sept., 2000). *Engineering-based paradigm for K-12 technology education.* Paper presented at the International Conference for Technology Education, Braunschweig, Germany.

Ritz, J.M. (1999). Addressing the shortage of technology education teaching professionals, *The Technology Teacher*, 59(1), 8-12.

Smith, K. (1998). *University of South Florida bachelor of science in technology education.* http://www.coedu.usf.edu/adltvoct/technoled/bsteched.htm.

Weston, S. (1997). Teacher shortage—supply and demand, *The Technology Teacher*, 57(1), 6-9.

The Implications of Standards for Technological Literacy for Teacher Licensure in Technology Education

Chapter 8

Mark E. Sanders
Virginia Tech

Len S. Litowitz
Millersville University

The role of technology teacher licensure[1] in the United States lies with each individual state. Licensure requirements that evolved throughout the 20th century were designed to ensure proficiency with both subject matter and pedagogy. Although the primary intent of teacher licensure has always been the improvement of teacher quality, teacher licensure prior to the 1900s sometimes strayed from this goal. An 1893 Arkansas law, for example, denied teacher licensure eligibility to atheists. The first teacher licenses in the early 1900s were blanket licensures covering all subjects and all academic levels. Even with licensure requirements established in most states, as late as the 1950s more than half of all elementary teachers in the United States had not graduated from college (Lucas, 1997, p. 51). The subject matter specific and level specific licenses we know today are a relatively recent development in education, having evolved in most states during the last 50 years.

---

[1] The terms "licensure" and "certification" are sometimes used interchangeably, sometimes not. For example, some states "certify" teachers instead of issuing "licenses." Others issue "certificates" initially and provide "licensure" upon completion of additional requirements such as master's level coursework and/or tenure. Still others use the term "licensure" when referring to the initial teaching credential, and use "certification" to refer to a more specific credential earned later in one's career. The term "licensure" is used throughout this document to refer to the process of issuing a teaching credential to those who meet a state's criteria for initial employment as a teacher. The term "certification" is used in historical context or when it appears within passages quoted from primary sources.

BENEFITS OF LICENSURE

While secondary level subject specific licensures have undoubtedly benefited all subjects by ensuring familiarity with subject matter and appropriate pedagogy, perhaps no field has benefited more from licensure requirements than has technology education. This is due, in part, to the unique laboratory-based nature of the technology education curriculum that has historically demanded appropriate instruction in the safe use of machinery and in laboratory management. Licensure has also helped to ensure that technology education teachers hold baccalaureate degrees and are well prepared in a broad spectrum of technical areas and pedagogy. Thus, technology education licensure has helped to differentiate technology education teachers from vocational trade and industry teachers, who may be licensed without a college degree, so long as they have occupational trade experience and complete a relatively limited number of college courses. Most recently, licensure requirements have helped to ensure that minimal subject matter knowledge in technology-related content has been provided to all pre-service teachers, regardless of their method of entry into the technology teaching profession. This has been especially important throughout the late 1990s as a shortage of fully qualified technology education teachers has led many persons with various backgrounds to pursue technology teaching positions via alternative methods of licensure.

SHORTCOMINGS OF LICENSURE

Teacher licensure has its shortcomings as well. Perhaps the most noteworthy is that despite a general increase in licensure requirements such as successful completion of the Praxis® exams, criminal record checks, an approved course of study at an accredited institution, and successful tuberculosis testing, there simply is no guarantee that a licensed teacher will be a successful teacher. At best, licensure ensures that individuals are minimally qualified to serve as teachers, by virtue of successful completion of a state's licensure requirements.

Licensure can be a double-edged sword; the same licensure requirements that have been adopted to ensure competence also limit the number of individuals qualified to teach technology education. In times of technology teacher shortages, as is currently the case, licensure requirements significantly extend the investment of time and money needed to become a technology education teacher. This undoubtedly dissuades some capable individuals from pursuing licensure in technology education.

Present state licensure requirements are not reflective of the instructional content standards outlined in the *Standards for Technological Literacy: Content for the Study of Technology* (*Standards for Technological Literacy*) (ITEA, 2000). As a result, many states are now considering, or will soon consider a revision of their technology education licensure requirements. But the process of changing state licensure requirements is a complex and politically charged task. On the one hand, the *Standards for Technological Literacy* suggests an expanded content base for technology education teachers. On the other hand, there is a grave shortage of technology education teachers, providing pressure to license new teachers under streamlined alternative licensing models. From yet another perspective, there is public pressure for universities to graduate students in four years, which has caused universities to impose limits on the number of credits required to earn baccalaureate degrees. Finding balance in the midst of these competing pressures makes licensure reform a very tricky business. If the various ramifications of licensure revision are not carefully considered, the revision process could result in a new set of problems, such as playing havoc with university course limits or simply making the licensure process unfeasible for a growing number of prospective candidates.

Because each state has its own unique licensure requirements, there are uneven licensing practices across the United States, therefore, some states do not honor licenses from others. In the absence of universal licensure reciprocity, teacher mobility is compromised, a problem that is exacerbated by the critical shortages of teachers in the field.

HOW TEACHER LICENSURE WORKS

The appointment of teachers was a local matter until the middle of the 19th century, when states began to provide funding for schools. The need for greater accountability of state spending on education led—as it generally does—to the development of a new state bureaucratic system generally referred to as the "state board of education." In the 1900s, county exams used for teacher "certification" gave way to state certification regulations based upon courses and clinical experiences successfully completed, and a prescribed distribution of credits (Gardner and Palmer, 1982, p. 20). Colleges, in turn, developed their teacher education programs in alignment with these state certification requirements.

Throughout this century, teacher education programs have been monitored at the state level. Since the 1920s, the conventional way to earn a teaching license in the United States was by graduating from a "state approved program" (Darling-Hammond, 1999, p. 238). Under this model, state boards of education, or related state agencies, establish a review process for teacher education programs within their respective states. Teacher education programs that meet state criteria are known as "approved programs." Students graduating from these approved teacher education programs are assured of meeting the credit hour/clinical experience requirements established for initial teaching licensure. Currently, 49 of the 50 states operate under the "approved program" model. In addition, most states require prospective teachers to pass the Praxis® exams—a nationally developed/administered test of professional and subject area knowledge—or equivalent state examinations before receiving their initial state teaching license.

Until the 1980s, teacher licensure regulations had been formulated independently by each of the 50 states, and these licensure regulations provided the framework for teacher education programs to become "state approved programs." Licensure was very much a "state's right," and thus licensing of technology education teachers, for example, varied substantially from one state to another. But all of that began to change in the 1980s.

Educational reform efforts over the past two decades have had a most significant impact on teacher education licensure, certification, and program accreditation practices. Public concern regarding the quality of education led to a chain-reaction of events in the late 1980s that has fueled these changes. Recommendations from *A Nation Prepared: Teachers for the 21st Century* (Carnegie Forum on Education and the Economy, 1986) led to the 1987 formation of the National Board for Professional Teaching Standards (NBPTS), which sought to identify what teachers should know and be able to do (Yinger, 1999, p. 98). That same year, the Council of Chief State School Officers sponsored the formation of the Interstate

Teacher Assessment and Support Consortium (INTASC), to encourage cooperation/collaboration among states interested in rethinking teacher licensure standards. The National Council for Accreditation of Teacher Education (NCATE), which had been established in 1952, stepped up its efforts to "partner" with states and professional associations in developing teacher education accreditation standards. In addition, *Tomorrow's Teachers*, the report of the Holmes Group (1986) reinforced the need for teacher education reform.

By the mid-1990s, the work of the NBPTS, INTASC, and NCATE resulted in a "remarkable consensus" regarding ideals and standards for teacher licensure, accreditation, and certification (Yinger, 1999, p. 98). *What Matters Most* (National Commission on Teaching and America's Future, 1996) referred to program accreditation, initial teacher licensure, and professional certification as the "three legged stool of quality assurance" in teacher education.

The significance of these collective efforts of the 1980s was that, for the first time, the development of professional guidelines and standards for teacher education resulted from national consensus guided by professional associations, rather than state agencies. NCATE had facilitated this shift through their state partnership program, in which they worked with states to develop a review process for teacher education programs that would seek to eliminate redundancy between state and NCATE reviews. By the end of the century, NCATE had established partnerships with 45 states and the District of Columbia to "conduct joint reviews of colleges of education (NCATE, 2000). These partnerships, according to NCATE "... integrate state and national professional teacher preparation standards, increase the rigor of reviews of teacher education institutions, and reduce the expense and duplication of effort that occurs when states and NCATE conduct two separate reviews." By 1997, 45 states were using NCATE standards to approve all of their teacher education institutions (Darling-Hammond, 1999, p. 243). There are, in fact, three types of state/NCATE partnerships (NCATE, "Three Types," 2000):

A. NCATE/State Based Partnership Framework, in which NCATE uses its standards to review the operation of the teacher education "unit." The state conducts a separate review of the content preparation programs. The state program standards are "subject to NCATE recognition based on optional program reviews by national specialized professional associations." There are currently 23 states and the District of Columbia in this type of NCATE partnership.

B. NCATE-Based Partnership Framework, in which NCATE reviews both the unit and content preparation programs using NCATE standards. The state then uses NCATE's review findings in determining whether or not the program is to be an "approved" teacher education program. There are 19 states in this type of partnership with NCATE.

C. Performance-Based Partnership Framework, in which NCATE conducts the review using a state-developed performance-based system that meets NCATE criteria. Three states are currently operating under this partnership option.

Some state boards of education are beginning to tell teacher education programs they will not be "state approved programs" unless they meet NCATE standards. Therefore, NCATE standards are influencing traditional teacher licensure requirements.

While all of these national associations worked in concert to facilitate change in teacher education, NCATE was the group that has had the most impact on technology education. From its inception in 1952, when NCATE was formed collaboratively by the American Association of Colleges for Teacher Education, the National Education Association, and state school officers, the intent was to promote quality and professional standards in teacher education programs. This was to be accomplished through voluntary membership of the various professional education associations and a system of peer assessment and self-regulation (Gardner and Palmer, 1982). Dues from these member organizations/schools supported NCATE's work.

In the early 1980s, using committees drawn from its member constituencies, NCATE established a new set of standards and guidelines for the accreditation process. This new set of standards addressed five key areas: a) knowledge base for professional education; b) relationship to the world of practice; c) students; d) faculty; and e) governance and resources (Gollnick & Kunkel, 1986, p. 23).

In 1986, the executive boards of the ITEA and its affiliate, the Council on Technology Teacher Education (CTTE) voted to join NCATE. Though membership dues were significant, the general feeling was that NCATE affiliation would benefit the image and stature of the profession in the long run. Moreover, NCATE accreditation procedures were seen as an opportunity to assist the field in its transition from industrial arts to technology education.

The CTTE was recruited to draft the first program guidelines for technology teacher education programs to be issued collaboratively by the ITEA, CTTE, and NCATE. These new guidelines took effect in 1987. Since that time, 35 technology teacher education programs have been approved by NCATE under these *ITEA/CTTE/NCATE Curriculum Guidelines* (ITEA, 1997).

PERCEIVED IMPACT OF THE *STANDARDS FOR TECHNOLOGICAL LITERACY* ON TEACHER LICENSURE

Though the *Standards for Technological Literacy*, was published in March 2000, review drafts had been circulated within the profession and beyond for about two years prior to their formal publication. Therefore, many in the profession had a reasonable preview of the *Standards for Technological Literacy* and by Summer 2000 had formulated an impression of their potential impact upon the profession. With that in mind, Sanders (2000) conducted a national study in July 2000 with a purposeful sample of leaders in technology education to get a sense of how they felt the *Standards for Technological Literacy* might influence teacher licensure. He developed and distributed a survey instrument to 50 state supervisors, 30 selected technology teacher educators (one from each of 30 different states around the United States), and 15 state technology education association officers. Thirty individuals, 32 percent response rate, representing 26 states completed and returned the survey.

One of the items on the survey asked, "In what ways, if any, do you think the *Standards for Technological Literacy* will impact technology teacher education licensure requirements in your state?" Nine respondents said they thought the *Standards for Technological Literacy* would have little or no impact on their state licensure requirements. Twelve respondents seemed cautiously optimistic, suggesting that the change was likely to be limited, and would take some time for these changes to occur. Their comments included, for example:

- "I can't see the Standards having an impact for years."
- "This is a long-term project. It will take five years to change."
- "No impact yet, due to the political process involved in making those changes."
- "We are currently updating licensure requirements, and the [*Standards for Technological Literacy*] will be an excellent resource as we determine specific competencies." [state technology education supervisor]

Several of these "cautiously optimistic" responses cited the indirect influence the *Standards for Technological Literacy* would have on licensure by first influencing the *ITEA/CTTE/NCATE Curriculum Guidelines* (ITEA, 1997):

- "The only impact may be indirectly, through the university program."
- "This will probably not effect licensure until changes are made at the university level."
- "Our [licensure] standards are based on NCATE. As it changes, we change."
- "[*Standards for Technological Literacy*] will probably have some impact over time, especially if the [*ITEA/CTTE/NCATE Curriculum Guidelines*] change."
- "Technology education licensure is aligned with [*ITEA/CTTE/NCATE Curriculum Guidelines*]. We are anxious to see the translation of *Standards for Technological Literacy* into [*ITEA/CTTE/NCATE Curriculum Guidelines*]."

The survey results underscore the fact that change in education never comes easily. It is most often the result of political action borne of public opinion. The current standards movement, which encompasses not only national standards in most school subject areas, but also state "standards of learning" in nearly every state across the United States is a political movement, with public support behind it. As such, there is reason to believe that standards will generate change in education, and there is considerable evidence of the influence of standards in nearly every subject matter area and at every level in the education hierarchy.

IMPLICATIONS OF *STANDARDS FOR TECHNOLOGICAL LITERACY* FOR TEACHER LICENSURE IN TECHNOLOGY EDUCATION

Determining the implications of *Standards for Technological Literacy* on future teacher licensure in technology education is fraught with conjecture. This is true; in particular, since *Standards for Technological Literacy* are content standards, identifying what K-12 <u>students</u> should know and be able to do. Inferring what <u>teachers</u> should know and be able to do from student content standards is tricky business. As Griffin (1999, p. 22) noted, "An issue for teacher educators and the profession at large as well as policymakers, then, becomes establishing the link between teacher standards and student standards, a difficult methodological and conceptual task." Nonetheless, developing teacher education pre-service standards is a logical next step, and in fact, is on the agenda of the Technology for All Americans Project.

For the past two centuries, it has been generally understood that teachers need two types of knowledge to be successful: subject matter knowledge and professional knowledge (Sosniak, 1999, p 186). They need to be comfortable with both content and pedagogy. Recent research (Shulman, 1986, 1987) suggests expert teachers also possess "pedagogical content knowledge"—a rich understanding of pedagogy that relates specifically and uniquely to their discipline, providing them with cognitive roadmaps that guide the assignments, assessments, and types of assistance they provide students. Teachers with pedagogical content knowledge can anticipate the kinds of difficulties their students will face, and teach accordingly. In addition, teachers need a working understanding of student behavior management, special needs issues, developmental stages of youth, legal issues, ethics, etc.

Since *Standards for Technological Literacy* are subject matter content standards, they provide considerable guidance as to the type of subject matter knowledge technology education teachers should understand (See Table 8.1). They do not, however, provide specific guidance with respect to

Table 8-1. Technology Content Standards

Chapter	Std #	Standard
3: Students will develop an understanding of the Nature of Technology. This includes acquiring knowledge of:	1	The characteristics and scope of technology.
	2	The core concepts of technology.
	3	The relationships among technologies and the connections between technology and other fields.
4: Students will develop an understanding of Technology and Society. This includes learning about:	4	The cultural, social, economic, and political effects of technology.
	5	The effects of technology on the environment.
	6	The role of society in the development and use of technology.
	7	The influence of technology on history.
5: Students will develop an understanding of Design. This includes knowing about:	8	The attributes of design.
	9	Engineering design.
	10	The role of troubleshooting, research and development, invention and innovation, and experimentation in problem solving.
6: Students will develop Abilities for a Technological World. This includes becoming able to:	11	Apply the design process.
	12	Use and maintain technological products and systems
	13	Assess the impact of products and systems.
7: Students will develop an understanding of The Designed World. This includes selecting and using:	14	Medical technologies.
	15	Agricultural and related biotechnologies.
	16	Energy and power technologies.
	17	Information and communication technologies.
	18	Transportation technologies.
	19	Manufacturing technologies.
	20	Construction technologies.

(ITEA, 2000, p. 15)

"professional knowledge," or the relationships between technology education subject matter and professional knowledge—the pedagogical content knowledge—that expert teachers regularly draw upon in their work. Accordingly, their initial impact upon technology teacher licensure will be primarily with respect to subject matter, and will most likely manifest in the form of course requirements. More specifically, *Standards for Technological Literacy* suggests the need for technology teacher education content to address the nature of technology, the interaction between technology and society, design principles and applications, and each of the technical areas identified in Chapter 7 of *Standards for Technological Literacy* as outlined in Table 8.1. While there are many ways to organize technology education curricula, the likely initial impact of the *Standards for Technological Literacy* is in the following three areas:

- Technical course requirements relating to Chapter 7 of *Standards for Technological Literacy*;

- One or more additional courses and/or additional content within existing courses that addresses the interactions among science, technology, society, and culture; and

- An increased emphasis on design and problem-solving in the curriculum.

There is, however, much more to technology teacher education than providing content knowledge. Professional teaching standards must also address pedagogical knowledge and pedagogical content knowledge. For example, the four "Standards for Professional Development of Teachers of Science," published as a component of the *National Science Education Standards* (National Research Council, 1996, pp. 55-73) clearly illustrate how different teacher education standards are from K-12 student content standards (see Table 8-2). Note that these science teaching standards contain few references to subject matter content, and focus, instead on professional knowledge for the relationship between content and pedagogy. Similarly, the current *ITEA/CTTE/NCATE Curriculum Guidelines* address technology education philosophy and instructional development and management techniques in addition to knowledge of content.

Table 8-2. Standards for the Professional Development of Science Teachers

Professional Development Standard A

Professional development for teachers of science requires learning essential science content through the perspectives and methods of inquiry. Science learning experiences for teachers must:

Involve teachers in actively investigating...

Address issues, events, problems, or topics significant in science...

Introduce teachers to scientific literature, media, and technological resources...

Build on teachers' current science understanding...

Incorporate ongoing reflection on the process and outcomes of understanding science through inquiry...

Encourage and support teachers in efforts to collaborate...

Professional Development Standard B

Professional development for teachers of science requires integrating knowledge of science learning, pedagogy, and students; it also requires applying that knowledge to science teaching. Learning experiences for science must:

Connect and integrate...

Occur in a variety of places...

Address teachers' needs as learners...

Use inquiry, reflection, and interpretation of research...

Professional Development Standard C

Professional development for teachers of science requires building understanding and ability for lifelong learning. Professional development activities must:

Provide regular and frequent opportunities for individual and collegial examination...

Provide opportunities for teachers to receive feedback...

Provide opportunities for teachers to learn and use various tools and techniques for self-reflection; support the sharing of teacher expertise...

Provide opportunities to know and have access to existing research...

Provide opportunities to learn and use the skills of research to generate new knowledge...

Professional Development Standard D

Professional development for teachers of science must be coherent and integrated. Quality pre-service and in-service programs are characterized by:

Clearly shared goals based on a vision of science learning...

Integration and coordination...

Options that recognize the developmental nature of teacher professional growth...

Collaboration...

Recognition of history, culture, and organization of the school environment...

Continuous program assessment...

Note: The dots (...) indicate abbreviated statements.

(NRC, 1996, pp. 55-73)

The ITEA's Technology for All Americans Project is currently in the process of developing *Professional Development Standards for Technological Literacy* for pre- and in-service technology education teachers. These professional development standards will undoubtedly be guided by *Standards for Technological Literacy* and address pedagogical issues that were not addressed in the standards document. These new professional development standards will in turn impact future revisions of the *ITEA/CTTE/NCATE Curriculum Guidelines* and state licensure regulations. So, while *Standards for Technological Literacy* have already begun to impact the thinking about state licensure regulations and technology teacher education curricula, their initial impact will be augmented by the ITEA's Technology for All Americans Project *Professional Development Standards for Technological Literacy*, scheduled for publication in 2003.

THOUGHTS AND RECOMMENDATIONS RELATING TO CHANGES IN STATE LICENSURE REQUIREMENTS

Standards for Technological Literacy poses both challenges and opportunities for those responsible for establishing technology education teacher licensure requirements at the state level and for technology teacher education programs that must meet those requirements. *Standards for Technological Literacy* provides a road map for some of the needed course and content alterations. At the same time, the content changes they foretell can call attention to the inadequacies of existing technology teacher education programs and state licensure requirements. That is, current technology teacher education programs and state licensure requirements will require revision to encompass the broad scope of new content suggested in *Standards for Technological Literacy*.

Change is not new to technology education, and there is reason to be cautiously optimistic about the profession's ability to continue to evolve. Over the past two decades, the field has made significant progress in educating students about the interactions between technology and society and about contemporary topics such as information and manufacturing technologies. Similarly, the technological problem-solving method is now widely used in the field, and technology education teachers across the

United States now consider the teaching of problem-solving to be the primary purpose of technology education, a significant departure from teaching tool skills, which was considered the primary purpose two decades ago (Sanders, 2001). *Standards for Technological Literacy* calls upon the profession to significantly expand its content base once again, which will require yet more change in the immediate future. In addition to *Standards for Technological Literacy* addressing content, such as the interaction between technology and society, problem-solving, design, energy and power, information and communication, and manufacturing technologies, *Standards for Technological Literacy* also identifies medical technologies, and agricultural and related biotechnologies as major headings, as well as the "core concepts of technology," (optimization and trade-offs, resources, systems, requirements, processes, and control) and a continuum of design and problem-solving activities (troubleshooting, research and development, invention and innovation, and experimentation) (ITEA, 2000, pp. 32-3, 34-43, 90, 139).

The new content areas identified in Chapter 3 (The Nature of Technology), Chapter 4 (Technology and Society), Chapters 5 and 6 (Design), and Chapter 7 (Medical Technologies, Agricultural and Related Biotechnologies) of *Standards for Technological Literacy* beg the question: How much content must a technology teacher be expected to know? Shulman, a champion of strong subject area knowledge, has conducted research on the relationship between subject area knowledge and teaching ability and has observed, "Very few of us simply know our field deeply or don't know our field deeply. Our fields are too complex for that kind of oversimplification. In fact, we know a real lot about some parts of our fields, and damn little about others, even when we are professors thereof" (1990, p. 3). This issue led Sosniak to ask, "Should we abandon the idea of a high school science teacher, and advocate instead that we certify teachers in more focused areas of physics or biology or chemistry.... What about mathematics? Should we argue for separate licenses for teachers of algebra, geometry, and statistics?" (Shulman, 1999, p. 190).

Those involved in the technology teacher education profession might also ask how much subject area content is <u>too much</u> to expect of pre-service teachers? Sosniak (1999, p. 190) supports this issue by stating: "It is hard to imagine how it could be possible to add more to already overburdened technology teacher preparation programs." He argues in favor of extending formal teacher education into the first years of teaching to provide additional time needed to address the increased professional knowledge and subject area content teachers are expected to ingest.

To those outside the teaching profession, it might seem logical that newly prepared teachers and those in teacher education programs should be prepared to deliver this content by taking pre-service course work in these content areas. There is, however, much work to be done before this might occur. A review of the 1999-2000 edition of the *Industrial Teacher Education Directory* (Bell, 1999-2000) revealed not one faculty member in a technology teacher education program with a teaching emphasis in medical technology, agricultural technology, or biotechnology. Even if new faculty with expertise in these areas were hired or if existing faculty taught these courses, incorporating additional course work into an already overcrowded curriculum would be extremely difficult. Most of the five technology teacher education programs currently recognized as exemplary by CTTE criteria already require credit in excess of the generally accepted 120 credit minimum for graduation and most offer no more than three hours of free elective credit. The already-overcrowded technology teacher education curriculum makes additional requirements a difficult proposition for students, faculty, and administrators.

One option would be to abandon some advanced level courses that provide depth in a particular content area such as communication and manufacturing in favor of adding new courses that provide an introduction to the new content areas specified by *Standards for Technological Literacy*, such as medical technology and biotechnology. The trend of curtailing depth of content in technology education has prevailed for the past century, and particularly in the last two decades. Further dilution of content via this "breadth versus depth" approach could jeopardize technology teacher education graduates' ability to effectively deliver high school level courses in subjects such as communication or manufacturing.

There are many important questions that must be addressed as technology teacher licensure requirements are revised in states across the United States. Among the questions to be asked and answered are the following:

- How much subject area content is enough to prepare competent "entry level" technology education teachers?

- How much professional teaching knowledge (such as knowledge of pedagogy, human growth and development, professional ethics, special needs students, diversity, etc.) is enough to prepare competent "entry level" technology education teachers?

- How much course work is too much to reasonably expect in a baccalaureate degree program?

- What is the proper balance between subject area content knowledge and professional teaching knowledge for technology education teachers?

RECOMMENDATIONS RELATING TO STATE LICENSURE REQUIREMENTS

Standards for Technological Literacy is serving as a catalyst for change at all levels of the profession. Though changing state licensure regulations is, as noted earlier, a complex and politically charged task, licensure regulations <u>can and will change</u> in the coming years. In view of the changes implied by *Standards for Technological Literacy*, the authors offer the following recommendations with respect to the evolution of state technology education teacher licensure requirements:

a. *Standards for Technological Literacy* and the Technology for All Americans Project's professional development standards should be used to revise the *ITEA/CTTE/NCATE Curriculum Guidelines*, because of the increasingly important role these guidelines play in most states with respect to the revision of teacher licensure requirements.

b. State departments of education should look to the *ITEA/CTTE/NCATE Curriculum Guidelines* when making decisions regarding state licensure requirements in technology education.

Given that the *ITEA/CTTE/NCATE Curriculum Guidelines* were developed and are revised every five years by the profession at large, they are the appropriate place to look for the "consensus" of the profession on teacher education program guidelines.

c. State departments of education should take stock of the research on the importance of pedagogy and pedagogical content knowledge with respect to teacher education and be sure these are effectively addressed when altering licensure requirements.

d. On whole, *Standards for Technological Literacy* has implications for more robust—rather than less comprehensive—teacher education programs. At the same time, the dire shortage of teachers has resulted in new "alternative licensure" models in many states in which the requirements for entry into the profession are radically reduced (Litowitz & Sanders, 1999). *Standards for Technological Literacy* provides further reason for state departments of education to consider/reconsider the long-range implications of these radically scaled-down licensure models.

e. Technology education initial licensure guidelines should place greater emphasis on design and problem-solving methodologies. Four of the 20 standards from *Standards for Technological Literacy* focus explicitly on design theory and practice. Tomorrow's technology education teachers will need to be comfortable with the "technological design and problem-solving" methodology as yesterday's industrial arts teachers were with the "project approach."

f. Because *Standards for Technological Literacy* significantly expands the content base of technology education well beyond what is currently being taught to prospective technology education teachers (without eliminating much, if any, of the currently taught content), and because teacher education programs are already "maxed out" with course requirements, "limited licensure models" (Litowitz & Sanders, 1999) should be considered. Specifically, the authors' recommend:

g. A Middle School (only) endorsement, with coursework emphasizing breadth of understanding rather than depth in any one technical area, and coursework and clinical experiences aimed at understanding the philosophy and pedagogy of middle school education. This endorsement might, for example, require one or two technical courses in five or more of the seven technical areas outlined by Chapter 7 of *Standards for Technological Literacy*, as well as sufficient coursework in pedagogy and clinical experiences to prepare technology education teachers to teach effectively in middle school settings.

h. Separate High School endorsements in each of four different "specialty areas": a) Medical, Agriculture, and Related Biotechnologies; b) Production Technologies (Manufacturing and Construction); c) Power/Energy/Transportation Technologies; and d) Information/Communication Technologies. These specialty area endorsements might require three or more courses in a particular technical area, such as information/communication technology. The requirements for one or more specialty area endorsements could be completed during a typical baccalaureate program, thus leading to initial licensure at the high school level in one or more technical areas. Additional "add on" endorsements for other technical areas could be added thereafter with additional coursework in those areas. This method of specialty area endorsement could reduce the overall number of technical courses required to teach technology education at the high school level, while providing graduates with sufficient technical background to effectively teach the subject areas for which they are endorsed.

The net result of implementing the two options noted above is a streamlined path to initial licensure that would nonetheless maintain the integrity of the baccalaureate technology teacher education program. These streamlined technology teacher education programs would be considerably more attractive and marketable to college freshmen and, even more importantly, to "internal transfer" students. Given the perennial shortage of technology education teachers, this is a critically important point, since: a) internal college transfers often account for the majority of students in our programs; and b) most internal transfers require five years or *more* to graduate from technology teacher education programs, because of the multitude of university and licensure requirements.

RECOMMENDATIONS ABOUT LICENSURE RELATING TO TECHNOLOGY TEACHER EDUCATION PROGRAMS

Technology teacher education programs will be expected to play a leadership role by infusing contemporary thinking (knowledge of standards and curricular and instructional change) within the profession that will allow for new licensure guidelines. With this in mind, and in view of the changes implied by *Standards for Technological Literacy*, the authors offer the following recommendations with respect to technology teacher education programs:

1. The field should recognize that technology education programs can play a large part in the development of a technologically literate citizenry, but they alone cannot be responsible for all technological literacy any more than English programs should be responsible for the development of all reading and writing skills or mathematics for all mathematical proficiencies. Technological literacy—as defined in the *Standards for Technological Literacy*—is bigger than the technology education profession, and other subject areas such as the biological sciences or earth sciences may best deliver some components of technological literacy.

2. In order to deliver on the goal of <u>technological literacy for all</u>, technology teacher education programs will need to develop courses that encompass content from new and emerging technologies which may be outside the current comfort level of the profession. These courses should be initially designed for delivery at the middle school level, where some states maintain requirements for technology education and technological literacy.

3. Technology teacher education programs need to consult with other departments across their campuses to determine what courses they offer that may be beneficial in addressing new content identified in *Standards for Technological Literacy*. On some campuses, it may be possible to require a limited number of courses in the general education block such as chemistry, biology, and science and technology studies, which could play an important part in the delivery of comprehensive technological literacy.

4. Technology teacher education programs should find ways to place greater emphasis on the principles and applications of design, which have received greater attention in *Standards for Technological Literacy* than ever before.

5. Technology teacher education programs should find ways to place greater emphasis on the impacts of technology upon our society. *Standards for Technological Literacy* implies greater emphasis in the cultural, social, and political and environmental impacts of technology, the role of society on the development and use of technology, the influence of technology on history, and the integration of technology in other fields.

THOUGHT-PROVOKING ACTIVITIES

Standards for Technological Literacy has begun to influence change throughout the profession. Until the last decade or so, the establishment of technology teacher licensure requirements and accreditation of teacher education programs was addressed individually within each of the 50 states. But in recent years, the various teaching professions/fields have enjoyed an opportunity for greater input into the revision of state licensure requirements, by virtue of their involvement with the standards movement and through their work with NCATE, which in turn has formed partnerships with most states. Perhaps now more than ever, the profession has an opportunity, and an obligation, to provide input and leadership with respect to technology teacher licensure. Those individuals and groups responsible for revision of licensure requirements might benefit from a review of questions such as those that follow, as they ponder the tricky business that lies before them.

1. What content is identified in *Standards for Technological Literacy* that is not currently addressed by existing licensure guidelines?

2. Are your state teacher education programs in a position to deliver a curriculum that can satisfy changes in licensure requirements?

3. Will revisions in licensure requirements reflect only changes in content, or will pedagogy also be addressed?

4. How much subject area knowledge is realistic to expect of pre-service teachers?

5. How will NCATE's role in state licensure and review of teacher education programs evolve over the next decade or more? NCATE's emphasis on "state partnerships" over the past decade has positioned them to play an increasingly important role in the development and administration of state licensure requirements. But the role that NCATE will play in the future licensure decisions and teacher education program reviews is not altogether clear right now, and how that role "plays out" in the future has implications worth considering.

REFERENCES

Bell, G. L. (1990). Teacher certification requirements for technology education in the United States. (Doctoral dissertation, Oklahoma State University, 1990). *Dissertation Abstracts International.* DAI, 51, no. 10A, (1990): 3388.

Bell, T. P. (Ed.). (1999-2000). *Industrial Teacher Education Directory (ITED),* CTTE and NAITTE, Department of Industry & Technology, Millersville University of Pennsylvania, Millersville, PA.

Carnegie Forum on Education and the Economy (CFEE). (1986). *A nation prepared: Teachers for the 21st century.* New York: Carnegie Council.

Darling-Hammond, L. (1999). Educating teachers for the next century: Rethinking practice and policy. In G.A. Griffin. (Ed.). *The education of teachers: Ninety-eighth yearbook of the National Society for the Study of Education,* (pp. 221-256). Chicago: University of Chicago Press.

Gardner, W., & Palmer, J. (1982). *Certification and accreditation: Background, issues, analysis, and recommendations.* Washington, DC: US Department of Education.

Gollnick, D. M., & Kunkel, R. C. (1986). The reform of national accreditation. *Phi Delta Kappan, 68*(4), 310-314.

Griffin, G. A. (1999). Changes in teacher education: Looking to the future. In G.A. Griffin (Ed.). *The education of teachers: Ninety-eighth yearbook of the National Society for the Study of Education,* (pp. 1-28). Chicago: University of Chicago Press.

Holmes Group. (1986). *Tomorrow's teachers.* East Lansing, MI: Author.

International Technology Education Association (ITEA). (2000). *Standards for technological literacy: Content for the study of technology.* Reston, VA: Author.

International Technology Education Association/Council on Technology Teacher Education/National Council for Accreditation of Teacher Education (ITEA/CTTE/NCATE). (1997). *ITEA/CTTE/NCATE Curriculum guidelines.* Reston, VA: International Technology Education Association.

Litowitz, L., & Sanders, M. (1999). *Alternative licensure models for technology education: Monograph #16 of the Council on Technology Teacher Education.* Reston, VA: Council on Technology Teacher Education.

Lucas, C. J. (1997). *Teacher education in America: Reform agendas for the 21st century.* New York: St. Martin's Press.

National Commission on Teaching and America's Future. (September 1996). *What matters most: Teaching for America's future.* New York: Author.

National Council for Accreditation of Teacher Education (NCATE). (2000). *State/NCATE partnerships.* Washington, DC: Author. Retrieved July 20, 2000, from the World Wide Web: http://www.ncate.org/partners/m_partners.htm

National Council for Accreditation of Teacher Education (NCATE). (2000). *Three types of state partnership.* Washington, DC: Author. Retrieved September 30, 2000, from the World Wide Web: http://www.ncate.org/partners/3types.htm

National Research Council (NRC). (1996). *National science education standards.* Washington, DC: Author.

Sanders, M. E. (2000). *Technology teacher education licensure survey.* Unpublished raw data. Blacksburg, VA: Virginia Tech.

Sanders, M. E. (2001). New paradigm or old wine: The status of technology education practice in the US. *Journal of Technology Education, 12*(2). 35-55.

Shulman, L. (1986). Those who understand: Knowledge growth in teaching. *Educational Researcher, 15*(2), 4-14.

Shulman, L. (1987). Knowledge and teaching: Foundations of the new reform. *Harvard Educational Review, 57,* 1-22.

Shulman, L. (1990). *Aristotle had it right: On knowledge and pedagogy. Occasional Paper #4.* East Lansing, MI: The Holmes Group.

Sosniak, L. A. (1999). Professional and subject matter knowledge for teacher education. In G.A. Griffin (Ed.). *The education of teachers: Ninety-eighth yearbook of the National Society for the Study of Education,* (pp. 185-205). Chicago: University of Chicago Press.

Yinger, R. J. (1999). The role of standards in teacher education. In G.A. Griffin (Ed.). *The education of teachers: Ninety-eighth yearbook of the National Society for the Study of Education,* (pp. 85-133). Chicago: University of Chicago Press.

Changes in Program Accreditation Guidelines for Technology Education

Anthony E. Schwaller

St. Cloud State University

In the field of technology education, accreditation has taken on a more important role. In the past 15 years, guidelines for accreditation of technology education programs have been implemented into many technology teacher education programs. More recently, through the efforts of many individuals in the field of technology education, the Technology for All Americans Project has developed *Standards for Technological Literacy: Content for the Study of Technology* (*Standards for Technological Literacy*) (ITEA, 2000). This chapter is written to help the reader explore accreditation agencies, their policies and procedures, and how the existing International Technology Education Association (ITEA), Council on Technology Teacher Education (CTTE), and National Council for Accreditation of Teacher Education (NCATE) curriculum guidelines might be better aligned to relate directly to *Standard for Technological Literacy*. Specifically, this chapter will identify the role and importance of regional and national accreditation standards and guidelines. It will examine various national and regional accreditation agencies to determine how these organizations relate to *Standards for Technological Literacy*. The role, policy, and procedures of the NCATE will be explained. Then, processes and procedures used by the CTTE for review of technology teacher education programs will be described and how *Standards for Technological Literacy* can be integrated into the *ITEA/CTTE/NCATE Curriculum guidelines* will be reviewed.

ROLE AND IMPORTANCE OF REGIONAL AND NATIONAL ACCREDITATION STANDARDS/GUIDELINES

Definition of Terms

To accomplish the objectives of this chapter, it becomes important to understand common terms and definitions about the components of accreditation. To begin, it should be noted that NCATE accredits colleges or units of education throughout the United States. Technology education programs, as part of this overall accreditation process, are then evaluated for program approval with guidelines that have been approved by NCATE.

The term accreditation can be defined in many ways. For example, accreditation can be defined as to ascribe or attribute to (Schwaller, 1997, p. 4). This means that when an educational program makes a decision to become accredited, it has agreed to ascribe to or agree to a certain set of standards or guidelines. In reference to technology education, programs should be designed to meet certain standards, guidelines, technological literacy skills, benchmarks, etc.

A second definition of accreditation is to supply with credentials or authority (Schwaller, 1997, p. 4). A technology education program that has adhered to a set of guidelines through the accreditation process will be looked upon by outside individuals as having attained a certain level of credentials, or a certain level of authority.

A third definition of accreditation is to attest to and approve as meeting a prescribed standard (Schwaller, 1997, p. 4). Technology education programs that have program approval through the accreditation process agree to meet a prescribed set of standards or guidelines. The set of guidelines for technology teacher education programs has also been developed, revised, and approved by NCATE three times over the past 15 years. This set of guidelines is part of the ITEA/CTTE/NCATE technology teacher education program review process. Thus, when a technology education program goes through the review process, it agrees to prepare its students to a certain set of guidelines, criteria, or literacy level.

A fourth definition to help define accreditation is to recognize an institution of learning as maintaining those standards requisite for its graduates to gain admission to other reputable institutions of higher learning or to achieve credentials for professional practice (Schwaller, 1997, p. 5). The key point in this statement is that educational programs that have program approval meet certain guidelines to achieve a certain level of professional practice. Programs that do not have program approval with a certain set of guidelines may or may not meet any level of professional practice, not necessarily those accepted by the profession.

Another definition to help understand accreditation is to grant approval to an institution of learning by an official review board after the school has met specific requirements (Schwaller, 1997, p. 5). The important part of this statement is that an official review has occurred from professionals other than from within the profession. In reference to technology education the guidelines have been reviewed by outside professionals in addition to professionals within the technology education field. Such practices can only serve to strengthen technology teacher education programs.

Advantages of Having Technology Education Guidelines

When technology education programs are reviewed for program approval, there are various advantages. Some of the more noticeable advantages are described by Brown and Race (1996) and can be applied to technology education. First, when a program receives program approval, there is an increase in professional respect from technology professionals both within the field and from outside the field. In the past, this has been a major problem for technology teacher education programs. Having program approval with a given set of guidelines enhances the respect given to technology teacher education professionals and programs from other departments and faculty. Second, in many cases, if a technology education program has approval related to a set of guidelines, it often increases the possibilities of resource allocation. Resource allocations may include faculty positions, supply dollars, equipment dollars, or physical space for laboratory classes. Third, advertising and marketing of the technology education program can also use the accreditation process and program approval as a means to draw students into the program. In many cases, stating that a technology teacher education program has approval with a regional or national accrediting association in a marketing or advertising brochure increases the likelihood of drawing more students into the program. Fourth, the profession of technology education has had a problem with image. Technology education professionals in the past, typically have not been overly concerned about how the profession is perceived by those outside of our discipline. To this end, having a technology teacher education program with program approval related to a set of guidelines will improve the image of the profession, the program, and the students. Fifth, having program approval related to a set of approved guidelines means that the departmental faculty knows exactly what level of proficiency, level of knowledge, competencies, and concepts each student should have acquired upon graduation from the program. Sixth, the technology education program that has program approval by ITEA/CTTE/NCATE means that students have improved job opportunities.

Other Accreditation Agencies

There are many accreditation bodies within the United States that accredit various education programs. However, few relate directly to technology teacher education programs. Business schools, medical school, as well as other fields of study all have accreditation agencies. One important group of education accreditation agencies is the regional accreditation bodies. These include the Middle States Association, New England Association, Northwest Association, Southern Association, Western, Association and the North Central Association (NCA). For example, many schools in the Mississippi Valley region are accredited by NCA. These accreditation bodies review the entire school rather than specific programs. Although these regional accreditation bodies do not directly accredit technology education programs, they do review and assess these programs and other curriculum areas within the university during the accreditation process. These regional accreditation bodies also accredit secondary and other post secondary schools throughout the United States. They observe the operation of the schools and review the curriculum for the total school. In many cases, consultants review the curriculum within specific disciplines. In terms of technology education, it is advisable to have consultants who are thoroughly familiar with the guidelines and standards for technology education.

There are also other educational accreditation bodies including the National Association of Industrial Technology (NAIT) and the ABET[1]. NAIT accredits Industrial Technology and ABET accredits engineering, engineering technology, and applied science programs. Applied science programs used to be known as related technology programs.

Another important accreditation body is called the National Board for Professional Teaching Standards (NBPTS). The NBPTS created the teaching profession's first standards-based professional certification system for what accomplished teachers should know and be able to do in the classroom. Performance assessments for 21 certificate fields are available. Performance assessments for each of these 21 fields challenge teachers to demonstrate that they know how their students grow and learn, know the subject they teach, and know how to teach it. They also assess if the teacher

---

[1] In the past ABET stood for Accreditation Board for Engineering and Technology. They have changed their name to ABET without the initials standing for anything.

can effectively manage and monitor student learning, can analyze and, when appropriate, revise teaching methods, and work effectively with parents and other school professionals.

In regards to technology education and the National Board for Professional Teaching Standards (NBPTS), presently the curriculum area of technology education is not one of the 21 certified fields available. However, efforts continue with the ITEA, CTTE, and the NBPTS to develop assessments and certification for the field of technology education.

NATIONAL COUNCIL FOR ACCREDITATION OF TEACHER EDUCATION

NCATE Organizational Structure

One of the largest and most influential accreditation agencies in the field of education is NCATE. It is the primary agency that sets and approves accreditation standards and guidelines for university level colleges or units of education throughout the United States. NCATE looks at standards or guidelines as a means for quality assurance within the total education profession. NCATE believes that every child in America has the right to be taught by a qualified teacher. NCATE also believes that if teaching is to become a truly respected profession, professional quality assurance is necessary.

NCATE's mission is two-fold (NCATE, 2001, p. 1):

1. Improvement of teacher performance through quality teacher preparation, and

2. Accountability to school children, their parents, and the public-at-large for quality teacher preparation.

The NCATE standards that are developed for education programs are designed to provide teachers with:

- A broad liberal-arts education
- An in-depth study of the teaching field
- A strong foundation of professional knowledge
- Structured, diverse clinical experiences
- Integration of preparation with practice
- Multiple measures of performance to evaluate skills and knowledge

In order to help accomplish these goals, NCATE is organized into four boards. The Executive Board consists of educational leaders from all sectors of education policymakers who make decisions about the operation of NCATE. The Unit Accreditation Board reviews the folios that have been prepared by units of education from across the United States to see if their particular program meets NCATE's college unit standards. The State Partnership Board helps to compare state licensure standards and certification with NCATE's standards. The Specialty Areas Studies Board (SASB) reviews and approves program standards/guidelines for specific disciplines such as the technology education specialty area guidelines.

Specialty Area Studies Board

The SASB reviews and approves specific subject matter area standards and guidelines, which includes guidelines for technology teacher education programs. The SASB consists of professional educators from different subject matter areas that conduct the rigorous review process. The specialty area programs that have NCATE approved standards and guidelines include (NCATE, 2001):

- American Alliance for Health, Physical Education, Recreation, and Dance
- American Association of School Administrators
- American Council on the Teaching of Foreign Languages
- American Educational Research Association
- American Library Association
- Association for Childhood Education International
- Association for Educational Communication and Technology
- Association for Supervision and Curriculum and Development
- Association of Teacher Education
- Council for Exceptional Children
- Council for Learned Societies in Education
- International Reading Association
- International Society for Technology in Education
- International Technology Education Association/Council on Technology Teacher Education
- National Association of Black School Educators

- National Association for the Education of Young Children
- National Association of Elementary School Principals
- National Association of School Psychologists
- National Association of Secondary School Principals
- National Council for the Social Studies
- National Council of Teachers of English
- National Council of Teachers of Mathematics
- National Middle School Association
- National Science Teachers Association
- Teachers of English to Speakers of Other Languages

Each of these professional specialty organizations has developed a set of standards or guidelines that have been approved by the SASB and are a part of the NCATE accreditation process. Hence, the technology teacher education program is a significant part of the total NCATE accreditation process.

The first set of guidelines for technology education were written by the CTTE Accreditation Committee and approved by the SASB in 1987. They were again revised and rewritten which the SASB approved in 1992 and 1997. According to NCATE policy, these guidelines must be revised, reviewed, and/or approved every five years. Future revisions of the technology teacher education guidelines will be aligned with *Standards for Technological Literacy*. This will ensure that future technology teachers are prepared to implement the standards in their elementary, middle, and secondary programs.

State Guideline Review Process

Over the past several years, more and more states have developed a partnership agreement with NCATE (NCATE, 1993). These partnership agreements are made through the State Partnership Board (SPB) of NCATE. They are made to reduce duplication of standards and guidelines used during state review of programs for the purposes of program approval and licensure and certification review processes.

Typically, each state has a set of specialty subject matter guidelines. In addition, there are the NCATE specialty area standards or guidelines. Written and approved by ITEA/CTTE/NCATE, the guidelines entitled *ITEA/CTTE/NCATE Curriculum Guidelines* (ITEA, 1997) are available as schools or colleges of education prepare program review folios. Thus, it is important that state partnerships work with NCATE and the SASB to have a common set of specialty guidelines or to make sure the state specialty guidelines are parallel and/or similar to the *ITEA/CTTE/NCATE Curriculum Guidelines*. Note that each state partnership agreement is different depending upon the specialty area guidelines and the state licensure process.

The CTTE Accreditation Committee has developed an NCATE approved process to review technology education state licensure guidelines. When a state requests to have its licensure guidelines reviewed by NCATE and CTTE, a process is followed.

1. The state contacts the Chairperson of the CTTE Accreditation Committee to request review of state guidelines or assistance in developing technology education guidelines similar to the *ITEA/CTTE/NCATE Curriculum Guidelines*.

2. The Chairperson of the Accreditation Committee forwards the name of a trained folio reviewer in that geographical area of the state to contact.

3. The ITEA/CTTE/NCATE folio reviewer and the state representative then meet to determine needed assistance. For example, state licensure guidelines may need to be written to be more in-line with *ITEA/CTTE/NCATE Curriculum Guidelines*.

4. The ITEA/CTTE/NCATE folio reviewer establishes a three-member committee consisting of two other regional folio reviewers to assist in the development or comparison between the specialty area and state licensure guidelines.

5. After review of the state licensure guidelines, the three-member committee may accept, reject, or encourage modifications of the state's guidelines. Depending upon the degree of comparison, they may continue to assist in the refinement of the state licensure guidelines.

6. Future university technology education program folios prepared for state review can now be either approved by the state licensure team or by the normal ITEA/CTTE folio review process, depending upon the exact wording of the NCATE and state agreement.

ITEA/CTTE/NCATE PROGRAM APPROVAL PROCESS

Institutions with technology teacher education programs, that wish to seek NCATE approval, are encouraged to respond to *ITEA/CTTE/NCATE Curriculum Guidelines*. To respond to the guidelines, each technology teacher education program must assemble a folio (ITEA/CTTE/NCATE, 1997). A folio is a document, roughly 100 pages in length, that shows evidence that a particular technology teacher education program meets the approved guidelines. Trained representatives from CTTE, called folio reviewers, review the folio and make recommendations to the SASB, which in turn, acts upon CTTE's recommendations. The specialty area review process is separate from the NCATE on-site unit or college of education accreditation process and precedes it by approximately one and one-half years.

Revising the Review Process

The *ITEA/CTTE/NCATE Curriculum Guidelines* and the folio process are revised every five years. Presently, technology teacher education program folios are sent through the college unit on campus and received by NCATE. NCATE sends the technology teacher education folios to the CTTE folio coordinator. The folio coordinator establishes a team of three regional folio reviewers. The team works together to agree on the strengths and weaknesses of the folio. Their report is sent to the folio coordinator.

The Folio Review Team

Each regional team folio reviewer is sent a copy of the folio being reviewed. The team members are selected based upon their regional location. After each member has reviewed the folio individually, the team communicates findings with each other. This is typically done at an upcoming regional conference, at a scheduled meeting place, by e-mail, and/or by a conference telephone call. The final team report, which is sent to the folio coordinator, stipulates the strengths and weaknesses of the technology teacher education program. The folio coordinator sends the final report back to NCATE. NCATE communicates accordingly with the technology teacher education program through the college unit on the particular campus.

Need for Training Folio Reviewers

To help assess technology teacher education programs and to assure that they reflect high standards and contemporary practices, folio reviewers need to be updated on programmatic changes for technology teacher education programs. This is especially true as the *ITEA/CTTE/NCATE Curriculum Guidelines* are revised to reflect *Standards for Technological Literacy*.

Training Reviewers

In the past, folio reviewers (both new and those needing updating) were trained at workshops at the annual ITEA conference. This process has been replaced with a two-on-one training session between two trained folio reviewers and the folio reviewer needing training. The CTTE Executive Committee, through consultation with the Accreditation Committee, first nominates individuals to become reviewers. This makes appointments more attractive to CTTE members.

After an individual is nominated and accepts the invitation to become a reviewer, the new folio reviewer is then assigned to a three-member review team to review technology teacher education folios. The two experienced reviewers provide guidance, explanations, and mentoring to the new reviewer during the folio review process. The new folio reviewer may work on several such folio review teams before being considered fully trained. This same process is used for updating reviewers as well.

Appeal Procedures

At times, technology teacher education programs may not agree with the folio review results and may appeal the findings. When this is the case, the folio coordinator, in conjunction with the CTTE President, identifies three experienced reviewers who become the Folio Review Appeals Committee. The Folio Review Appeals Committee does a detailed review and assessment of the folio documentation and the appeal. The Folio Review Appeals Committee reports its actions to the folio coordinator. The folio coordinator corresponds with the appealing institution, CTTE President, and NCATE to make judgments regarding the appeal. If further clarification is required, the CTTE President intervenes and makes the final appeal decision.

Continuing Program Approval

ITEA and CTTE believe that program review is a continual process. As such, procedures are in place for an interim five-year review for technology teacher education programs that have program approval through the ITEA/CTTE/NCATE approval process. The goal of the interim five-year review is to assure that technology teacher education programs are continually assessing their performance and making appropriate changes. The college unit is notified by NCATE that the technology teacher education program needs to submit the interim five-year review. It is the college's responsibility to notify faculty in the technology teacher education program of the forthcoming review at least 12-18 months before the report is due to NCATE.

For the interim five-year review, the institution, through the technology teacher preparation program, submits a report addressing the following questions.

1. Describe the progress toward addressing each specific guideline found to be "not met" or not addressed during the last folio review.

2. Describe progress toward addressing each weakness/recommendation noted during the last folio review.

3. Describe changes in the program since the last folio review and explain how those changes might impact program approval with the curriculum guidelines of the specialty organization.

4. Describe institutional/programmatic circumstances or special considerations that were or were not included in the initial folio review, which might help the folio reviewers better understand the program.

5. Describe changes in resources such as faculty, technology, etc., and explain how these changes have impacted the program.

6. Describe added faculty resources, new emphasis, or areas of study for the continued development of this program since the last folio review.

KNOWLEDGE BASE FOR TECHNOLOGY EDUCATION

A subject area can be defined as having a stand-alone knowledge base validated by research. A sound knowledge base is important because it validates that the standards and guidelines are valid for the particular field. Within the field of technology education, there has been continuous research for the technology education knowledge base.

Jackson's Mill Curriculum Theory

In the field of technology education, there is documented history of changing its knowledge base from the study of industry to technology. Today, it is the study of technology.

The technology education profession has undergone curricular and programmatic changes since the *Jackson's Mill Curriculum Theory* (*Jackson's Mill Project*) was published in 1981 (Snyder & Hales, 1981). This research and the supporting documents called for far-reaching changes. One major change was the recognition of technology as a viable knowledge base. A second was the way technology education was structured and delivered at the elementary, middle, and high school and post-secondary levels.

The knowledge base and guidelines established for technology teacher education programs have been refined since their adoption in 1987. The first and second editions of the *ITEA/CTTE/NCATE Curriculum Guidelines*, that were approved by the SASB in 1987 and 1992, relied heavily on the research, recommendations, and conclusions provided by the *Jackson's Mill Project*.

Conceptual Framework for Technology Education

After the *Jackson's Mill Project*, the knowledge base and research used to revise the guidelines that were approved in 1997 by SASB were based upon *A Conceptual Framework for Technology Education* (Savage & Sterry, 1991). The knowledge base was established through research conducted by practicing technology education teachers, teacher educators, administrators, and other leaders working with the ITEA. This refined knowledge base has allowed technology education programs to increasingly focus instruction on critical technological analysis and technological problem solving, rather than on product and materials processing related instructional methodologies. The identified knowledge base organizers for developing curriculum were the technological systems of communicating, constructing, manufacturing, and transporting.

Additional Research for a Technology Knowledge Base

Since 1990, there have been several published documents that have contributed to the knowledge base of technology education. One was the 44th CTTE Yearbook, *Foundations of Technology Education* (Martin, 1996). This document, researched and written by leaders in the profession, presented a complete review of the most current thinking in the field of technology education pertaining to the bases for technology education, curriculum theory, professional practices, and leadership. A second was *A Rationale and Structure for the Study of Technology* (*Rationale and Structure*) (ITEA, 1996). This research publication outlined the rationale and structure for the study of technology and was the knowledge base for *Standards for Technological Literacy.*

The CTTE has also developed other yearbooks that have recently contributed significantly to the knowledge base for technology education. Some of the more important titles include:

- Kemp, W. H., & Schwaller, A. E. (1988). *Instructional strategies for technology education.* New York: Glencoe McGraw-Hill.

- Liedtke, J. A. (1990). *Communication in technology education.* New York: Glencoe McGraw-Hill.

- Dyrenfurth, M. R., & Kozak, M. R. (1991). *Technological literacy.* New York: Glencoe McGraw-Hill.

- Wright. J. R., & Komacek, S. (1992). *Transportation in technology education.* New York: Glencoe McGraw-Hill.

- Seymour, R. D., & Shackelford, R. L. (1993). *Manufacturing in technology education.* New York: Glencoe McGraw-Hill.

- Wescott, J. W., & Henak, R. M. (1994). *Construction in technology education.* New York: Glencoe McGraw-Hill.

- Custer, R. L., & Wiens, E. A. (1996). *Technology and the quality of life.* New York: Glencoe McGraw-Hill.

- Rider, B. L. (1998). Diversity in technology education. New York: Glencoe McGraw-Hill.

- Martin, E. G. (2000). *Technology education for the 21st century: A collection of essays.* New York: Glencoe McGraw-Hill.

The Technology for All Americans Project as a Knowledge Base

The information presented in the *Rationale and Structure* (ITEA, 1996) was the basis for the development of *Standards for Technological Literacy* (ITEA, 2000). This project developed national technology standards for K-12 technology education programs. The National Science Foundation (NSF) and National Aeronautics and Space Administration (NASA) funded this project. The project took approximately four years to complete and was presented to the technology education profession at the ITEA Conference in Salt Lake City, April 2000.

RECOMMENDED CHANGES BASED UPON *STANDARDS FOR TECHNOLOGICAL LITERACY*

Standards for Technological Literacy provides standards and benchmarks for curriculum development in grades K-2, 3-5, 6-8, and 9-12. Thus, the technology teacher of all grades must be completely familiar and schooled in *Standards for Technological Literacy.*

Comparisons between ITEA/CTTE/NCATE Curriculum Guidelines and Standards for Technological Literacy

ITEA/CTTE/NCATE technology teacher education curriculum guidelines were approved by SASB in 1987, 1992, and 1997. All university technology education programs that have been reviewed through the folio process in the past have been reviewed in comparison with these guidelines. There are 33 guidelines, which can be subdivided into five major areas. These include:

1. Philosophy—These two guidelines assess whether the technology teacher education student has a sound technology education philosophy, which is congruent with the most recent research on knowledge bases.

2. Interdisciplinary Nature—This guideline measures the study of depth and breadth in other related disciplines that the teaching candidate has in mathematics, science, history, social studies, etc., so he/she can better study and teach technology education.

3. Technological Knowledge—These 13 guidelines assess the technology teacher candidate's knowledge about technology in general and the systems of communication, construction, manufacturing, and transportation technology, including tools, materials, machines, appropriate concepts, and problem solving and design.

4. Managing and Evaluating—These 13 guidelines assess technology teacher candidate's knowledge about teaching skills including selecting instructional content and strategies, implementing laboratory

management, developing objectives and lesson plans, the using standards, developing and following a professional development plan, etc.

5. <u>Success as a Technology Teacher</u>—These four guidelines assess the technology teacher education candidate's ability to teach in the classroom including managing activities, applying multicultural and global perspectives, and incorporating values and ethics related to the study of technology.

If a comparison is made between *Standards for Technological Literacy* and the *ITEA/CTTE/NCATE Curriculum Guidelines*, there are certain parallels. All of *Standards for Technological Literacy* deals with technological content in the following areas:

- <u>Nature of Technology</u>—Characteristics, concepts, and relationships of technology.
- <u>Technology and Society</u>—Social/cultural and environmental effects and influences of technology.
- <u>Design</u>—The attributes of design, design processes, and research and development.
- <u>Abilities for a Technological World</u>—Applying and using designs and assessing impacts.
- <u>The Designed World</u>—Medical, agricultural and related biotechnologies, energy and power, information and communication, transportation, manufacturing, and construction technologies.

Blending Standards for Technological Literacy with ITEA/CTTE/NCATE Curriculum Guidelines

As part of the ITEA's Technology for All Americans Project, additional funding was provided in 2001 for the project to develop a set of *Professional Development Standards for Technological Literacy*. Thus, it is important to blend the following three components into future *ITEA/CTTE/NCATE Curriculum Guidelines*:

- *Standards for Technological Literacy* (ITEA, 2000)
- *Professional Development Standards for Technological Literacy* (proposed to be published in 2003 by ITEA/Technology for All Americans Project)

- Existing technology education folio guidelines from ITEA/CTTE/NCATE.

It should also be noted that NCATE has changed the format concerning how specialty area guidelines or standards are written. Future ITEA/CTTE/NCATE technology education curriculum guidelines or standards need to be performance-based, thus including observable outcomes that can be demonstrated by technology teacher education students. In addition, guidelines are now called standards and are defined as broad statements that are supported by a set of performances or performance indicators. The following are being proposed as technology teacher education standards and performance indicators for future folio development and program approval.

Standard 1—Nature of Technology

Technology education teacher candidates understand the nature of technology, its characteristics and core concepts, and how technology relates to other disciplines by creating meaningful learning experiences that analyze the nature of technology.

Performances

The technology teacher candidate will:

1. Identify and describe technology.

2. Identify the characteristics and scope of technology including the relationship between people and technology, and the relationship between the natural and human-made world.

3. Apply the core concepts of technology including systems, resources, requirements, optimizations and trade-offs, processes, and controls.

4. Identify the relationship among technologies and the connections between technology and other disciplines.

Standard 2—Technology and Society

Technology education teacher candidates understand the relationship between technology and society, the effects of using technology, and the role technology plays in our society by creating meaningful educational experiences in a technology education classroom.

Performances

The technology teacher candidate will:

1. Define the cultural, social, economic, and political effects of technology.

2. Analyze the effects of technology on the environment.

3. Identify the role of society in the development and use of technology.

4. Analyze the influence of technology on history.

Standard 3—Technology and Design

Technology education teacher candidates understand the design process as related to technology products by creating meaningful learning experiences through the technology education curriculum.

Performances

The technology teacher candidate will:

1. Define the importance of design in the human-made world and the attributes of design.

2. Describe engineering design processes and principles.

3. Analyze the role of troubling-shooting, research and development, invention and innovation, and experimentation in the process of problem solving.

Standard 4—Abilities for a Technological World

Technology education teacher candidates understand how to apply, use, and assess the design process by creating meaningful design experiences in a technology education curriculum.

Performances

The technology teacher candidate will:

1. Apply design processes and the processes for solving technological problems.

2. Use and maintain technological products and systems, including identifying how various technologies work, working safely using technological tools, and using common technological symbols.

3. Assess the impact of technological products and systems including collecting data, identifying trends, and troubleshooting to maintain technological systems.

Standard 5—The Designed World

Technology education teacher candidates understand the components and systems of the major technologies used in our society today and are able to implement these technologies into a technology education curriculum.

Performances

The technology teacher candidates will:

1. Incorporate medical technologies into the technology education curriculum.

2. Design technology education curriculum that includes agricultural and related biotechnologies.

3. Use energy and power technology in the curriculum.

4. Apply information and communication technologies into the curriculum.

5. Use transportation technology content when designing curriculum.

6. Use manufacturing technology content when designing curriculum.

7. Incorporate construction technology into the curriculum.

Standard 6—Curriculum

Technology education teacher candidates design, implement, and evaluate effective curricula based upon *Standards for Technological Literacy*.

Performances

The technology teacher candidates will:

1. Engage in collaborative long term planning (scope and sequence) to create curriculum for the future.

2. Select, develop, and evaluate curriculum and instructional materials.

3. Integrate content from other fields of study with technology.

4. Improve curriculum by using multiple sources of information.

5. Maintain a dynamic curriculum by incorporating current technological developments.

Standard 7—Effective Teaching
Technology education teacher candidates use a variety of effective teaching practices that enhance and extend the learning of technology.

Performances

The technology teacher candidates will:

1. Base instruction on a contemporary teaching philosophy consistent with *Standards for Technological Literacy*.

2. Apply the principles of learning and student differences to the delivery of instruction.

3. Select and use a variety of instructional strategies.

4. Use materials, tools, equipment, and processes to enhance student learning about technology.

5. Analyze teaching performance to improve instruction using self-reflection, student outcomes, and other inputs.

6. Exhibit enthusiasm to create meaningful and challenging learning experiences that lead to positive student attitudes toward technology.

Standard 8—Learning Environment
Technology education teacher candidates design, create, and manage learning environments that promote technological literacy.

Performances

The technology teacher candidates will:

1. Create a resource rich learning environment that provides for varied educational experiences.

2. Provide an environment that encourages, motivates, and supports student innovation, design, and risk taking.

3. Provide an environment that recognizes and accommodates diversity of students.

4. Create and maintain a learning environment that accommodates varying learning behaviors, controls discipline, and maintains classroom procedures and rules.

5. Design, manage, and maintain a physically safe technology-learning environment.

6. Create and manage a flexible learning environment that is adaptable to the future.

Standard 9—Professional Growth

Technology education teacher candidates value and engage in comprehensive and sustained professional growth to improve the teaching of technology.

Performances

The technology teacher candidates will:

1. Build an increased understanding of the knowledge base and processes of technology.

2. Continue to implement improved instructional practices that promote technological literacy within the students.

3. Demonstrate a personal commitment to continuous professional growth.

4. Collaborate with others to promote one's own growth by contributing to the profession.

5. Assume leadership roles to promote the study of technology and technology education.

6. Participate in professional organizations and promote technology organizations for students.

This suggested guide or model of the ITEA/CTTE/NCATE standards and performances includes a total of nine major standards with 44 performances or guidelines to help assess these standards. This model will be used to guide the development of new accreditation standards.

SUMMARY

As the technology education field continues to grow and mature, it becomes important for technology teacher education programs to meet a set of approved technology standards and guidelines. This is done through the NCATE accreditation processes. In addition, the technology education knowledge base continues to expand. The most recent contribution to the technology education profession has been the research completed in the ITEA's Technology for All Americans Project and the resultant documents. In the future, *Standards for Technological Literacy* will be implemented into the ITEA/CTTE/NCATE standards and guidelines revision and approved by the SASB. This will move the technology education teaching profession into the future. To do this, a model has been presented that includes a total of nine standards and 44 performance indicators to assess the technology teacher education program and students. It is suggested that this model be used to revise the *ITEA/CTTE/NCATE Curriculum Guidelines.*

THOUGHT-PROVOKING ACTIVITIES

The technology teacher education programs that have been reviewed and have program approval with the existing *ITEA/CTTE/NCATE Curriculum Guidelines* must submit an interim report to the profession every five years listing how the program has changed or improved. In addition, technology teacher education programs continue to prepare their folios for future review by NCATE. In this chapter, a total of nine standards and 44 performance indicators were presented. Consider that your technology teacher education program is either getting ready for a CTTE specialty subject matter review or preparing for the five-year interim report. To this end, compare your technology teacher education program to these nine standards and 44 performance indicators. Use a scale of 1 to 5 with 1 meaning that your students are not meeting the performance indicators and 5 meaning that your students are fully meeting the performance indicators. Evaluate your program against the nine standards and 44 performance indicators. After completing your review, do you believe your technology teacher education program would receive program approval with the new standards and performances? What would need to change in your program to assure program approval with the nine standards and 44 performance indicators? Also, along with each performance indicator describe student assignments that illustrate each performance indicator has been accomplished. Reviewing your program against these standards and performance indicators, and identifying student assignments that verify how guidelines are being met will help prepare for future ITEA/CTTE/NCATE folio reviews and interim reports.

REFERENCES

Banta, T. W., Lund, J. P., Black, K. E., & Oblander, F. W. (1996). *Assessment in practice*. San Francisco: Jossey-Bass Publishers.

Brown, S., & Race, P. (1996). *Assess your own teaching quality*. London: Kogan Publishing.

Custer, R. L., & Wiens, E. A. (Eds.). (1996). *Technology and the quality of life: Forty-fifth yearbook of the Council on Technology Teacher Education*. New York: Glencoe McGraw-Hill.

Dugger, W. E., Jr., Bame, A. E., Pinder, C. A., & Miller, D. C. (1985). *Technology standards for technology education programs*. Reston, VA: International Technology Education Association.

Dyrenfurth, M. J., & Kozak, M. R. (Eds.). (1991). *Technological literacy: Fortieth yearbook of the Council on Technology Teacher Education*. New York: Glencoe McGraw-Hill.

International Technology Education Association (ITEA). (1988). *Technology: A national imperative*. A Report by the Technology Education Advisory Council. Reston, VA: Author.

International Technology Education Association (ITEA). (1996). *A rationale and structure for the study of technology*. Reston, VA: Author.

International Technology Education Association (ITEA). (2000). *Standards for technological literacy: Content for the study of technology*. Reston, VA: Author.

International Technology Education Association/Council on Technology Teacher Education/National Council for Accreditation of Teacher Education (ITEA/CTTE/NCATE). (1997). *ITEA/CTTE/NCATE Curriculum guidelines*. Reston, VA: International Technology Education Association.

Kemp, W.H, & Schwaller, A. E. (Eds.). (1988). *Instructional strategies for technology education: Thirty-seventh yearbook of the Council on Technology Teacher Education*. New York: Glencoe McGraw-Hill.

Liedtke, J. A. (Ed.). (1990). *Communication in technology education: Thirty-ninth yearbook of the Council on Technology Teacher Education*. New York: Glencoe McGraw-Hill.

Martin, E. (Ed.). (1996). *Foundations of technology education: Forty-fourth yearbook of the Council on Technology Teacher Education.* New York: Glencoe McGraw-Hill.

Martin, E. (Ed.). (2000). *Technology education for the 21st century: Forth-ninth yearbook of the Council on Technology Teacher Education.* New York: Glencoe McGraw-Hill.

National Council for the Accreditation of Teacher Education (NCATE). (1993). *Conditions and procedures for state/NCATE partnerships.* Washington, DC: Author.

National Council for the Accreditation of Teacher Education (NCATE). (1998). *Technology standards, procedures and policies for the accreditation of professional education units.* Washington, DC: Author.

National Council for the Accreditation of Teacher Education (NCATE). (2001). *Professional standards for the accreditation of schools, colleges, and departments of education.* Washington, DC: Author.

Ravitch, D. (1995). *National technology standards in American education.* Washington, DC: The Brookings Institution.

Rider, B. L. (Ed.). (1998). *Diversity in technology education: Forty-seventh yearbook of the Council on Technology Teacher Education.* New York: Glencoe McGraw-Hill.

Savage, E., & Sterry, L. (1991). *A conceptual framework for technology education.* Reston, VA: International Technology Education Association.

Schwaller, A. E. (1997, November). *The relationship between accreditation and assessment.* Speech presented at the 84th Mississippi Valley Technology Teacher Education Conference. Nashville, TN: Mississippi Valley Technology Teacher Education Conference.

Seymour, R. D., & Shackelford, R. (Eds.). (1993). *Manufacturing in technology education: Forty-second yearbook of the Council on Technology Teacher Education.* New York: Glencoe McGraw-Hill.

Snyder, J. F., & Hales, J. A. (Eds.). (1981). *Jackson's mill industrial arts curriculum theory.* Reston, VA: International Technology Education Association.

St. Cloud State University. (1996). *Assessment handbook, working toward a culture of assessment.* St. Cloud, MN: SCSU Assessment Office.

Waetjen, W. B. (1992). *Shaping the future of the professional. Critical issues in technology education* (pp. 25-30). Camelback Symposium, A Compilation of Papers. Reston, VA: International Technology Education Association.

Wescott, J. W., & Henak, R. M. (Eds.). (1994). *Construction in technology education: Forty-third yearbook of the Council on Technology Teacher Education.* New York: Glencoe McGraw-Hill.

Wiens, A. E. (1994). *Technology as liberal education.* Reston, VA: International Technology Education Association.

Wright, J. R., & Komacek, S. A. (Eds.). (1992). *Transportation in technology education: Forty-first yearbook of the Council on Technology Teacher Education.* New York: Glencoe McGraw-Hill.

Technology Teacher Education's In-Servicing of Technology Education Teachers

John R. Wright
University of Southern Maine

The undergraduate experience in technology teacher education is an intensive four-year experience that concentrates on how to teach technology to children. It represents a minimum of 120 semester hours or up to 2000 contact hours. Increasingly, technology education teachers earn additional hours in graduate programs that could add another 30 semester hours or 450 contact hours. Upon graduation, technology education teachers can expect their school system to provide an average of 12 contact hours of in-service education each year for the rest of their working careers. In most cases, that in-service experience will be broadly focused and rarely dedicated to the teaching of technology education. What's wrong with this picture?

In a dynamic discipline such as technology, the pressure to keep pace provides stress that can burn technology education teachers out at a faster rate than other colleagues with more stable subject matter areas do. Add to this dilemma recent professional changes and the new challenge of implementing *Standards for Technological Literacy: Content for the Study of Technology* (*Standards for Technological Literacy*) (ITEA, 2000) and the "world begins to tilt" for the average public school technology education teacher. This issue is so critical to the technology education profession that major efforts are being planned by national and state professional associations to provide regular workshops to implement the new *Standards for Technological Literacy* at conferences and special in-service seminars. But, it is also time for the technology teacher educators to actively provide opportunities for classroom teachers beyond the typical offering of credit courses and invite them to campus for enhancement of philosophical, technical, curricula, and instructional skills based on *Standards for Technological Literacy*.

This chapter explores the issues of technology education teacher in-service education and the role of the university in providing this service. It will also cover the various types of in-service education and the advantages of each. Some types of in-service education may be used to in-service teachers for implementing *Standards for Technological Literacy.* Once accomplished, attention will be given to the issue of national *Standards for Technological Literacy* and how best to provide public school teachers with the necessary knowledge and tools to implement the new goals and objectives for achieving technological literacy. The chapter concludes by discussing three case studies, including one university that has successfully in-serviced over 250 technology teachers during the past ten years.

EFFECTIVENESS AND SHORTCOMINGS OF IN-SERVICING TECHNOLOGY TEACHERS

Typical public school in-service education consists of a day or two in the fall and again in the spring when teachers gather to hear an invited outside consultant present a topic of interest. Usually the topic is broad (e.g., student discipline, drugs in the schoolhouse, or sexual harassment) so that all teachers can participate. In the afternoon, teachers retreat to their academic departments where common issues are discussed and preparations are made for the incoming students. Sometimes, academic departments also provide in-service by reviewing a document (i.e., national or state standards), or using a state consultant, an outside consultant, or a teacher educator to conduct a work session. These sessions are much more focused and may include some role-playing of activities and discussions about curricula and instructional strategies. On occasion, technology education teachers have also been able to visit other programs in neighboring towns and/or visit a local industry to view the latest technological innovations. All these forms and styles of in-service are useful and effective for updating teachers about current events. However, they fall drastically short in providing enough material or experience to change a teacher's behavior. The in-service experiences are simply too short and too shallow to cause sustained change.

According to Harris and Bessent (1969, p. 4) the need for in-service is not something new and has been described in the literature for well over 30 years. However, there are some fundamentally important reasons for providing in-service programs:

- Pre-service preparation of professional staff members is rarely ideal and may be primarily an introduction to professional preparation rather than professional preparation as such.

- Social and educational change makes current professional practices obsolete or relatively ineffective in a very short period of time. This applies to methods and techniques, tools, and substantive knowledge itself.

- Coordination and articulation of instructional practices require changes in people. Even when each instructional staff member is functioning at a highly professional level, employing an optimum number of the most effective practices, such an instructional program might still be relatively uncoordinated from subject to subject and poorly articulated from year to year.

- Other factors argue for in-service education activities of rather diverse kinds. Morale can be stimulated, but improvement of any dynamic kind does not occur.

The typical model used for in-service education is called direct teaching. That is, a professional consultant "teaches" the faculty about a topic. "Because direct teaching is currently much of what the public and many districts consider staff development, it is important that teachers, administrators, and policymakers become aware of new and broader conceptions of professional development. At present, many districts have one to seven days of in-service education in the school year where teachers are introduced to new ideas (e.g., math standards, new forms of assessment). Some school districts conduct workshops on themes or particular subjects. They often hire consultants to handle implementation of these ideas. While learning about new ideas that affect both the content and the processes of teaching is important, ideas unrelated to the organization and context of one's own classroom have a hard time competing with the daily nature of work—even when teachers are excited about and committed to them (Lieberman & Miller, 1999, p. 5). Figure 10-1 describes direct teaching, learning in school, and learning out of school as methods for organizing future professional development for teachers.

There are a number of collaborative opportunities available to school districts. With the increasing capability of on-line linkages between schools and universities, networks have been developed that approach a new way of delivering in-service education at all levels. But breaking the traditional mold, according to Lieberman (1995, p. 5), is very difficult, but it must be done to get past the following limitations:

Figure 10-1. Organizing for Professional Development

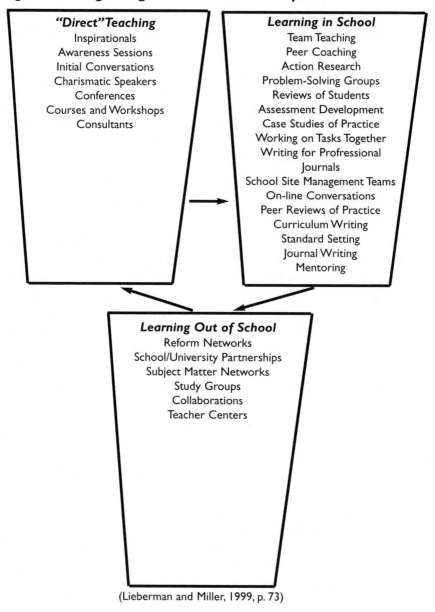

"Direct" Teaching
Inspirationals
Awareness Sessions
Initial Conversations
Charismatic Speakers
Conferences
Courses and Workshops
Consultants

Learning in School
Team Teaching
Peer Coaching
Action Research
Problem-Solving Groups
Reviews of Students
Assessment Development
Case Studies of Practice
Working on Tasks Together
Writing for Profressional
Journals
School Site Management Teams
On-line Conversations
Peer Reviews of Practice
Curriculum Writing
Standard Setting
Journal Writing
Mentoring

Learning Out of School
Reform Networks
School/University Partnerships
Subject Matter Networks
Study Groups
Collaborations
Teacher Centers

(Lieberman and Miller, 1999, p. 73)

- Teacher development has been limited by a lack of knowledge of how teachers learn.
- Teachers' definitions of the problems of practice have often been ignored.
- The agenda for reform involves teachers in practices that have not been part of the accepted view of teachers' professional learning.
- Teaching has been described as a technical set of skills leaving little room for invention and the building of craft knowledge.
- Professional development opportunities have often ignored the critical importance of the context within which teachers work.
- Strategies for change often do not consider the importance of support mechanisms and the necessity of learning over time.
- Time and the necessary mechanisms for inventing as well as consuming new knowledge have often been absent from schools.
- The move from "direct teaching" to facilitating "in-school learning" is connected to longer-term strategies aimed at changing not only teaching practice but also the school culture.
- Networks, collaborations, and partnerships provide teachers with professional learning communities that support changed teaching practices in their own schools and classrooms.

In technology education, the changeover from industrial arts has put a great deal of pressure on the public school teacher. Pre-service education prior to 1980 was focused on the traditional areas of content. Unless a teacher was able to return back for a master's degree during the 1980s, it is likely that his/her background is not sufficient for teaching the new content areas of technology education without some assistance. Lieberman (1995) calls for including practice in in-service education especially for technology education. In fact, in-service education for implementing *Standards for Technological Literacy* will be much more successful if there is a component that deals with hands-on activities for teachers.

MOTIVATING TECHNOLOGY TEACHERS TO IMPLEMENT *STANDARDS FOR TECHNOLOGICAL LITERACY*

The primary motivation for implementing *Standards for Technological Literacy* is to increase the technological literacy of students. Having said that, the reality of why teachers will be interested in adopting *Standards for Technological Literacy* will be much less lofty. In practice, the difficult issue of decreasing enrollments continues to plague many public school programs. In state after state, the closing of programs and the continuing trend of not replacing retiring teachers is a red flag indicator that the relevance and value of industrial arts curricula in the public school is being questioned. Programs that have changed to technology education are able to reverse this trend and create a new excitement for both students and teachers. Challenges remain for the profession as science teachers are using technology activities to motivate their students, and computer teachers are being called technology teachers making the role of technology education less clear to administrators and parents.

It is interesting to note that governors are in a high technology frenzy trying to attract the "clean, high paying high tech companies" to locate in their states. Workforce readiness needed to sustain such a movement heavily relies on a technological literate workforce and it is a "no-brainer" to make the connection to programs in technology education—yet, technology education has not gained on the workforce development forefront. Never-the-less, most technology education teachers will be motivated to implement *Standards for Technological Literacy* if they:

- Feel comfortable with the new content and teaching strategies,
- Can convince their colleagues and administrators that all students need this type of education,
- Believe that enrollment increases will occur with the new curriculum offerings, and
- Can secure some assistance in the change process.

State supervisors can play an important role in securing funding that rewards the implementation of *Standards for Technological Literacy*. They can also play an important role in convincing state officials and local administrators that *Standards for Technological Literacy* are an essential component of general education and the basic incubator for the future needed by a high technology workforce. If this is possible, new funding to support the implementation of *Standards for Technological Literacy* could be forthcoming from the coffers of economic development and/or labor as well as education. New funding would be a major motivator for teachers and administrators to implement *Standards for Technological Literacy*.

Teacher burnout and boredom are also motivators for implementing *Standards for Technological Literacy*, especially for those teachers who are still teaching industrial arts content. The national technology education demonstration centers funded by the United States Office of Education in the early 1990s found that bored and turned-off industrial arts teachers were re-vitalized when they changed over to technology education. Some of these teachers, as was the case in the state of Connecticut, put off plans to retire because the new content was such fun to teach and they enjoyed the new self-image of being a technology education teacher (Wright, 1992). School administrators need to capitalize on *Standards for Technological Literacy* as a vehicle for changing traditional programs into meaningful curricula that can enhance their district's offerings.

MONDAY MORNING UNITS OF INSTRUCTION

Things they do to help students understand technological concepts motivate technology teachers. Therefore, the activities become an important aspect for implementing *Standards for Technological Literacy*. During the past 10 years a number of excellent design briefs have been developed to create problem-solving situations for students at all levels. An excellent source for such "Monday morning" ideas is the student activities section of *The Technology Teacher* (ITEA) produced for public use by technology education faculty of Old Dominion University. Another source of activities can be found in the university where future teachers are generating new instructional materials as part of their teacher education program. This is particularly true when locating materials in the bio-related technology area.

The least developed areas for teaching materials and student activities are bio-related and transportation. The works of Dr. Ernie Savage at Bowling Green State University and Dr. John Wells at West Virginia

University in bio-related technologies have been beneficial for understanding the role of technology education. Dr. Paul DeVore (retired) at West Virginia University, Dr. Myron Bender (retired) at University of North Dakota, and Dr. Stan Komacek at California University of Pennsylvania provide an excellent array of philosophical and curricula positions along with a number of Monday morning activities to support the teaching of transportation and energy. ITEA also has excellent resources for Monday morning ideas providing a number of support materials including action videos, curriculum materials, and student activity kits.

For the past ten years, the ITEA annual conference has featured a Technology Festival that provides an opportunity for teachers to share ideas, curriculum, student activities, and instructional strategies. Additionally, commercial vendors have been sharing ideas in special interest sessions as well as on the show floor where the latest supplies, kits, and equipment can be viewed. More and more states have adopted the concept of the technology festival and most provide opportunities for vendors to show their equipment, supplies, and educational kits at annual conferences.

Most recently the Internet has been a resource used to share ideas and exchange teaching strategies. To participate, log-on to the professional organizations, universities, state agencies, vendors, or free float by searching titles such as technology education, design, problem-solving, transportation, communication, information, energy, construction, manufacturing and bio-technology. One distinct advantage of this resource is its international orientation bringing concepts and practices from a number of participating countries.

INSTRUCTIONAL STRATEGIES

The implementation of the *Standards for Technological Literacy* requires a mental transformation from that of a "fountain of knowledge" to that of a "facilitator of knowledge." Technology is a dynamic discipline that grows exponentially rather than arithmetically. *Standards for Technological Literacy* support the "process" approach for implementing content. This is best exemplified by the use of design briefs and setting up problem-solving situations that allow students to use technical means to solve problems. As students go through the discovery process of solving problems, the teacher becomes a facilitator who helps students understand technology. Does that mean that the teacher no longer stands up and teaches the content? No, content is still important because information is the foundation of technology and problem-solving.

But the real question is what to teach. At Eastern Illinois University (1976-80) a number of graduate students under the direction of Dr. Ronald E. Jones began the task of building content organizers for the Illinois Technology Education State Plan. Using a taxonomy approach, the students classified the technical, social, cultural, and systems relationships of transportation, communication, production, and energy. In the process, they learned the importance of logic when organizing content. Now technology teacher educators and technology education teachers can use the logic identified in *Standards for Technological Literacy* to determine content, instructional strategies, and student learning experiences. If students understand the "logic" of technology and the logic of a technological context (e.g., information and communication), then the logic will be transferable to other technologies.

At about the same time as the British educators were experimenting with a process approach for studying design and technology, and using a design brief approach that set up student problem-solving situations, the "Conceptual Framework" (Savage & Sterry, 1990) group met in 1986. The leaders were divided between "process" and "content" instructional strategies. What resulted was the blending of process and content called the technological method. This method is still valid with the new *Standards for Technological Literacy* and is a powerful way to provide instruction for the study of technology (See Figure 10-2).

One negative aspect of using a number of high impact design and problem-solving activities is placing less emphasis on "stand-up" content teaching. The temptation to simply run one activity after another is often too much to resist. But, if the teacher is to teach content, the complex question of what to teach and what is important must be addressed.

> Thankfully, in *Standards for Technological Literacy*, we have a tool to help us address the mismatch between dependency and understanding. Through an arduous four-year process, involving many levels of review and countless revisions, the International Technology Education Association has successfully distilled an essential core of technological knowledge and skills we might wish all K-12 students to acquire (ITEA, 2000, p. v).

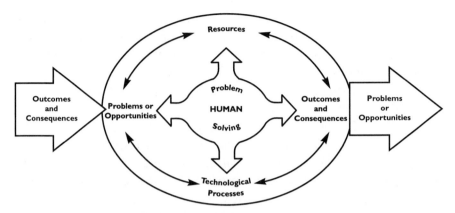

Figure 10-2. The Technological Method (Savage & Sterry, 1990)

Standards for Technological Literacy is based on the premise that all students should become technologically literate. In the process of acquiring literacy there are a number of ways we could approach the development for students. For instance, technical literacy is important for students in Applied Technology programs where the focus is on career skill sets. However, if the purpose is general:

> ...[T]hen technological literacy is important for all students, even those who will not go into technological careers. Because technology is such an important force in our economy, anyone can benefit by being familiar with it. Corporate executives and others in the business world, brokers and investment analysts, journalists, teachers, doctors, nurses, farmers, and homemakers all will be able to perform their jobs better if they are technologically literate" (ITEA, 2000, p. 10).

"Efforts toward implementation of technology education have aroused considerable interest in the curriculum area and have fostered the rapid growth of contemporary resource materials. However, the process of implementing a technology education program is a complex undertaking. It also requires a change in philosophy, curriculum, and instructional practices" (Larkin, 1999, p. 100). *Standards for Technological Literacy* "pull all the bits and pieces" together so that a united approach to the study of technology can be undertaken by the profession. Perhaps the most frustrating aspect of implementing a technology program is the design or redesign of the laboratory facilities. The use of "soft" materials in K-8, and "high tech" equipment in 9-12 can be a difficult transition if careful planning is not undertaken during the transition.

IN-SERVICE LABORATORY ACTIVITIES

Technology education teacher in-service has taken many forms. Many different types of in-service facilities have been used with success in bringing about change in the profession. Four key elements in bringing about change are for participants to want to change, to conceptualize the "logic" of technology and the logic of a technological context (e.g., energy and power, information and communication), to develop strategies for implementing the change in their facilities, and to have enough in-service time to make the desired change.

Understanding the "logic" of technology can result in a technology education teacher being successful in a variety of instructional facilities. Can technology education be taught in a traditional industrial arts laboratory? Absolutely! In fact, Dr. Paul DeVore (retired) and Dr. David McCrory at West Virginia University conducted a series of experiments from 1973-80 called Project Open that demonstrated that technology education could even be taught successfully in a general classroom with minimum technical support. However, the optimal situation will be realized if laboratory design is intentional and focused on intended learning outcomes.

Elementary school programs are easily served by portable technology centers that provide students with a variety of basic tools and materials. These centers are stored when not in use allowing the elementary teacher a great deal of flexibility in a limited (usually self-contained classroom) facility. Soft materials (e.g., paper, foam board, cardboard) can be processed easily on regular tables as students sketch their ideas and construct their design solutions.

Middle schools can provide additional flexibility by creating general technology laboratories. These laboratories should have the capability to engage students in medical, biological, agricultural, energy and power, information and communication, transportation, manufacturing, and construction technologies. Portable and modular configurations are useful because of their flexibility and multiple use capability. Technology islands can be used for utilities, computers, and storage, allowing students to bring a variety of technologies together. Also useful is a basic modeling area where students have access to material processing equipment as they construct their experiments, working models, and design solutions. Additionally, there are a number of commercial vendors who will provide facility design services and modular solutions for middle schools.

Technological system laboratories best serve high schools. The most popular are production, transportation, communication, biotechnology, energy, and materials processing. A more recent trend is the senior level research and development laboratory where pre-engineering classes can be taught. Instrumentation and equipment becomes more complex and computerized, and students work with both soft and hard materials. Students do all types of design and problem solving activities, which include troubleshooting, research and development, invention, innovation, experimentation, and procedural development. Students' technological interests can be used as the medium for student learning. Students are required to study a given technological context in a technological, social, and cultural setting.

THE IN-SERVICE ROLES OF TECHNOLOGY TEACHER EDUCATORS

University professors conduct a great deal of public school in-service work, usually on a consultant basis where they contract with schools for on-site short-term seminars and workshops. A second area of in-service, usually longer in duration and more outcomes-oriented, is funded by grants. These grants can be awarded to the school district or the university, depending on the type of grant and/or the proposal writer. In the consensus publication, *A Rationale and Structure for the Study of Technology* (ITEA, 1996), the authors challenge teacher educators to "...expand their teacher preparation and research in the field of teaching technology so that issues can be addressed with knowledge and understanding" (p. 44). Additionally, "In-service programs must be developed to teach technology educators how to implement *Standards for Technological Literacy* "...[and] "[t]hose who educate technology teachers should review and revise undergraduate and graduate programs..." (ITEA, 2000, p. 201). This is a call for technology teacher educators to move beyond their credit-bearing pre-service roles and get involved as a university in the implementation of *Standards for Technological Literacy* in the public schools using both traditional and innovative in-service models.

The process of change is never smooth, rational, or linear. When things do not go well in schools that are transforming, they develop the courage to regroup, plan again, and find ways out of the confusion. Despite conflict, which sometimes seems ubiquitous, teachers learn how to make it productive – rather than destructive. Sometimes it takes external help to teach people how to talk to one another in a way that works, rather than expressing interpersonal differences. If people can collaborate, then they can make progress. Having many perspectives is critical to school and teacher transformation (Lieberman & Miller, 1999, p. 90).

Technology teacher educators have the distinctive advantage of knowing a number of technology teachers, since most of them are graduates of their university. The support of teacher educators is also reassuring in that it is acceptable to change what they were taught as undergraduates. Teacher educators are also experienced change agents and understand the change process and all its implications. By strategically working with innovators, communicators, laggards and adopters, professors can move the change process along in an orderly and professional manner. By serving as a driving force for change, teacher educators can reduce peer pressure for opposing points of views.

In a sense, the technology teacher education program has the professional responsibility to re-train alumni who were taught methods of yesterday and who struggle with implementing *Standards for Technological Literacy* new content and teaching strategies. Because *Standards for Technological Literacy* reflect a philosophy of technological literacy for all Americans, just about everyone in the profession benefits from in-service education on the *Standards for Technological Literacy*.

IN-SERVICE MODELS FOR TECHNOLOGY EDUCATION

The following is a description of university initiated in-service models for public school technology teachers. The programs were developed to help teachers change from industrial arts to technology education. They represent a pro-active approach to advance the technology education agenda in West Virginia, Connecticut, and the northeastern region of the United States. There are many other models that could be featured in this section of the chapter, but these three models are unique and different than the traditional approaches highlighted by Lieberman. These actual case studies can serve as models for universities who want to provide assistance to public schools that want to implement *Standards for Technological Literacy*.

Project Open

In 1973 West Virginia University's Technology Education Program entered into an agreement with two public school districts to provide assistance in changing their industrial arts programs to technology education over a three-year period. The curricula, in-service initiative was called Project Open and was the first comprehensive change model of its type in technology education. Under the leadership of Dr. Paul DeVore (retired) and Dr. David McCrory, two change models were designed to work in two totally different situations.

A consultant model was established for the school that had an existing program (combination of middle/high school) with two seasoned teachers. The university consultant (doctoral student) provided 20 hours each week of in-service to help teachers make the conversion and to provide intensive assistance in curricula and instructional strategies. During the summer months, the consultant prepared teaching materials for the next academic year. Over a three year period, seven courses were developed, new teaching materials were developed, and the facility was completely renovated to allow the teachers to teach communication, transportation, manufacturing, and construction technologies with emphasis on technological impacts and consequences.

A second model was called a direct implementation approach where two doctoral students teamed together to teach and support a new program in a standard middle school classroom space. During the fall semester, one of the doctoral students went to a secondary school to begin teaching general technology. The other team member remained at the university and provided curricula and instructional support. During the half-year holiday break, the team flip-flopped and reversed roles of teacher and supporter. After three years, courses in technology education were implemented and the classroom was retrofitted to accommodate the teaching of technology and its impact on humankind.

Over the next 15 years, the Project Open in-service models served a number of public schools. The programs were totally funded by the public schools and made an impact in all parts of the West Virginia and parts of Southwestern Pennsylvania. This change model would be ideal for those universities that have advanced graduate degree programs and a resource for school districts in need of curriculum development to align them with *Standards for Technological Literacy.*

Technology Teacher Enhancement Center

Dr. John Larkin launched the Technology Teacher Enhancement Center (TTEC) at Central Connecticut State University (CCSU) during Fall, 1991. This long-term in-service approach modeled after the successful Schenely Teacher Center in Pittsburgh, Pennsylvania. The basic concept was to provide long-term enhancement programs to revitalize experienced practicing teachers so that they can bring new innovations into the field.

The CCSU program provided 12 all-day in-service sessions that focused on the implementation of technology education at middle and high school levels. National experts provided minds-on, hands-on sessions which were topical in nature and comprehensive in practice. Each presenter was required to provide action-oriented activities, design briefs, and/or other teaching materials that could be used on Monday mornings. Topics included philosophy, outcome assessment, transportation, biotechnology, communication, production, facility design, teaching methods, and national and state standards. Each teacher was able to accumulate a large amount of resources, argue and debate the positive and negative aspects of technology education, and talk to each other about issues related to teaching public school technology education.

In the eight years that the TTEC was offered, over 250 technology education teachers were in-serviced. This resulted in program change and refinement in Connecticut's schools, teacher bonding and networking, and an increase in enrollments at CCSU in the undergraduate technology teacher education program. Another unique feature was that the university cost-shared the program with the public schools using Perkins Funds allocated to the local education agencies. Dr. Larkin received re-assigned time to organize and coordinate the program. Most schools sent at least two teachers to the TTEC. A few districts in-serviced all their teachers. The success of the model lies in the long-term (12 consecutive Friday's) commitment of the school districts and the ability of the university to bring national experts to deliver the program.

Northeast Technology Education Consortium

In 1991 the United States Office of Education requested research funded proposals (RFPs) to develop four national technology education demonstration centers. The concept was to develop centers of excellence that technology education public school teachers could visit and see technology education in action with actual teachers and students. A secondary goal of the program was to develop new instructional and curricula materials, and facility designs.

CCSU took the initiative to organize several universities and public schools into a consortium for the purpose of responding to the RFP. University faculty, public school teachers, and state supervisors met in Auburn, MA, and agreed to participate in the project. CCSU wrote the final proposal.

The proposal was funded and the Northeast Technology Education Consortium (NETEC) was created to develop the centers of excellence. Two public schools in New York were selected: one in the city and the other in an upstate affluent community. A rural regional school was selected in Rhode Island and a small rural middle school was selected in Vermont. Rounding out the NETEC schools was a medium sized city school in Maine. The schools were selected because of their commitment to teaching technology and their willingness to accept large amounts of visitors over several years. The state supervisors tried to select schools that were regionally accessible to all northeast teachers.

The demonstration schools received large amounts of in-service education organized by Bill Boudreau, the Director of NETEC and delivered by consortium members. A large number of vendors provided assistance by donating over $700,000 worth of equipment to the schools and in-service time to help the NETEC teachers learn to use and teach the new technology. NETEC teachers also designed and developed new facilities that were state-of-the-art for teaching technology education.

When visiting teachers arrived at a NETEC demonstration site, they were given in-service by the teachers, allowed to visit the laboratories, and watched live classes while teachers taught and students did their work. In many cases, the students were the best ambassadors for technology education. During the first three years of the project over 1,000 teachers visited the NETEC sites. Some state supervisors organized field trips to NETEC sites using school buses to help cut travel costs. Teachers in the northeast still visit NETEC demonstration schools.

The advantage of this in-service model was its ability to show technology education in action. Many teachers are reluctant to change because they fear technology education will not work. NETEC demonstrated that technology education does work in all situations; city to rural, and rich to poor, and every teacher can teach and engage students in the study of technology.

RECOMMENDED CHANGES FOR TECHNOLOGY TEACHER EDUCATORS FOR IN-SERVICING TECHNOLOGY TEACHERS

Technology education is at an interesting crossroad in its history. After 20 years of philosophical dialogue, curricula change, and instructional experimentation, the ITEA has put forth the most comprehensive and collaborated set of national standards, entitled *Standards for Technological Literacy*, in the history of the profession. What is profound about the technology education movement is that the leadership came from states and public schools rather than technology teacher educators who had been the primary innovators in the past (Wright, 1999). But now, it is time for teacher educators to "step up to the plate" and get behind the implementation of *Standards for Technological Literacy*.

It is time for teacher education program faculty, chairpersons, and deans to provide resources for post-service education. In a non-traditional manner, like CCSU, teacher educators should be given reassigned time, with credit toward tenure and promotion, for working with teachers and public schools to assure proper implementation of *Standards for Technological Literacy*. Never before has the profession needed comprehensive post-service education more than now, and never before has the profession needed the support of technology teacher educators more than now.

Teacher educators also need to revise methods and curriculum courses to address *Standards for Technological Literacy*. Student teachers should be given the opportunity to implement *Standards for Technological Literacy* and cooperating teachers should be in-serviced on *Standards for Technological Literacy* before being allowed to supervise new teachers. Technology teacher education graduate programs need to be revised. The role of the teacher education program is significant in both pre-service and post-service technology education.

"The conventional view of staff development as a transferable package of knowledge to be distributed in bite-sized pieces needs radical transformation and rethinking. It carries not only a limited conception of teacher learning, but one grounded in a set of assumptions about teachers, teaching, and the process of change that does not match current research or practice" (Grimmett & Neufield, 1994, p. 592). The days of <u>individual curriculum plans</u> by innovative teacher educators are over. The new generation of curriculum leaders must work collaboratively with the ITEA to assure high quality curriculum for all Americans. Fortunately, the technology education profession has many distinguished technology educators who serve as role models for all... but technology educators must take the lead and reform traditional programs and outdated practices (Wright, 1999, p. 197). They must be ready to meet the challenge to make sure that *Standards for Technological Literacy* are at the core of what the profession is all about.

The role of technology teacher educators in in-servicing technology teachers on how to implement *Standards for Technological Literacy* is significant. Traditional methods of providing consulting to public schools have their limitations in terms of time, costs, and effectiveness. The teacher education programs have a professional responsibility to its alumni to keep them abreast of new changes in the profession. This responsibility goes beyond an occasional newsletter or presentation at the state conference. It must be a comprehensive, pro-active approach to bring everyone on-board.

In-service based on long term commitments between the university and public schools is long overdue. This chapter has argued that the one-day, "start-up and shutdown" models used in the past are not intense or comprehensive enough to cause real change in the classroom. Long-term funded and unfunded projects between the teacher education program and public school technology programs must be designed to help implement *Standards for Technological Literacy*. Teacher educators must get as committed to post-service education as they are for pre-service education. And university administrators must value fieldwork as important, scholarly, and acceptable for consideration in promotion and tenure decisions if the profession expects professors to seriously meet the challenge.

In the past 20 years, state supervisors, professional associations, and public school teachers have taken the lead for the development and implementation of technology education. It is time for teacher educators to "step up to the plate" of action and provide meaningful in-service educational opportunities based upon *Standards for Technological Literacy*. At a time when teacher education enrollments are modest, it would appear to be ideal for the profession to dedicate itself to *Standards for Technological Literacy* leadership. The stars appear to be lined up and our profession has never been better organized. The expectations are high and the potential enormous. The profession needs a new generation of technology teachers and teacher educators to enhance the team that's out there everyday. If everyone pulls, the load is light.

THOUGHT-PROVOKING ACTIVITIES

1. What is the value of long-term in-service education? What barriers must be removed in order to provide the necessary time away from school?

2. If you were the curriculum coordinator, how would you provide opportunities for technology teachers to become familiar with the *Standards for Technological Literacy*?

3. How would you plan a five-day retreat for technology teachers to learn about *Standards for Technological Literacy*? Provide a topical outline for the five-day session.

4. What assets do you think teacher educators have to assist in the implementation of *Standards for Technological Literacy*?

5. What methodologies would you employ to provide in-service for public school technology teachers?

REFERENCES

Gilberti, A.F., & Rouch, D. L. (Eds.). (1999). *Advancing professionalism in technology education: Forty-eighth yearbook of the Council on Technology Teacher Education.* New York: Glencoe McGraw-Hill.

Grimmett, P., & Newfield, J. (1994). Teacher development and the struggle for authenticity. In A. Lieberman (Ed.). *Practices that support teacher development transforming conceptions of professional learning.* [On-line]. Available: http://amazon.com [2000, Sept.].

Harris, B.M., & Bessent, W. (1969). *In-service education.* Englewood Cliffs, NJ: Prentice-Hall.

International Technology Education Association (ITEA). (1996). *A rationale and structure for the study of technology.* Reston, VA: Author.

International Technology Education Association (ITEA). (2000). *Standards for technological literacy.* Reston, VA: Author.

Larkin, J. C. (1999). Developing effective in-service for technology education. In A.F. Gilberti, & D.L. Rouch (Eds.). *Advancing professionalism in technology education, Forty-eighth yearbook of the Council on Technology Teacher Education,* (pp. 97-119). New York: Glencoe McGraw-Hill.

Lieberman, A. (1995). Practices that support teacher development: Transforming conceptions of professional learning. [On-line]. Available: http://amazon.com [2000, Sept.].

Lieberman, A., & Miller, L. (1999). *Teachers-transforming their world and their work.* New York: Teachers College Press.

Savage, E., & Steery, L. (1990). *A conceptual framework for technology education.* Reston, VA: International Technology Education Association.

Wright, J.R. (1992). *Northeast technology education consortium (final report).* Technology Education Demonstration Program V-230A00080/CFDA 84.230. Washington, DC: US Office of Adult and Vocational Education.

Wright, J.R. (1999). Teacher professionalism in technology education. In A.F. Gilberti, & D.L. Rouch, (Eds.). *Advancing professionalism in technology education, Forty-eighth yearbook of the Council on Technology Teacher Education,* (pp. 181-198). New York: Glencoe McGraw-Hill.

Cooperative In-service by Teacher Educators and State Departments of Education

Bryan Albrecht
Wisconsin Department of Public Instruction

Ken Starkman
Wisconsin Department of Public Instruction

Douglas Wagner
Florida State Department of Education

Ron Barker
Georgia State Department of Education

Teachers have long been expected to be change agents. They are expected to carry out the broad mission of public education, i.e., implement programs, enforce policies, conduct evaluations, and develop new curriculum to implement in public education. Now increasingly, they are expected to assume leadership roles in school reform.

One aspect of this leadership is the implementation of local, state, and national standards. Technology education teachers are expected to implement *Standards for Technological Literacy: Content for the Study of Technology* (*Standards for Technological Literacy*) (ITEA, 2000). It must be remembered that teachers continue to be the link between curriculum and learning. Key to this linkage is teachers staying current with educational reform efforts like *Standards for Technological Literacy*. This document provides the foundation for curriculum design and classroom innovation. Proper understanding of the purpose and use of standards is the role of teacher educators and state departments of education.

This chapter examines the role that technology teacher educators and state department of education supervisors of technology education can play in the preparation of technology education teachers and establishing collaborative partnership in implementation of *Standards for Technological Literacy*. Specifically, this chapter presents major partnership concepts with examples from three states: Wisconsin, Florida, and Georgia. Some major ideas and concepts outlined support the implementation of

Standards for Technological Literacy as they relate to establishing a collaborative partnership, marketing, and funding teacher in-service, and innovative instructional strategies. Best practices in states committed to implementing *Standards for Technological Literacy* and that offer a diverse approach to the in-servicing of teachers are also examined.

RELATIONSHIP BETWEEN TEACHER EDUCATION AND STATE DEPARTMENTS

Wisconsin

Wisconsin has a long collaborative relationship between its technology education teacher preparation programs and the State Department of Public Instruction. History reveals a very close working relationship between faculty at both the University of Wisconsin-Stout and the University of Wisconsin-Platteville teacher educator institutions and the state department. Much of this is due to the leadership of the faculty at both universities in the early days of the profession, and it continues today in the research and educational design of contemporary technology education programs.

Florida

Florida also has had a long institutionalized relationship between its technology education teacher preparation programs and the Florida Department of Education. Teacher educators and state department staff have been the driving force of the leadership programs for the state serving on the prestigious State Technical Committees, Council for Supervisors, and numerous executive committees of the profession. This combined vision for the advancement of the field is necessary in moving technology education forward in Florida.

Georgia

Just as cooperative relationships have been established in Florida and Wisconsin, the State of Georgia has expanded technology teacher in-service by partnering with the ITEA Center to Advance the Teaching of Technology and Science (CATTS). The CATTS consortium of states has focused on the development of resources to implement *Standards for Technological Literacy.*

ESTABLISHING A COLLABORATIVE PARTNERSHIP

As the role of teachers change and the impact of technology plays an even greater role in the content for the curriculum and its delivery, it is increasingly clear that the knowledge and skills teachers need to succeed can only be acquired through greater investments in teacher preparation and continued professional development. Success in today's classroom requires high levels of knowledge and a broad range of skills. Current education reform also creates a broader range of roles for teachers in developing standards-based curriculum and assessments of student performance related to these standards.

Local education agencies and state departments of education must partner with colleges and universities in the development and support of teacher pre-service and in-service programs that support the changing needs of the classroom teachers and the implementation of *Standards for Technological Literacy*. It is clear that at least four essential elements contribute to successful collaboration when implementing *Standards for Technological Literacy*. These include:

- Strong relationships built upon shared beliefs. A common set of shared beliefs is foundational to the "message sent to the field." Classroom teachers must see and hear a clear and consistent message whether it comes from their continued professional education or from state directives. The belief is simple. The research and knowledge base for curriculum and instructional methodologies rests in the hands of the university faculty with proven expertise and the opportunity to extend curriculum capabilities. The continued connection to local schools and assessment of program improvement is the responsibility of state department staff.

- A common vision for technology education and teacher preparation. Each partner must have a common understanding of each other's role. Strategies that can help reach this common vision are shared roles on program and state advisory committees, jointly developed and sponsored teacher pre-service and in-service, and cooperative research and funding initiatives that support technology education and the *Standards for Technological Literacy*.

- A common knowledge base and curriculum that supports the teaching of technology. Critical to providing effective professional in-service is a common understanding of *Standards for Technological Literacy* that makes up the knowledge base for technology education. Technology education programs have evolved from a rich history and a wide variety of implementation models found within local schools. One thing that is consistent in the standards is the base for technological literacy and the content knowledge for all programs. State leadership has set the direction for local schools in curriculum, implementing the standards, and learning assessment. Ensuring the success of this direction, university teacher educators must adopt the standards and integrate them into pre-service and in-service programs.

- Establishing goals, implementing the standards, and identifying program expectations. While each of these efforts can stand alone, the strength comes from the integration of these for implementing *Standards for Technological Literacy* and their accompanying instructional resources into all aspects of state department and university initiatives. State staff and teacher education faculty rely on each other to support and reinforce *Standards for Technological Literacy.*

The culminating success of these four elements result in the achievement of established goals. State departments of education staff and teacher educators should work together to ensure teacher support, resource development, technical assistance, and financial commitment.

A major educational reform effort such as the infusion of *Standards for Technological Literacy* into the existing state department and teacher education institutions staff development activities is possible because of the attitudes of the shared partnership. State departments of education provide leadership in critical areas described such as funding, program approval and guidance, and leveraging political change. Teacher educators share in this responsibility by undertaking supportive research and reforming undergraduate and graduate programs to reflect *Standards for Technological Literacy.*

Standards for Technological Literacy serve as a road map for reform. They trace a strong history and will lead to a new and exciting future. State leadership is critical and can be established by embracing *Standards for Technological Literacy* in the process of teacher preparation, continued professional development, teacher certification, and overall general public awareness.

MARKETING AND FUNDING

Marketing is certainly an aspect that cannot be neglected. Public awareness, teacher engagement, and school district support are all aspects of marketing *Standards for Technological Literacy*. Wisconsin, as well as Florida and Georgia, has leveraged the leadership of state department staff and university faculty to connect *Standards for Technological Literacy* to the existing state standards. Providing models of standards-based curriculum design and demonstrating student achievement based on those standards is essential. Teacher in-service through state-called meetings, professional association conferences, university conferences, informational web pages, listserves, and workshops provide vehicles to communicate the value and inspire leadership at the local level for the use of the national standards. Teachers throughout the state can participate in meetings, conferences, and email exchanges with state leaders to discuss the process of standards reform. State resources provide additional support for teachers and teacher educators to attend national meetings to expand their vision for the implementation of *Standards for Technological Literacy*. In Wisconsin, a cadre of leaders have developed supportive resources such as a matrix for the integration of *Standards for Technological Literacy* with mathematics, science, language arts, and social studies standards, a scope and sequence for program development, a series of professional development experiences, a model curriculum, and assessment tools for technology teachers. Each of these resources helps to demonstrate to teachers and administrators the valuable role standards play in connecting educational content and teacher preparation.

Like many states, the current environment for education in the State of Florida is legislatively controlled by elected officials who need to hear a constant message from the field in regards to technology education. It is important that the message be one that moves technology education forward. This is only possible if the stakeholders in the profession work together and relay the message precisely and systematically.

A good example of the results of a unified voice has been the tremendous amount of legislative approved funds (over 55 million dollars) in the 1990s, plus countless millions from local sources for the re-design and renovation of old industrial arts laboratories into trend setting, state-of-the-art technology education facilities. Efforts in marketing are critical to gaining overall support for *Standards for Technological Literacy*. These efforts must be built upon knowledge that technology education administrators, teacher educators, and teachers are the creators, designers, and implementers of *Standards for Technological Literacy*.

TEACHER IN-SERVICE

With financial support from the State Department of Education and the expertise of teachers and teacher educators, Georgia has begun the process of comprehensive reform in technology education. This effort includes the development of state content standards, adoption of standards-based curriculum, and systematic training of technology education teachers. The in-servicing of teachers is a comprehensive venture between the state department, professional associations, and teacher educators. A variety of strategies have been implemented to address the growing need to expand the in-servicing options. Traditional university course offerings and conference workshops continue to provide quality experiences for teachers. New models of in-servicing such as distance education, the use of the internet, and industry training all provide excellent resources for teacher in-servicing.

To assist in the development and implementation of *Standards for Technological Literacy*, Georgia has joined the ITEA CATTS consortium. With CATTS, it is necessary to establish a model that will provide systemic and on-going in-service training. Teacher educators may be excellent trainers in such a model as they directly impact pre-service as well as in-service experiences. In every case, a common understanding and collective partnership between teacher educators, state staff, and contracted in-service providers is critical to the overall success of the process.

Another example of how state departments of education can successfully collaborate with teacher educators is to work together to leverage or influence administrators or institutions in a philosophical change, which will move technology education forward. In Florida, hundreds of thousands of dollars have been used for the design and implementation of university courses that meet current teacher certificate demands and for implementing *Standards for Technological Literacy*. A change, that could take years if universities had to complete the work themselves, can be reduced to weeks. Many new ideas have been tried in Florida, but the most successful one is the benefits from the strong partnerships between the teacher educators and the state department of education.

In Wisconsin, the process of teacher in-service is just that, a process. Teacher educators and state department staff continually work together to provide innovative opportunities for teachers. One unique model that has proven successful is the Wisconsin Staff Development Initiative. This is a National Science Foundation and local business partnership funded effort that brings together mathematics, science, and technology teachers, training them in curriculum development, standards implementation, and curriculum integration.

Teachers are the catalysts for change and *Standards for Technological Literacy* will serve as a guide to innovation and continued curriculum development. In-servicing teachers should include a collective outreach that extends the role of teacher educators and state department staff to assist in teacher training. State professional associations, business and industry technology training opportunities, local leadership, and integrated in-service opportunities with other subject matter areas are all influenced by *Standards for Technological Literacy*. Teacher educators and state departments must provide leadership to all entities that impact teacher training.

INNOVATIVE INSTRUCTIONAL STRATEGIES

In Wisconsin, new initiatives have been created around equity and technological literacy for all students. Efforts led by teacher educators and the state staff have created a bold, new vision for the inclusion of young women in the teaching of technology. The Technology Action Coalition to Kindle Lifelong Learning Project provides training and information to increase the number of girls and young women in technology education through virtual resources over the Internet. National research was conducted and a knowledge base was created that led to the identification of five factors that influence whether young women will participate in technology education. The technology curriculum and instruction proved to be important factors in getting young women to participate. More specifically, the effort must include connecting subject matter to procedures and subject matter across a variety of curricular areas. *Standards for Technological Literacy* allows the profession to connect the curriculum and lead to the measurement of student success.

A second innovative strategy is the Wisconsin Technology Articulation Initiative. Teacher educators, state staff, and local school districts have partnered to create a two college credit course titled Exploring Technology. This course is designed to teach concepts of technological literacy and provide high school students with college credit. The course is based on the state standards for technological literacy and links student experiences in high school with future experiences they will gain in college. With technological literacy as the expected outcome, the content standards drive the curriculum and its delivery.

In Florida, the state legislature approved a program where one student from every public and private high school in the state is eligible to receive a college scholarship to become a technology education teacher. The program also covers tuition reimbursement for any current teacher (in any field) to take a university level class in technology education. Last, under the Loan Forgiveness Program, new teachers in technology education can receive up to $10,000 to repay student loans. These programs would not be possible without a strong partnership between teacher education and state staff, which has been cultivated over the decades. No one entity can work independently; collaborative efforts have been the key to success in Florida.

SUMMARY

States are using the framework of *Standards for Technological Literacy* to redefine teacher certification standards, local program funding initiatives, and university teacher educator programs. *Standards for Technological Literacy* can serve as an important catalyst to connect state departments and teacher educators. This chapter was designed to showcase selected, best practices and spark creativity in building relationships. It is important to remember that any partnership takes a commitment and continuous dedication to achieve success. Teacher educators and state department staff are critical to the overall success of implementing *Standards for Technological Literacy*. Only by establishing a strong positive network of professionals at all levels within each state will the profession achieve the vision of technological literacy for all our children.

Throughout this chapter, the authors have learned that there are many factors that impact the success of implementing *Standards for Technological Literacy*. Personal commitment, financial support, and innovative practices were described through the examples provided by Wisconsin, Florida and Georgia. The ideas presented will continue to serve as guiding principles in future reform. Foremost among these is the need to focus on building collaborative partnerships between teacher educators and state department of education staff members. The second is the necessity to fully involve and support teachers in the development, training, and preparation of programs that implement *Standards for Technological Literacy*. Finally, there is the need to be "champions" of innovation and provide the leadership to challenge the traditions of our profession.

Change comes slowly. Even so, technology educators face a challenging task as we strive to make the technology curriculum relevant to the lives of students. *Standards for Technological Literacy* provides a roadmap for future professional updating.

THOUGHT-PROVOKING ACTIVITIES

1. Collaboratively plan a series of four evening workshops led by state staff and teacher education faculty that could be provided regionally within states to introduce *Standards for Technological Literacy* to technology education teachers.

2. Plan an agenda for a meeting between technology teacher educators and state department staff to plan for the introduction of *Standards for Technological Literacy* to parents, public school administrators, and technology education teachers. Plan an agenda for a press conference. Develop a press release to advertise the events.

3. What state level activities should occur during the next several years to implement *Standards for Technological Literacy*?

4. Outline a state plan for developing and using assessment tests to measure the technological literacy of students in your state.

REFERENCES

Balistreri, J., Daugherty, M., Gray, R., & Valesey, B. (1998). *ROAD MAPS: Perspectives for excellence in technology education programs.* Reston, VA: International Technology Education Association.

Danielson, C. (1999). *Enhancing professional practice.* Alexandria, VA: Association for Supervisors and Curriculum.

Grif, G. (1999). *The education of teachers.* Ninety-eighth Yearbook of the National Society for the Study of Education. Chicago, IL: University of Chicago Press.

Harriss, D. (1996). *How to use standards in the classroom.* Alexandria, VA: Association for Supervision and Curriculum Development.

International Technology Education Association (ITEA) (2000). *Standards for technological literacy: Content for the study of technology.* Reston, VA: Author.

Loughran, J., & Russell, T. (1997). *Teaching about teaching.* Washington, DC: The Falmer Press.

Lusi, S. (1997). *The role of state departments of education in complex school reform.* New York, NY: Teachers College Press.

Teacher Education and National Organizations: Their Relationships in Preparing Standards-Oriented Technology Teachers

Chapter 12

Kendall N. Starkweather
International Technology Education Association

"To improve is to change; to be perfect is to change often."
Winston Churchill

National organizations such as the International Technology Education Association (ITEA) and its councils are a powerful force in determining the direction that technology teacher education will take in preparing and in-servicing the next generation of teachers. The mission and energy from national organizations have the power to transform a profession that was unnoticed into one that is a major focus of society, a segment of a profession that is passive into one that comes alive, and a field that was formerly positioned on the sidelines into one more centrally focused in people's minds. The creation and implementation of *Standards for Technological Literacy: Content for the Study of Technology* (*Standards for Technological Literacy*) (ITEA, 2000) will succeed because of the ability of people, their institutions, and relationships with other principle groups working together to advance education. The result is a higher focus on teaching technology education, credibility for creating a content area, and recognition for advancing the profession and education in general.

Just as people need nurturing and opportunities to grow and excel, professional fields such as technology education need a similar type of nurturing. National organizations play a significant role in providing opportunities and nurturing technology education for its worth as a viable part of the educational system. Organizations are involved in the funding of projects and directions, creating standards or guidelines for the profession, providing professional development and forums to discuss issues, advancing policy and promoting the field, assisting in the positioning of the profession within the entire arena of education, and representing the institutions and programs in situations where advocacy is important.

There are many types of national organizations, each with its own personality, that play a role that is specifically unique and in line with their expertise. Often these organizations will "team up" to provide a bigger alliance for gaining additional support. Their intent is very genuine in working with others to improve a particular function or part of society. Table 12-1 lists the types of national organizations that exist, their general focus/mission, and selected examples of organizations that fall into each of the categories.

Table 12-1. Types of National Groups Working with Standards

National Group	Focus/Mission	Selected Examples of Group
Unions	Represent teachers as workers	National Education Association American Federation of Teachers
Foundations	Address initiatives outlined in their charters for giving	Rockefeller, Ford, Sloan
Trade Associations	Promote selected occupations, technology, or industry	Society of Manufacturing Engineers American Society of Mechanical Engineers Institute of Electrical & Electronic Engineers
Educational Associations	Advance policy, administrations, or curriculum	International Technology Education Association National Science Teachers Association National Council of Teachers of Mathematics American Society of Engineering Education
Alliances/Coalitions	Provide forums for initiatives on issues/ topics that are directly addressed by an individual organization	Triangle Coalition for Science & Technology Education Alliance for Curriculum Reform
Governmental Agencies	Represent national initiatives on topics deemed important by government	Department of Education National Science Foundation National Aeronautics & Space Administration National Academy of Science National Academy of Engineers

It is important to note that each of these organizations has its own operating procedures and policies. They are regulated by bylaws, established governing guidelines, and unique policy acceptance procedures. Their bylaws and mission statements provide direction that is often described in credos. They have elected or appointed boards of governors, directors, or trustees who help them frequently adjust the nature of initiatives for projects, activities, and giving.

Technology teacher education is no different from other areas of education in enjoying the support of national organizations. Although technology education teaching is not comprised of large numbers when compared to the whole field of education, it enjoys the same respect and attention experienced by the other fields in terms of licensing, standards, and practices that come primarily as a result of national organizations working on its behalf.

For example, the Council on Technology Teacher Education (CTTE) and the International Technology Education Association joined with the National Council for the Accreditation of Teacher Education (NCATE) to create a certification process that provides guidance for technology teacher education as well as many other fields of education. The end result has been a strengthening of both technology education as well as other subject areas. CTTE/ITEA is comprised of professionals from higher education institutions who help set the *ITEA/CTTE/NCATE Curriculum Guidelines*. Therefore, ITEA/CTTE/NCATE becomes the mechanism or avenue for improving technology teacher education as a result of its involvement in initiatives that create improvement and change. This is only one example of how national organizations work to improve technology teacher education while strengthening higher education.

Few educators ever realize the significant role that national organizations play in their formal and informal education. Educators who are actively involved in forging new directions as well as refinement of successful practices do realize that they make a difference in their profession and teacher education by being active in organizations. While the majority of teacher preparation is designed and delivered by a teacher education institution, that institution and the people preparing or in-servicing teachers have a relationship with all types of organizations. This relationship directly affects the nature of course offerings, offers teacher enhancement for the institution, creates standards, develops instructional materials, and more that support the whole education process. Ordinarily, the teacher in training or in-service never realizes the effects of such relationships although all who are involved profit from the interaction.

The role of an association such as ITEA as it relates to teacher education and standards for the profession is one of being a change agent. Members of the association and profession work to adapt the standards. They create materials, resources, and models to be tried and implemented. They work to research a more effective teaching and learning situation and use the association as a vehicle for trying to advance their ideas through professional development. Members also use an association for positioning and conducting advocacy campaigns that will strengthen the field's status and impact. In a standards-based education, the association becomes the mechanism for sharing and advancing common ideas about philosophy, leadership, promotion, and implementation.

ITEA members, with the assistance of other agencies, created *Standards for Technological Literacy*. CTTE and other councils within the Association were actively involved in this process. Years of work were put into the original proposal. Countless meetings with potential supporters and funding groups were initiated and conducted. Once the support was created and the funding secured, work to complete *Standards for Technological Literacy* was advanced.

These steps were taken because of the necessity to change technology education from its current status into a curriculum positioned to better serve the profession and education. Change in technology education has not been swift, nor has the thinking that has gone into a lot of change reflected deep thought of what students should "know" and "be able to do" as it relates to the study of technology. Rather, much of the change has been as a result of an entrepreneur mentality with a genuine intent to do right. Unfortunately, many of the changes reflected a mentality with the teacher as a "follower" rather than a "thinker" and "leader" in determining the content being delivered in their programs.

THE STATUS OF TECHNOLOGY EDUCATION BEFORE *STANDARDS FOR TECHNOLOGICAL LITERACY*

A status review of technology education and technology teacher education before the advent of *Standards for Technological Literacy* would show many programs unaltered in decades of existence. This stagnation in the secondary schools has resulted in suffering enrollment for once popular courses such as woods, metals, and drafting. These programs have lost stature in today's school curriculum and as a result have either been altered or dropped from educational programs. Ultimately, it has become obvious to many students and their parents that these courses were not appropriate for a curriculum to reflect technology.

Technology educators have experimented with various curricula, such as the *Jackson's Mill Curriculum Theory* (Snyder & Hales, 1981), in attempts to produce the first generation of technology education while closing the last generation of industrial arts. These changes have been slow, but in all fairness to industrial arts and technology educators, more change has happened within the field than all of the other areas of the school curriculum. Educational reform in the United States has not been known for its quick impact.

The field of technology education has also suffered from the lack of consistency and accountability. This would stand to reason, for a field that has not had a rationale and structure for the study of technology and devoid of content standards from which to use as a basis for a common ground, certainly could not be expected to have any accountability (ITEA, 1996). The result has been a poor attempt at creating a research base for continuing to build the profession, study factors pertaining to teaching and learning, and proving the worth of technology education.

At the university level, entire departments have either been closed or subsumed into other departments for various reasons. One main reason has been the failure to stay on the leading edge of the latest practices that could advance the field. University departments that led the profession in ideas and innovation during the 1960s decade are nonexistent or without direction at the turn of the century. These departments, to regain the position that they once held as a leader in the profession, have exhibited little effort. Departments have seemingly taken on the characteristic that plagues the university tenure system. That is, once tenure has been reached, research, creativity, and educational innovation have decreased. At times, university departments have been rudderless in their attempts to provide leadership to the profession.

Research pertaining to the worth of technology education can easily be described as "an extremely small stream with little water worth drinking." Fewer research institutions have been able to sustain a strong research program that could prove the worth of technology education, evaluate practices in teaching and learning, or create models that could be replicated in any area of the profession. University departments have neither tried to establish nor promote their expertise in any aspect of technology education. Research seems to have been limited to surveys on the status of or feelings about a particular aspect of technology education.

Further, serious questions arise as to any advancement in teaching and learning practices at the university level. Only recently have departments experimented with new delivery techniques that have mostly related to educational or instructional technology. Few university technology programs have made adjustments for the delivery of education through the Internet.

One could easily conclude from this foregoing discussion that the profession has been without direction. It would seem that the passion and enthusiasm for teaching technology has waned! It has not! The field of technology education has had to endure all that has happened to the entire field of education. In other words, the big picture as it pertains to education has not been pleasant with resulting effects on technology education. Such ills of education as policy, funding, public perception, and more have not been kind to educators.

Dissatisfaction with education during the 1980s, for example, caused a whole series of studies that called for reform. The public became critical of education and the resulting years have been filled with unhappiness with the performance of students in the classroom. The standards movement spun out of the need to describe performance that students should attain and the need to adjust educational practices to better educate our population. Technology education teaching was one of the last curriculum areas to create standards and attempt to identify what students should "know" and "be able to do" as it pertains to the study of technology.

AN OPPORTUNITY TO REINVENT A SUBJECT MATTER AREA

The funding of the ITEA Technology for All Americans Project, by the National Science Foundation (NSF) and the National Aeronautics and Space Administration (NASA), was in itself a signal to technology educators of new things to come. This was the first time that either of these two science, technology, engineering, and mathematics (STEM) oriented agencies had funded a major project dealing with technology education.

The nature of the project would, for the first time, create *A Rationale and Structure for the Study of Technology* (*Rationale and Structure*) (ITEA, 1996). This rationale would serve as the basis from which to build content standards for the field. The field had never created content standards in all of its years of existence. Instead, the field had used an activity-based, career orientation and often was considered a subset of vocational education. This subset was only partially successful in positioning the field.

With NSF and NASA funding, new opportunities for structuring the field and strengthening its position within the field of education arose. The *Rationale and Structure* could be used as a basis for creating content. The field of technology had an opportunity to position itself as a subject matter area alongside the mathematics and science content areas. Technology education teaching also had an opportunity to more closely align its content with engineering, architecture, and other high technology areas.

These types of opportunities for repositioning a subject matter area based upon its content, created a crucial time in the history of the field. None of this would have happened without ITEA members and staff working with other national organizations who could see a need for improving teaching and learning about technology, a new basis for the field to build upon, and positioning a field to make a larger contribution to K-12 education in the country.

The progress of the standards project attracted additional attention in the STEM content areas as the project utilized fellow educators to capitalize on their expertise and experiences in building standards from their subject matter areas. Contacts with the Center for Science, Mathematics, and Engineering Education (CSMEE), National Research Council (NRC), National Academy of Science (NAS), and the National Academy of Engineering (NAE) created relationships and support not anticipated at the beginning of the project. The strong ties with NSF and NASA were continued and strengthened.

ITEA was successful in obtaining additional funding for a formal review of the standards as a step towards gaining approval from these communities. The NRC, on behalf of the academies, conducted the detailed review that approved *Standards for Technological Literacy*. The National Academy of Engineers conducted its own review on behalf of the engineering community. These steps toward approval from agencies outside the field were major historical accomplishments toward recognition, integrity, and respect for *Standards for Technological Literacy* content-oriented direction. The input from these national organizations serving in their role toward the promotion of education helped the technology education profession tremendously.

DELIVERING STANDARDS-BASED CURRICULUM AND INSTRUCTION

National organizations exist in education to influence curriculum and instruction and to help teachers. Foundations, associations, and governmental agencies typically fund projects that follow preset goals or directions that have been determined by their governing bodies. Alliances and coalitions provide initiatives that advocate set directions that promote standards and their use. Education is influenced by all these organizations, which are the motivators, organizers, directors, and funding agencies of teacher education initiatives, and research that affects the implementation of standards. Teacher educators are often members of these organizations and are stakeholders in the directions taken.

The advent of *Standards for Technological Literacy* gave reason for ITEA and CTTE members to work with credentials and licensing groups that set criteria for technology teacher education institutions. This work must be coordinated because it affects teachers at the K-12 grade levels as well as in higher education.

Governmental agencies were also contacted to create an awareness of the standards and to encourage their use in advancing work related to technology education teaching. Such agencies help determine educational statistics, terminology, research, and legislation.

ITEA created the Center to Advance the Teaching of Technology & Science (CATTS) as a part of its commitment and mission to implement the standards. There also was a commitment to strengthen, broaden, and deepen the subject matter and pedagogical knowledge of teachers.

The Center has given leadership and support to improve the results of learners studying technology and science as it pursues four continuing goals: Research on Teaching and Learning, Curriculum Development,

Teacher Enhancement, and Curriculum Implementation and Diffusion (ITEA, 1999).

The intent of these goals is described as follows:

- Research on Teaching and Learning. The Center plans and conducts research on the factors that underlie effective teaching and learning of technology and science at all levels. CATTS projects have included research with NASA on micro-gravity activities to be used in technology and science. Other projects include aerospace missions and unique topics pertaining to NASA and education. In work of this nature, CATTS research writers coordinate the needs of the association and profession with major initiatives being funded by agencies, foundations, or corporations. The result is research on teaching and learning that helps technology and science teachers.

- Curriculum Development. The Center plans and develops curriculum and instructional materials that incorporate appropriate content, instructional delivery, student activities, and assessments. For example, CATTS has worked with ITEA's Technology for All Americans Project in creating and providing in-service for promoting *Standards for Technological Literacy* at the elementary, middle school, and high school levels.

- Teacher Enhancement. The Center plans and develops programs to strengthen the preparation of teachers at all grade levels to effectively include the study of technology and science within the school curriculum. ITEA/CATTS has conducted professional development workshops on implementation of *Standards for Technological Literacy*, activities for the technology classroom, and children's engineering. Work with the children's engineering workshops has been done in conjunction with the National Association of Elementary School Principals (NAESP). ITEA has also made an electronic version of its journal, *Technology & Children*, available to NAESP members to support the teacher enhancement work.

- Curriculum Implementation and Diffusion. CATTS also utilizes a consortium to identify needs, develop interest, generate support, and maintain a commitment to advance the teaching of technology and science. Through the consortium, organizations and agencies can build alliances and pool resources, whereby expediting solutions to their respective needs for high quality professional development.

- Alliances are established among public agencies, institutions, organizations, and private businesses to facilitate the development of relevant products and services. A contractual agreement and fee entitles consortium members to receive deliverables, e.g., instructional activities, curriculum guidelines, professional development workshops, etc. Grants are also used to support the Center's activities and to supplement the consortium's low fees.

- This consortium work has resulted in the largest technology curriculum development effort in the profession within the last 30 years with teacher enhancement and leadership being provided to consortium states throughout the United States. Plans and activities are being implemented to create a new series of technology courses at the secondary level including additional work with activities at the elementary level.

- ITEA conducts extensive work beyond CATTS and other project efforts on a continual basis with ongoing professional development programs. For example, *Standards for Technological Literacy* has been the major focus of the last four major conferences with general session and special workshop sessions designed for teacher education. Publications and extensive worldwide web activities are aimed at implementing *Standards for Technological Literacy* and helping teacher educators in every way possible.

THE CHALLENGES AHEAD

Most technology educators have not even begun to realize the true potential of their field. They have not realized the possibility of their field being a core subject. Years of thinking in a career rather than a content direction has led technology education teachers to be trapped into thinking that they are in a vocational career subject matter area when they have an opportunity to teach the major technology content and become a major player in the overall education of students. The traditional thinking gives security and stifles efforts to mature the field into its full potential.

The advent of technology with the beginning of the Internet era has caused changes in society resulting in an increased awareness about the effects of technology on our lives. The last time that technological change of this magnitude affected society may have been with the creation of electricity and the light bulb. Such inventions create profound changes in work patterns and family relationships. The major institutions in society such as economic, religious, governmental, and education are impacted as well as the major organizations that operate within these contexts.

It is widely known that technology has changed society over the past centuries. The innate human ability to innovate has led to those changes. However, the field of education has not until recently addressed the importance of learning more about technology. To the average member of society, technology has been so sophisticated that it seems like magic or so basic that it has been overlooked. Science has often been given credit for many technological advances with such terms as "rocket scientist" when perhaps the more accurate term would have been "rocket engineer or technologist."

Interest in teaching about technology has risen. The *Rationale and Structure* and *Standards for Technological Literacy* have brought focus to the technology curriculum. Technology teacher education has a unique opportunity to reinvent itself into a dynamic subject matter area. If technology teacher educators do not take advantage of this window of opportunity, others will probably teach the subject matter area. The choices are simple: either technology teacher educators study technology, focus on this subject matter area, and understand how to implement *Standards for Technological Literacy*, or stand idly by as other areas of education attempt to teach technology according to their own interpretations.

Technology teacher educators can easily be leaders in learning innovation. There is no secret formula or special prerequisites. All that is needed is an intense desire to study, lead, and implement what can be the most dynamic subject area ever.

The environment exists to reposition the study of technology in people's minds and in schools throughout the nation. National organizations such as ITEA, engineering associations, and many more, as well as governmental agencies such as the NAE, NASA, NSF, and more are helping to bring about those changes. Now, technology teacher education institutions must look at their programs, assess their higher education role, and provide solid leadership.

The real danger facing higher education institutions is the potential for apathy in providing leadership. *Standards for Technological Literacy* provides a focus on technology that is not technical education, vocational education, skills preparation, or career education. The focus is on the study of technology! Technology education cannot reach its full potential unless teacher educators realize their important role in focusing the profession on the study of technology.

The biggest challenge for technology teacher education is shedding its traditions and moving forward with the positioning starting from the creation of *Standards for Technological Literacy*. For example, many technology education teachers of today are actually teaching more specific technical education under the title of technology education without any realization of this practice. The field has the burden of having a large number of teachers who are unfamiliar with the content associated with the study of technology. Many teacher educators actually teach about vocational education while calling it technology education. The rest have been muddling together the purposes of technical, technology, career and/or vocational education, which does not help any of these areas reach their potential.

Educational administrators, fellow teachers, parents, students, and countless other decision makers will need to be educated pertaining to the changes that have occurred in the field. Work in this area has already begun with writing efforts such as the 63 pages of the National Association of Secondary School Principals (NASEP), *The Bulletin*, devoted entirely to technology education (NASSP, 1999). Many more activities will be completed in the future as a result of interactions with other national organizations. For example, ITEA now has a partnership with the (NAESP) to co-produce professional development and provide *Technology and Children* to NAESP members. With these thoughts in mind, it is obvious that professionals will use association work to strengthen teacher education in the years ahead.

Failing to address these challenges by technology teacher educators and technology education teachers will result in the field never fully realizing its potential for becoming one of the most dynamic and exciting subject matter areas in the school curriculum. A prime opportunity exists to take the profession through the following steps (See Figure 12-1) in the creation of solid technology education programs.

Figure 12-1. Continuum for Creating Technology Programs

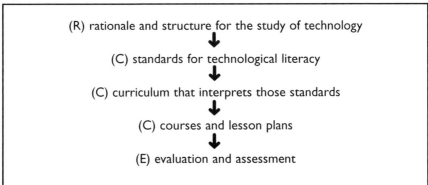

(R) rationale and structure for the study of technology
↓
(C) standards for technological literacy
↓
(C) curriculum that interprets those standards
↓
(C) courses and lesson plans
↓
(E) evaluation and assessment

Each of these steps is significant for the profession. The association and every teacher education institution have their hands full with the amount of work to be completed. The opportunities for leadership from every institution exist. The future of the field depends upon how well each department rises to the challenges of using *Standards for Technological Literacy* to improve their positioning, research base, teacher quality, teaching and learning, and positioning of the field as a strong viable part of everyone's general education. The time span to take advantage of these opportunities is limited. Technology teacher education institutions that do not react will lose their position in the field and be replaced by others who may not be in the teacher preparation business at this time.

Table 12-2 describes selected major thought patterns that must evolve or change for technology teacher education to assume a leadership role. Associations can and will help with these positioning challenges. However, these changes will occur more quickly if teacher educators take on an active posture in implementing *Standards for Technological Literacy*.

As technology teacher educators consider the changes that must be made in their field, they must focus on the opportunities and not dwell on the perils of creating change. As Henry Kissinger (1999, p. 73) noted:

> For any student of history, change is the law of life. Any attempt to contain it guarantees an explosion down the road; the more rigid the adherence to the status quo, the more violent the ultimate outcome will be.

Table 12-2. Positioning of Technology Teacher Education

From	To
Thinking along traditional lines	➜ Thinking as a change agent
Owned and taught primarily by technology educators	➜ Owned and taught by various subject area educators with leadership provided by technology educators
Passive existence with few major initiatives beyond special projects	➜ Leadership potential in philosophical, curriculum, research, teacher enhancement, assessment, etc.
Grouping primarily with vocational offerings and administration	➜ Grouped with math, science, and engineering curriculum and administration
Manipulative skills dealing with careers	➜ Thinking, problem solving, innovation, and manipulative skills
Focus on splintered set of activities with inconsistent curriculum	➜ Focus on teaching/learning curriculum, activities, and research
No consistent course content unless technical or career emphasis	➜ Opportunity for consistent course offerings (nationwide)
No systemic accountability in place	➜ Teacher/learning measuring capability on national/international level
Vendor-driven philosophy, materials, and direction	➜ Teacher educator/teacher driven with standards as the basis

Technology teacher educators must become the change agents and leaders who help take the national organizations, their own institutions, and profession toward the true role that technology education should play in an education appropriate for a technological society. What is at stake at this point in history is whether technology educators have the enthusiasm and drive to provide the leadership for the changes to be made.

The intellectual capability is present, the obvious directions have been identified, and national organizations are doing their part. Now, the time has come for technology teacher educators to take advantage of the opportunities before them or face the consequences of playing an insignificant role in the future of the field. The students in our society will be the real winners when the opportunities are addressed. The following scenario identifies the future direction for national organizations implementing *Standards for Technological Literacy* and technology teacher educators' important role in advancing the profession. These thought provoking questions should stimulate your thinking about what needs to take place in the future.

SCENARIO

The advancing technological world has caused remarkable developments, which are already transforming business, communications, and lifestyles. There is no reason to believe that education will not also undergo a tremendous change to reflect the rest of the world. Associations and teacher education institutions will take on different mentalities, partly to survive and partly as a result of changes coming from the outside world.

Teacher education will not only become more electronic, it will change because of the remarkable developments of the electronic revolution. Computers and video power will be everywhere making the current computer age seem very basic as more developments continue to change our environment. This will affect what we traditionally thought to be outstanding on-site technology teacher preparation programs. The context and delivery of teacher education will have no borders, different guidelines, and competition from businesses that were not in existence at the turn of the century.

Knowledge, skills, and natural resources are today considered a source of comparative advantage for any nation. The strong educational system of the future will place emphasis on knowledge and skills as a part of a country's social investment. The strong countries will be those which use the computer as a tool to reinvigorate their science and technology base. The importance of natural resources in the strength of a country will slowly wane.

Computing in the future will be everywhere because of the ability to plant more knowledge into smaller spaces. This will cause our society to go from being observers to choreographers of nature with the advances in genetics, biotechnology, and every other type of technology. How can teacher education not change in this type of world?

Teacher education of the future, as compared with today or past years, will definitely be considered non-traditional—non-traditional in terms of its setting, requirements, timing, instructional systems, delivery, and standards. The essence of human nature will also change as is already evident with one's ability and often desire to be in touch no matter where they may be on or around our planet.

There will always be a starting point for knowledge and skills in whatever times we may live, a need for a rationale and structure for the study of technology even as technology and people change, and a need for standards from which to set goals and measure progress. Human teachers will be needed even as we become sophisticated enough to create robots with higher skills and intelligence.

With those teachers comes a compelling challenge to produce students with the ability to lead the next generation of thinkers for our civilization. Technology teacher education will be faced with the task of not only creating teachers who can impart experiences and knowledge of the scientific and technology world, but they must also be able to use the computer tools available everywhere for delivering that knowledge.

The role of organizations and teacher educators in this type of world will be necessary as long as there is learning to take place. There will be a need to constantly re-establish standards and develop experiences for learning. There will also be a need for visions by educators to adapt to the changing environment, roles of technology teacher educators, and organizations in the educational systems of the future.

THOUGHT-PROVOKING ACTIVITIES

With those thoughts in mind,

1. How do we design education that can effectively prepare members of our society to be technologically literate?

2. What are the effective ways to produce teachers with an understanding of technology content and the ability to be quality teachers?

3. How can education be designed to effectively teach technology in all subject areas and settings other than schools such as museums, fairs, home, and more?

4. What strategies can be utilized to create consistent measures of student learned knowledge about technological capabilities at the local, state/provincial, national, and international levels?

5. What should be the design and benefits of future technology teacher organizations and teacher education institutions?

SUMMARY

A significant step has been taken at this point in technology teacher education. *A Rationale and Structure for the Study of Technology* has been developed. *Standards for Technological Literacy* exists where they were absent in the past. The groundwork or foundation to build a stronger curricular area is in place.

The profession can expect *Standards for Technological Literacy* to be revisited and adjusted in the future. We can expect new players and systems of content delivery as "dot com" companies seek to improve education. We can expect more attention being played to technology education teaching as other than the traditional technology teachers start to address the content. As these changes evolve, national organizations will continue to promote the core beliefs of the profession, work with existing university and professional development personnel, while taking advantage of opportunities resulting in a better technology education for all.

REFERENCES

International Technology Education Association (ITEA). (1996). *Rationale and structure for the study of technoloogy.* Reston, VA: Author.

International Technology Education Association (ITEA). (1999). *A guide to develop standards-based K-12 technology education.* Reston, VA: Author.

International Technology Education Association (ITEA). (2000). *Standards for technological literacy: Content for the study of technology.* Reston, VA: Author.

International Technology Education Association (ITEA). (2000). *Teaching technology: Middle school, strategies for standards-based instruction.* Reston, VA: Author.

International Technology Education Association (ITEA). (2001). *Exploring technology: A standards-based Middle school model course guide.* Reston, VA: Author.

International Technology Education Association (ITEA). (2001). *Teaching technology: High school, strategies for standards-based instruction.* Reston, VA: Author.

International Technology Education Association/Council on Technology Education/National Council for Accreditation of Teacher Education (ITEA/CTTE/NCATE). (1997). *ITEA/CTTE/NCATE Curriculum guidelines.* Reston, VA: International Technology Education Association.

Kissinger, K. (1999, October). Reader's digest quotable quotes. *Readers Digest,* 73.

National Association for Secondary School Principals (NASSP). (September, 1999) *The bulletin.* Reston, VA: Author.

Snyder, J.F., & Hales, J.A. (Eds.). (1981). *Jackson's mill industrial arts curriculum theory.* Reston, VA: International Technology Education Association.

Providing Education to Implement *Standards for Technological Literacy*

Chapter 13

William E. Dugger, Jr.
International Technology Education Association
Technology for All Americans

John M. Ritz
Old Dominion University

Everett N. Israel
Adjunct Professor, Illinois State University

Standards for Technological Literacy: Content for the Study of Technology (*Standards for Technological Literacy*) (ITEA, 2000) presents a vision for the content of technology to prepare technologically literate students. In order to deliver this vision, all teachers of technology (technology education, science, social studies, etc.) must become knowledgeable of the subject's content, methods of delivery, and students needs for studying technology. In the preparation of qualified and licensed teachers, the teacher education program must take an active role in preparing the best teachers possible to deliver the content presented in the 20 standards in *Standards for Technological Literacy*. This active role of the universities is vital and fundamental for the successful delivery of technological literacy to each student.

This yearbook has provided the best thinking of the Council on Technology Teacher Education to transition teacher education to the next phase, using the *Standards for Technological Literacy* as the knowledge base for the preparation of future technology education teachers. In Section 1 of this yearbook, the authors provided an overview of the role of standards in education. Educational reform and the need for improving learning created a need for educational standards. In technology education, the opportunity and financial support were garnered through the efforts of the International Technology Education Association and its members. Although *Standards for Technological Literacy* have provided new knowledge to be delivered through technology education, if the profession does not act, nor act intelligently and conclusively, it can encounter many stumbling blocks and not realize the power that can result from a planned reform effort. Also in this section, the authors examined the standards that have been developed for other school subject areas. These were reviewed and those that have a close relationship with the study of technology were explained. This information should help technology educators see that they are not in the standards arena alone but can work with colleagues from other teaching areas to use their subjects to support the development of technology education teachers.

The authors of Section 2 provided the background research that was used to establish *Standards for Technological Literacy*. Through funding by the National Science Foundation (NSF) and the National Aeronautics and Space Administration (NASA), an opportunity was created for the members of the technology education professions. *Rationale and Structure for the Study of Technology* (1996) provided the knowledge base from where the *Standards for Technological Literacy* were developed. The chapter on *Standards for Technological Literacy: Content for the Study of Technology* summarized the standards and suggested how they can be used in the re-design of technology teacher education programs.

Section 3 authors provided ideas for the actual integration of *Standards for Technology Literacy* into technology teacher preparation. Visions were created of what a technology teacher education program should consider in its re-design. Models for how the curriculum for teacher education should change to deliver *Standards for Technological Literacy* were suggested. The authors did not limit their thinking to one model, but proposed several that teacher educators can consider as curriculum changes are prepared for the future education of teachers. Also within this section, several alternatives were explored that have been successful in the preparation of teachers from non-traditional perspectives. Futuristic visions were also set forth, one that used mentors and electronic means for the preparation of technology education teachers. This was done in hopes of reducing the shortage of licensed technology education teachers.

Licensure and accreditation are two external factors that regulate the preparation of teachers. Authors of Section 4 addressed the implications that *Standards for Technological Literacy* have on future technology education teacher licensing. With the re-design of teacher education programs, teacher educators must be cognizant of adhering to accreditation standards. Within this section, a vision was set forth of what the *ITEA/CTTE/NCATE Curriculum Guidelines* might look like in the near future. This vision can assist with the re-design of teacher preparation curriculum.

Since many practicing technology teachers were not schooled in implementing *Standards for Technological Literacy*, ideas were set forth in Section 5 for providing in-service education for re-designing the delivery of technology education for K-12 teachers. The role of teacher education in providing effective in-service strategies for implementing *Standards for Technological Literacy* was discussed. Also, the authors reviewed cooperative arrangements between departments of education, schools systems, and universities in providing in-service training so practicing teachers can become aware of and develop curriculum, courses, instruction, and activities using *Standards for Technological Literacy*. Since a majority of our teachers already teach, the importance of in-service education was addressed. Finally, this section reviewed the role of national associations in developing cooperative relationships for the profession and the development of instructional materials and professional development for technology teacher education.

With this yearbook, the stage has been set for technology teacher education to deliver the *Standards for Technological Literacy*. The authors provided ideas for the re-design of technology teacher education. In this final chapter, the editors build upon these ideas and suggest some planning strategies that can be used for integrating *Standards for Technological Literacy* into technology teacher preparation.

STRATEGIC FRAMEWORK FOR IMPLEMENTING *STANDARDS FOR TECHNOLOGICAL LITERACY*

Each technology teacher education program should prepare a written strategic framework for integrating and implementing *Standards for Technological Literacy* into its undergraduate program. The strategic framework for implementing *Standards for Technological Literacy* should include the following steps:

1. Orient technology education faculty to *Standards for Technological Literacy.*

Most technology education faculty need an orientation to the complete *Standards for Technological Literacy.* The department chair/program leader should organize a workshop for this purpose. An International Technology Education Association (ITEA) staff person, a Technology for All Americans Project staff member, or Standards Specialist who has been trained in the philosophy and content of *Standards for Technological Literacy* can conduct the workshop. A minimum of one-day should be devoted to orienting the technology teacher education faculty to the standards. These workshops should focus on the relationships between *Standards for Technological Literacy* and the *ITEA/CTTE/NCATE Curriculum Guidelines* (ITEA/CTTE/NCATE, 1997). It is possible that a state agency may provide financial support for a technology teacher education faculty workshop. This allows all technology teacher educators in one state to become oriented to *Standards for Technological Literacy* and to discuss implementation into teacher education programs.

2. Work to gain consensus on *Standards for Technological Literacy* by the faculty.

Once the technology teacher education faculty has been given an orientation to *Standards for Technological Literacy,* they need to discuss the implementation of these standards within the technology teacher education program. The faculty must gain consensus on implementing the standards in the program. The department chair or some designee should lead the faculty through this consensus gaining process in order to assure that all items are discussed and the faculty is given an opportunity to resolve concerns. By doing this and gaining consensus, each faculty member has a degree of ownership in the decisions for implementing the standards in their technology teacher education program.

3. Convert the technology teacher education program to be based on *Standards for Technological Literacy.*

Standards for Technological Literacy provides the content basis for the study of technology. It presents the content of what every child should know and be able to do in order to become technologically literate. The standards provide a rich basis for the content at the teacher education level, since graduates should be prepared to deliver this content in grades K-12. The knowledge base for the content, which is presented in *Standards* 1-10, is important for their infusion into the coursework of the undergraduate degree program. The content developed around the categories of the Nature of Technology, Technology and Society, and Design provides a rich cognitive and effective foundation for the study of technology. Likewise, the knowledge and abilities presented in *Standards* 11-20, which deal with Abilities for a Technological World and The Designed World, provide the basis for much of the hands-on laboratory-based content for the technology teacher education program. These 20 standards should provide the foundation for what should be offered in the technology teacher education courses. Also, activities provided for by the Technology Education Collegiate Association (TECA) can provide co-curricular experience for the students based on the Standards. The professional clinical experiences can provide rich real world experiences and should be based on *Standards for Technological Literacy*. Likewise, the pedagogical courses typically offered by the department or the college can be designed so that they include the 20 content standards for technological literacy.

It is important that other majors outside of the technology teacher education program learn about *Standards for Technological Literacy* in hopes that they will deliver technology content within their classes. This is certainly true for such pre-service candidates as science, mathematics, social studies, language arts, and history teachers.

It also may be possible to select certain university core requirements, which complement *Standards for Technological Literacy*. Such possible courses could include History of Technology, Technology and Society, Science, Technology, and Society (STS), as well as related engineering and computer science courses.

A committee should modify the existing technology teacher education program based on *Standards for Technological Literacy*. This modified curriculum should cut across all areas of the undergraduate degree program including technology courses, clinical experiences, pedagogy courses and experiences, and university core requirements. The committee should work to develop a comprehensive plan for revising the undergraduate degree curriculum, which is within the acceptable timeframe of the university.

It is also essential to contact personnel in state departments of education licensure area to make sure that the proposed changes will meet the state licensure requirements. The program leader must meet with key people at the state department to secure approval for the proposed changes.

4. <u>Gain college/university support of the new technology teacher education program.</u>

Once the committee has studied the revision of the undergraduate degree program, it needs to take the recommendations through the committee process within the college and/or university for approval. This usually is an arduous process that takes time and effort to navigate the changes through the curriculum approval process successfully. The committee should be prepared to argue for reasons why the changes in the program are necessary and why it will produce better-qualified teachers.

The committee must be prepared to inform other faculty and administrators within the college and university about what is involved in the study of technology and why everyone needs to be technologically literate. This should be perceived by technology teacher education faculty as an opportunity, instead of a problem, for educating key university personnel about the importance for all citizens becoming technological literate.

5. <u>Implement new program.</u>

Once the college or university has approved the modified technology teacher education program, the department leader and other faculty need to implement the program. This involves informing and educating students about proposed changes. Previous program graduates and department alumni should be made aware of the program changes and the benefits of implementation. Also, those who hire graduates or supervise technology education student teachers must be informed of the rationale for and the change in the teacher education program.

An implementation schedule should be developed so that the proposed program can be phased into the undergraduate degree program over a period of time. Undergraduate degree advisors should be trained on the new degree requirements and how to advise students in the degree program. Off campus teachers and others who work with undergraduate technology education majors in clinical experiences should be informed of program changes so they are familiar with both what has been done and why the modifications occurred.

6. <u>Recruit new majors.</u>

It is imperative that the technology teacher education faculty recruits new majors as soon as possible. Many times because change is underway, it becomes more difficult to take time to recruit majors. Strategies should be developed to recruit high school graduates, transfers from other academic departments, and transfers from community colleges and other universities. It is critical to work with key teachers around the state or region who have historically recruited students to enroll in the university technology teacher education program. Since there is a major national shortage of technology education teachers, it is mandatory that every technology teacher education faculty recruits future technology education teachers.

7. <u>Market this new program to key stakeholders.</u>

The new program needs to be marketed to key stakeholders, e.g., other faculty within the college and university, the university's administration, potential new majors, and as previously stated, alumni. Key stakeholders also include school systems that hire graduates from the undergraduate degree program as well as teachers who worked as student teacher supervisors and other clinical supervisors. Marketing the new program to state department personnel is also imperative in an effort to gain support, which may result in possible funding for standards-based reform. Last, it is important to market the new program to other teacher education programs nationwide. This may be done through ITEA's Council for Technology Teacher Education (CTTE) Web sites and/or department and/or university Web sites. Other universities can review program changes in the new technology teacher education program.

8. <u>Evaluate the program.</u>

It is imperative that the undergraduate degree program be periodically evaluated. This can be done through formal means, such as formal accreditation processes or through informal means such as self-evaluation procedures. It is recommended that the program leader initiate an internal review to assess progress four to five years after program modification is implemented. Questions need to be answered, such as "Were the changes beneficial to producing high quality graduates in technology education?" Also, evaluation should include the opinions of graduates as well as key stakeholders that hire undergraduate degree majors. The results of this evaluation should be formulated into a report so that faculty within the department as well as those in the college or university administration can see the effects of the revision and changes over this time period. This report will also be useful when preparing documentation for an ITEA/CTTE/NCATE program review.

9. Revise on regular basis.

Based on the evaluation and input received over the four to five year period, it is imperative that the undergraduate degree program be revised on a regular basis. The evaluation data provide a rich resource for further improving the undergraduate degree program. The faculty should focus on what works and what does not, and further changes should be made to improve the undergraduate degree program. Evaluation through either internal review or external accreditation provides an excellent means for further refinement of the pre-service technology teacher education program.

HOW THE THREE COMPANION STANDARDS WILL ASSIST THE IMPLEMENTATION PROCESS FOR *STANDARDS FOR TECHNOLOGICAL LITERACY*

ITEA's Technology for All Americans Project is unique on a worldwide scale because no other agency or association has developed standards for technological literacy. As a result, there is an acute need for a cadre of teachers, curriculum developers, teacher educators, and administrators who can effectively lead educational reform and implementation in technological studies.

The National Science Foundation (NSF) and the National Aeronautics and Space Administration (NASA) have funded the ITEA's Technology for All Americans Project, from 2001-2003, to develop three additional sets of standards in Phase III of the project. The goals for Phase III that follow outline the necessary leadership skills to make technological literacy a reality.

The goals for Phase III include:

1. To develop student assessment standards based on *Standards for Technological Literacy*.

2. To develop professional development standards (in-service and pre-service) based on *Standards for Technological Literacy.*

3. To develop program standards that are used as criteria to assess the overall quality of and conditions for technology programs in schools, based on *Standards for Technological Literacy.*

4. To develop a cadre of teachers, curriculum specialists, and administrators who can effectively lead reform in education and implement *Standards for Technological Literacy* (NASA initiative).

A Rationale and Structure for the Study of Technology (Rationale and Structure, 1996) and *Standards for Technological Literacy: Content for the Study of Technology (Standards for Technological Literacy,* 2000) will create the need for educational reform in technology education. An implementation strategy is being developed to help educators bring about the desired change in technology education based upon the standards. Technological literacy will not become a reality for all students until critical support documents proposed in Phase III are created for student assessment, program development, and professional development standards. ITEA's Center to Advance the Teaching of Technology and Science (CATTS) also helps in this important implementation process.

Other standards, such as the *National Science Education Standards* and *Principles and Standards for School Mathematics,* in addition to content standards, have developed standards, which addressed assessment, programs, and professional development standards.

<u>Assessment Standards</u>

Assessment is the systematic, multi-step process of collecting information on student learning, understanding, and capability and using the results to inform instruction.

The vision articulated in *Standards for Technological Literacy* emphasizes that assessment is central to providing feedback in the study of technology. As an integral part of the learning process, assessment should be ongoing (formative) rather than simply marking the end of a learning cycle (summative). The assessment process should be at the school level to inform students and teachers about their progress toward technological literacy. The data should provide a measure of the effectiveness of the program goals, instructional strategies, classroom practices, planned curricula, learners, and report student progress. In other words, assessment should not only be a measure of students' learning outcome, but also an integral part of the entire instructional process. Finally, assessment will offer information to high stakes policymakers concerning the success of implemented policies.

Assessment must reflect the vision of educational reform in technological studies. Central to this vision is an agreed-upon content that is based on what every student should know and be able to do with technology. The primary goal of assessment is to advance students' learning and to inform teachers as they make instructional decisions. Assessment involves a multi-phased process of systematically collecting and interpreting educational data. The data can be used in the classroom to plan curriculum and instruction and to guide learning. The data will determine whether special and/or gifted students are gaining meaningful experiences in the study of technology. The data also may be used to validate the development of an educational philosophy. Regarding policy, assessment data can assist policymakers in monitoring the effectiveness of specific policies and procedures. This may determine the allocation or reallocation of resources to meet future needs. In terms of teacher preparation, the data can be used for establishing credentials and licensing future teachers.

Assessment standards provide criteria to judge the progress toward the vision that all students should be technologically literate. Assessment standards do not develop assessment instruments; rather, they should specify parameters for good practice. The end use of the assessment standards directly affects students, parents, teachers, educational policymakers, and administrators. In the broader spectrum, institutions for higher education are affected by the assessment process in terms of pre-service and in-service for teachers.

Professional Development Standards

Professional development is a continuous process of lifelong professional learning and growth – from pre-service in undergraduate years to in-service through the end of a professional career.

The professional development standards directly relate to the carefully planned pre-service and in-service of all teachers in grades K-12. The colleges and universities who are preparing the future teachers will be involved in putting these standards into practice. Because the study of technology is a vital field of education, those in charge of all teacher education programs need to revise their curricula and teaching methodologies to reflect the vision of *Standards for Technological Literacy*.

The study of technology is a continuously changing field of study, and teachers must, therefore, be well prepared and have the ability and desire to stay informed and current on technological advances throughout their careers. The professional development standards will provide the guidelines for in-service training for school teachers already in the classroom and laboratory.

Because many states are experiencing a shortage of qualified and licensed teachers, in-service and pre-service training is essential. The professional development standards will address the education of technology education professionals, as well as other educators, including those at the elementary school level and in other school disciplines.

Program Standards

The program standards include the totality of the program (courses) of study, curriculum and assessment, teaching, equipment and resources, and the teaching/learning environment across grade levels in a school or school district.

The International Technology Education Association's Technology for All Americans Project will develop program standards for the study of technology. Program standards deal with all elements for teaching technology across grade levels within schools. The technology program should be coordinated to promote interdisciplinary learning.

The program standards are grounded in the assumption that thoughtful design and implementation of technology programs at the school and district level are necessary to provide comprehensive and coordinated experiences for all students across all grade levels. Because coordinated experiences result in effective learning, the program standards must be synchronized with *Standards for Technological Literacy*. The study of technology should be developmentally appropriate for every student, and it should be coordinated with science, mathematics, the humanities, social studies, geography, career and technical education, and all areas of the school curriculum. The technology program must extend beyond the domain of the school to involve the community, business and industry, school-to-work programs, as well as professionals in engineering and other careers related to technology.

VISION FOR THE FUTURE

We live in a world that is increasingly dependent on technology. Technology has been a growing human endeavor since the first chipped edge flint tool was created by our ancestors approximately 1.5 million years ago in what is now Kenya. Today, technology exists to a degree unprecedented in history. Furthermore, technology is evolving at an extraordinary rate with new technologies being created and existing technologies being improved and extended each day.

Surprisingly, there is much confusion in today's society about what technology actually is. Some people think that technology is just computers or information technology. Unfortunately, this is a myopic view of what other people consider a very powerful presence in all our lives. In its simplest terms, technology is how humans have modified our natural world. This includes not only computers and information technology, but also medical technologies, agricultural and related biotechnologies, energy and power technologies, transportation technologies, manufacturing technologies, and construction technologies. Also, it is essential in the 21st century for a person to know the nature of technology, to have an understanding of technology and society, and to be educated in design and problem solving. Knowledge of and abilities in all of these areas provide the basis for a person to be technologically literate. Our citizenry needs to be technologically literate in order to make wise decisions about technology in the future. These decisions should be based on a quality education related to the study of technology rather than through emotion or happenstance. Technology teacher education programs at colleges and universities play a very important role in developing the technological literacy of teachers and, in turn, their students.

Our role as citizens will be very different ten or twenty years from now. People have a choice about how technology affects their future. They can march into the future with their eyes open and decide for themselves how technology will affect them, or they can remain ignorant of technology and its effects on their lives. A vision for the future is that technological literacy, provided through the study of technology as presented in *Standards for Technological Literacy*, will enable people to make conscious and educated choices.

By understanding the role that standards play in education, teacher educators are better prepared to develop teacher education programs that produce competent teachers. *Standards for Technological Literacy* can serve as a basis for program improvement. This yearbook had this goal in mind throughout its preparation. It has suggested ideas for program improvement. Suggestions have also been made for changes in teacher preparation, licensure, program accreditation, and in-service education. The editors hope that the ideas set forth by this yearbook's authors will assist technology teacher educators in the re-design of their programs, which can provide the education to deliver *Standards for Technological Literacy* throughout the education community.

REFERENCES

American Association for the Advancement of Science (AAAS). (1992). *Benchmarks for science literacy.* Washington, DC: Author.

International Technology Education Association (ITEA). (1996). *A rationale and structure for the study of technology.* Reston, VA: Author.

International Technology Education Association (ITEA). (2000). *Standards for technological literacy: Content for the study of technology.* Reston, VA: Author.

International Technology Education Association/Council on Technology Teacher Education/National Council for Accreditation of Teacher Education (ITEA/CTTE/NCATE). (1997). *ITEA/CTTE/NCATE Curriculum guidelines.* Reston, VA: International Technology Education Association.

National Council of Teachers of Mathematics (NCTM). (1989). *Curriculum and evaluation standards for school mathematics.* Reston, VA: Author.

National Council of Teachers of Mathematics (NCTM). (1991). *Professional standards for teaching mathematics.* Reston, VA: Author.

National Council of Teachers of Mathematics (NCTM). (1995). *Assessment standards for school mathematics.* Reston, VA: Author.

National Council of Teachers of Mathematics (NCTM). (2000). *Principles and standards for school mathematics.* Reston, VA: Author.

National Research Council (NRC). (1996). *National science education standards.* Washington, DC: National Academy Press.

INDEX

Index

Principles and Standards for School
Mathematics (*continued*)
relationship to *Standards for Technological
Literacy*, 39
Problem solving, design, and technology,
105-109
Procedural development, 108
Process approach, 196
Process standards, 63, 109
Producing abilities, 110
Professional development standards, 1,
246-247
in National Science Education Standards,
14
Professional knowledge, 149, 150
Program standards, 247
Project Open, 199, 202-203

R

*Rationale and Structure for Standards for
Technological Literacy*, 47-57, 177, 200,
238
defining technological literacy in, 51-52
dimensions of technology in, 50-55
funding of, by NSF and NASA, 48, 177-178,
224-226
in preparing students for a technological
world, 49-50
purpose of, 49-50
taxonomic organizers in, for the study of
technology, 55-56
*A Rationale and Structure for the Study of
Technology*, 4
Research and development, 107, 110
Restructuring the technology teacher education curriculum, 99-119
*ROAD MAPS: Perspectives for Excellence in
Technology Education Programs*, 83-86

S

Science
education standards in, 12-30
Benchmarks for Science Literacy, 1, 12,
44, 101
comparison of, with other standards,
39-40
content of, 21, 22-29
goals of, 19-20
history of AAAS Project 2061 in leading to, 18-19
organization and structure of, 20-21

relationship of, to *Standards for
Technological Literacy*, 21, 30
National Science Education Standards, 1,
101
comparison of, with other standards,
39-40
content of, 14-17
goals of, 12-13
history of development of, 12
organization and structure of, 13-14
relationship to *Standards for
Technological Literacy*, 17
strategic framework for standards-
based reform in, 5
technology, engineering, and mathematics
(STEM) oriented agencies, 225
Science content standards, in National
ScienceEducation Standards, 14
Science education program standards, in
National Science Education Standards, 14
Science education system standards, in
National Science Education Standards, 14
Science for All Americans, 12, 18
Science teacher standards, in National
Science Education Standards, 14
Science/Technology/Society Approach, 90
Scope, Sequence, and Coordination Project,
12
Secondary grades
development of alternative teacher educa-
tion programs for, 134-135
in-service laboratory activities for, 200
Social institutions, influence on technology,
104
Society, Science, Technology, and Society
7(STS), 241
Society, technology and, 104-105
Southern Association, 169
Standards. *See* Education standards
Standards-based education, participants in, 8
Standards-based reform, strategic framework
for, 5
Standards for Technological Literacy, 1, 238
accuracy and thoroughness of, 1
alternative models for teaching in, 122
as the basis for future technology teacher
education programs, 79-97
benchmarks in, 65-67
blending with *ITEA/CTTE/NCATE
Curriculum Guidelines*, 179-184
brief tour of, 61-62
comparison of, with other standards,
39-40

256

Index

Technology education (*continued*)
status of, before *Standards for Technological Literacy*, 222-224
Technology Education Collegiate Association (TECA), 241
Technology for All Americans Project, 4, 153, 156, 227, 244
as a knowledge base, 177-178
Phase III of, 77, 244-247
Technology teacher education models, 113-114
imbedded program model, 117-119
stand-alone program model, 113, 114-117
capstone courses, 115
design courses, 114-115
producing courses, 115
teaching technology courses, 114
using and assessing courses, 115
stand-alone program model variations, 116-117
core concept model, 117
integrated, multidisciplinary model, 116
Technology teacher education programs
alternative, 121-138
evaluation of, 92-93
future laboratories in, 91-92
impact of *Standards for Technological Literacy* on, 75-77
implementing, 83-86
leadership roles for faculty in, 76-77
restructuring curriculum for, 99-119
Standards for Technological Literacy as basis for, 79-97
Technology teacher educators
in-service roles of, 200-201
recommended changes for, for in-servicing technology teachers, 205-207
Technology Teacher Enhancement Center at Central Connecticut State University, 203
Technology teachers
in assessing achievement, 113
competence for, 100-102
in determining program and course content, 112-113
in developing and presenting courses, 113
developing and using philosophy by, 112
in fostering technological literacy, 86-87
motivating, to implement *Standards for Technological Literacy*, 194-195
need for qualified, 122-123
preparing standards-oriented, 219-235

role of teacher education and national organizations in preparing standards-oriented, 219-235
technology teacher education's in-servicing of, 189-207
Texas A&M University, adoption of interdisciplinary model at, 125-126
Thinking outside of the box, 107, 108
Third International Mathematics and Science Study (TIMSS), 2
3M Corporation, 108
Tomorrow's Teachers, 145
Troops to Teachers Program, 123-124
Troubleshooting, 107, 110
Tuberculosis testing, 142

U

United Kingdom Open University Model, 128-130
University of Maryland, Eastern Shore, alternative program offered by, 127
University of South Florida, Florida 2 plus 2 program at, 124-125
Using abilities, 111

V

Video streaming, 137
Vignettes, in *Standards for Technological Literacy*, 67
Virginia Department of Education, special license for middle school technology teachers offer by, 124
Virtual model program for teacher preparation, 135-137

W

Western Association, 169
West Virginia University, Technology Education Program at, 202-203
What Matters Most, 145
Wisconsin
innovative instructional strategies in, 215-216
relationship between teacher education and state department of education in, 210, 213, 215
Staff Development Initiative in, 215
Technology Articulation Initiative in, 216